AK-47

OTHER BOOKS BY LARRY KAHANER

Nonfiction

Values, Prosperity, and the Talmud:
Business Lessons from the Ancient Rabbis

The Quotations of Chairman Greenspan:
Words from the Man Who Can Shake the World

Competitive Intelligence:
How to Gather, Analyze, and Use Information
to Move Your Business to the Top

Say It and Live It:
The 50 Corporate Mission Statements
That Hit the Mark (coauthor)

Cults That Kill:
Probing the Underworld of Occult Crime

On the Line:
How MCI Took on At&T—and Won!

The Phone Book:
The Most Complete Guide to the Changing
World of Telephones (coauthor)

Fiction

Naked Prey
(pseudonym Larry Kane)

AK-47

The Weapon That Changed
the Face of War

Larry Kahaner

John Wiley & Sons, Inc.

Published by John Wiley & Sons, Inc., Hoboken, New Jersey
Published simultaneously in Canada

Design and composition by Navta Associates, Inc.

For general information about our other products and services, please contact our Customer Care Department within the United States at (800) 762-2974, outside the United States at (317) 572-3993 or fax (317) 572-4002.

Wiley also publishes its books in a variety of electronic formats. Some content that appears in print may not be available in electronic books. For more information about Wiley products, visit our web site at www.wiley.com.

Library of Congress Cataloging-in-Publication Data:

Kahaner, Larry.
  AK-47 : the weapon that changed the face of war / Larry Kahaner.
    p. cm.
  Includes bibliographical references and index.
   ISBN-13 978-0-471-72641-8 (cloth: alk. paper)
   ISBN-10 0-471-72641-9 (cloth: alk. paper)
1. AK-47 rifle. I. Title
  UD395.A16K 2006
  623.4'424—dc22

                                                        2006004501

Printed in the United States of America

10 9 8 7 6 5 4 3 2 1

In some places, an AK-47 assault rifle can be bought for as little as . . . a bag of grain. They are easy to use: with minimal training, even a child can wield one. They are easy to conceal and transport. Since they require little maintenance, they can last for decades.

— UN SECRETARY-GENERAL KOFI ANNAN

That rifle hanging on the wall of the working-class flat or labourer's cottage is the symbol of democracy. It is our job to see that it stays there.

— GEORGE ORWELL

I'm proud of my invention, but I'm sad that it is used by terrorists. I would prefer to have invented a machine that people could use and that would help farmers with their work—for example, a lawnmower.

— MIKHAIL T. KALASHNIKOV

CONTENTS

Acknowledgments   ix

Author's Note   xi

Introduction   1

1   Protecting the Motherland   9

2   A Reputation Born in the Rice Paddies   29

3   Pandora's Box   55

4   The African Credit Card   75

5   The Kalashnikov Culture Reaches Latin America   103

6   Kalashnikov and His Gun Visit America   133

7   The United Nations Takes On the True Weapons
    of Mass Destruction   169

8   AK versus M-16: Part 2   187

9   The Second Selling of the AK   209

Epilogue: The Last Days of the AK?   227

Notes   235

Index   247

ACKNOWLEDGMENTS

I have many people to thank for their help in researching and writing this book. Some of them spent a great deal of their time with me; others helped me over some rough spots, offering ideas or a different way of looking at things that moved me along.

I am grateful for early assistance from: Glen Senkowski, A Troop, 1st Squadron, 9th Cavalry, who offered stories about his Vietnam War experience when he often used an AK instead of his army-issued M-16; Doug Wicklund, Senior Curator, National Firearms Museum, who showed me his personal AKs as well as those in the museum and pointed out their salient features; Duncan Long, firearms author, who posited his ideas on the AK's success; Mark Schwartz, who offered insights on combat tactics of World War II; Rachel J. Stohl, Senior Analyst, Center for Defense Information, whose research on the importance of small arms helped me better understand their impact; William Addison Hurst, one of Kalashnikov's hosts on his first trip to the United States; Rick Davis, who offered technical insights on the AK; Mark Bromley, Research Associate, Arms Transfers Project, Stockholm International Peace Research Institute (SIPRI); Matthew P. Caulfield, Major General, U.S. Marine Corps (ret.), Executive Director, Helmets to Hardhats; Vadim Dabrov, creator of www.ak47-guide.com, a useful e-book source about the Kalashnikov Museum; the staff of the Small Arms Survey, produced by the International Action Network on Small Arms, for sharing their data; moderators and members of the Guns Network, whose web site www.ak-47.net was a great source of quick answers about the minutiae of the AK; Larry Zilliox, President, Investigative Research Specialists, LLC, for his help in unearthing government documents; and Karl Bickel, Senior Policy Analyst, Department of Justice, for insights on police and assault rifles.

Thanks go to those in my writer's group, which has been meeting monthly for almost fifteen years: Allen Appel, Audie Appel, Dan Stashower, John McKeon, and Marc Smolonsky, all authors and writers in their own right; Doug Starr, a longtime friend who keeps me from stepping into literary hot water; Adam Firestone, who spent time with me at the National Rifle Association range so I could understand better the shooting profiles of the M-16 and AK; special thanks go to Charlie Cutshaw, firearms expert and journalist, for his technical reading of the manuscript; my agent, Gail Ross, of the Gail Ross Literary Agency and her creative director, Howard Yoon, for understanding the importance of this book and propelling the project to completion; my editor, Eric Nelson, for his insights and wisdom; and my wife, Robin Latham, herself an accomplished author and writer, for her editing and support.

AUTHOR'S NOTE

Despite repeated requests, Mikhail Kalashnikov declined to be interviewed for this book.

Now in his eighties, Kalashnikov has become a sympathetic and tragic figure. He continues to grant shorter interviews to newspapers and magazines, often at public events, allowing him to advertise his brand of vodka, refute critics of his weapons' global destructive power, and drum up business for the Russian arms makers that he represents with his new celebrity status.

Fortunately, the story of Kalashnikov, the AK-47, and its effect on world history is available from open-source material, as well as from private and confidential sources I have cultivated. I drew on all of these for the information in this book.

INTRODUCTION

O N MARCH 23, 2003, under the cover of darkness, thirty-two U.S. Army Apache attack helicopters flew into Baghdad in advance of coalition forces moving northward on the ground toward the capital city. The choppers were on a search-and-destroy mission to find Saddam Hussein's elite Republican Guard, who reportedly were deployed in a semi-circle to protect the southern part of town. In the hours leading up to this mission, Saddam's main artillery positions had been pounded by American surface-to-surface missiles and ATACMS rockets carrying 950 half-pound bombs. The remaining enemy forces would then be wiped out by these low-flying $22 million machines, equipped with 30mm cannons and state-of-the-art Longbow radar systems that could direct Hellfire antitank missiles at multiple targets.

Yet as the Apaches settled into position, something unexpected happened. The lights on the outskirts of Baghdad shut off, as if hit by a blackout. Then, just as mysteriously, they came back on two minutes later.

The U.S. Army pilots did not realize the lights were a signal to attack.

What happened next shocked even the most seasoned combat veterans. The Apache helicopters were attacked from all directions by the world's most prolific and effective combat weapon, a device so cheap and simple that it can be bought in many countries for less than the cost of a live chicken. This weapon, depicted on the flag and currency of several countries, waved defiantly by guerrillas and rebels around the world, has changed the geopolitical landscape of the post–cold war era. It has been responsible for more than a quarter million deaths every year. It is the undisputed firearm of choice for at least fifty legitimate standing armies, along with untold numbers of disenfranchised fighting forces ranging from international insurgents and terrorists to domestic drug dealers and street gangs.

It is the AK-47 assault rifle.

As the Apaches hovered in position, they took thousands of rounds of gunfire from Iraqi ground troops. Thirty-one of the thirty-two helicopters sustained damage; all had to abort their mission. One was downed and two pilots captured. Pentagon officials do not know if the chopper was shot down or suffered mechanical problems. A pilot who made it back safely said, "It was coming from all directions. I got shot front, back, left, and right." Springfield, Massachusetts, pilot Bob Duffney, who flew combat helicopters in the 1991 Gulf War, added, "In Desert Storm, we didn't have a firefight like this."

For all of the billions of dollars spent by the United States military on space-age weapons and technology, the AK still remains the most devastating weapon on the planet. Its banana-shaped magazine gives this gun a familiar silhouette that makes it a symbol of third world rebellion and power. Unlike the scourge of land mines in the world, the eighty to one hundred million AKs manufactured and distributed since the rifle's invention in 1947 pose a more dangerous threat because they can be easily transported, repaired, and used by roving bands of assailants. The AK has made possible coups in Africa, terrorist raids in the Middle East, and bank robberies in Los Angeles. It has become a cultural icon, its signature shape defining in our consciousness what a deadly rifle is supposed to look like.

Why has the AK earned such a legendary reputation? The gun has few moving parts so it hardly ever jams. It is resistant to heat, cold, rain, and sand. It doesn't always shoot straight, but in close combat its awesome firepower (600 rounds a minute) and reliability give it a nod over more sophisticated weapon designs, such as the M-16. American GIs in Vietnam reported that AKs buried in rice paddies for six months or more, unearthed filthy and rusted shut, fired perfectly after kicking the action bolt with the heel of a boot.

In scenarios played throughout the world's hot spots like Iraq, Somalia, Sudan, Sierra Leone, and the Gaza Strip, low-tech AKs are besting superior military training and weaponry. In Iraq, for example, insurgents recently have inflicted demoralizing casualties on U.S. troops mainly with simple tactics such as bombings, kidnapping, and massive small-arms fire with AKs. American troops are hamstrung, forced to fight street to street where the AK allows an everyday citizen to be just as deadly as a professionally trained, well-armored, and physically fit U.S. soldier. Because explosions kill enough people to make newspaper headlines, most Americans think that's how Iraqis and U.S. troops are killing and dying. In fact, small arms still kill more people in Iraq than the touted improvised explosive device.

Why the U.S. military as a whole has been so slow to recognize this "new" face of war remains a mystery, because individual soldiers, those on the ground, understand it. "It's somewhat frustrating," Colonel Bill Wolf, former commander of the army's 11th Aviation Regiment, said. Referring to long-standing U.S. policies about civilian casualties, he added, "We can't take out a street block because of the way we go to war."

This "way we go to war" doesn't work anymore, and some would argue it never did once the Russian assault rifle spread throughout the world and became as ubiquitous as the common cold. Today's wars are small, hot conflicts in urban areas, where sophisticated and expensive weapons are no match for AK-carrying rebels who need little training and know the local terrain better. This sentiment was expressed by Major General William J. Livsey Jr., the commandant of Fort Benning, the infantry head-quarters and school, in the early 1980s. The military was going through a monumental change at the time because computer chips were being integrated into the first generation of smart weapons. The army was enamored of the complexity and promise of these smart weapons. "Despite all the sophisticated weapons we or the Soviets come up with, you still have to get that one lone infantry-man, with his rifle, off his piece of land. It's the damn hardest thing in the world to do."

The AK has shifted the balance of power in warfare by allow-ing small factions, not armies, to overthrow entire governments. Charles Taylor, a Liberian-born, U.S.-educated preacher, proved this in 1989 when he and a ragtag cadre of a hundred men armed with AKs, stormed the presidential palace in Liberia and con-trolled the country for the next six years. By issuing AKs to anyone who swore allegiance to the new regime, Taylor stayed in power with bands of thug soldiers, all of whom were allowed to pillage their defeated enemies as payment for their loyalty.

On the other side of the continent, Mozambique's flag and coins display an AK as homage to the weapon that brought this nation its freedom. Ironically, the United Nations estimates that the coun-try is awash in millions of undocumented AKs left behind from civil war. As long as the AKs remain, the seeds of instability stay rooted in Mozambique's land.

War has changed; it no longer *has* to be about border disagree-ments, ideology, or political differences. Through the power of AK assault rifles, factions can roam through a country, terrorize its citizenry, and grab the spoils.

They can even keep a superpower at bay.

Consider the U.S. Rangers in Mogadishu during the now

famous "Black Hawk Down" incident in 1993 (later made into a Hollywood film by the same name). Eighteen American soldiers were killed and many more wounded during several days of bitter street fighting that eventually led to the resignation of the secretary of defense and a total U.S. troop withdrawal from Somalia. Yusuf Hassan of the BBC's Somali service, who covered the action, said during one of his broadcasts, "It [the film] was sort of portraying the Americans as heroes, when in fact they had *all* the technology. It was a high-tech war against people who only had AK-47 rifles." (To be fair, they also had rocket-propelled grenades and a variety of machine guns.)

Despite this thrashing in Somalia, the message never seems to reach decision makers: superpowers with superweapons are no match for a determined warrior with an assault rifle. Afghani general Mohammad Yahya Nawroz and U.S. Army lieutenant colonel Lester W. Grau wrote for the Foreign Military Studies Office a case study entitled "The Soviet War in Afghanistan: History and Harbinger of Future War?" in which they posited that well-equipped nations do not want to wage war with the United States, because U.S. weapons are technically superior. Oddly, less capable nations have a stronger position. "At present, the countries that have a large supply of high-tech weaponry are few and unlikely to go to war with the United States in the near future. Now, the only effective way for a technologically less-advanced country to fight a technologically-advanced country is through guerrilla war. Guerrilla war, a test of national will and the ability to endure, negates many of the advantages of technology." Written in 1996, their report apparently fell on deaf ears, as the United States has now become bogged down in Iraq and Afghanistan.

In a stroke of irony, the world's most advanced and destructive weapon, the atomic bomb, led the way for the low-tech AK. Because of the A-bomb's guarantee of mass global destruction, the two cold war superpowers declined to wage direct war. Instead, they invented the "proxy war" that employed third-world countries with poorly trained combatants to carry the superpowers'

ideologies. These countries used fighters who possessed little or
no training but were armed with cheap, durable, and easy-to-
obtain AKs. Hot little wars started quicker and lasted longer,
fueled by these indestructible weapons that anyone—trained or
untrained—could fire immediately and become as deadly as a
highly trained soldier. When a specific war ended, the AKs were
gathered up and sold by arms brokers to fighters in the next hot
spot. This scenario has occurred over and over, especially in Africa
and the Middle East. Just as the A-bomb changed the face of modern warfare, so did the AK.

On a cultural level, the AK is a symbol of anti-Western ideology, seen daily on the front pages of our newspapers. AKs built by
the Soviet Union were offered to countries that shared the dream
of worldwide Communist domination. Although they were supposed to be sold, the Soviet Union ended up giving millions away
free to Soviet bloc nations and allowing others to manufacture the
gun on their own soil. Nowadays, in destabilized areas, owning an
AK is a sign of manhood, a rite of passage. Child soldiers in
Congo, Myanmar, Sri Lanka, and dozens of other countries
proudly display their AKs for all to see. Stock video footage of a
white-robed Osama bin Laden shows him firing an AK, a message
to the world that he is the true antiestablishment fighter. Saddam
Hussein was captured with two AKs beside him in his hidey-hole
in the ground. He too was so enamored with the weapons that he
built a Baghdad mosque sporting minarets in the unique shape of
AK barrels. His son Uday commissioned gold-plated AKs.

And what of its designer? During World War II, young tank
soldier Mikhail Timofeevich Kalashnikov, the son of peasants, was
convalescing from a gunshot wound inflicted by Nazis pushing
east. In his hospital bed, he sketched the simplest automatic
weapon possible and later was given the opportunity to build it.
His goal was to help the Soviet army defeat the Germans and
quickly end the war.

Now eighty-five, tiny, feeble, nearly deaf, losing control of his
right hand because of tremors, Kalashnikov thinks about the terri-

ble gift he has given the world and it often haunts him. "I wish I had invented a lawnmower." At other times, this financially poor man, who receives no royalties for his invention, is defiant and aloof, blaming others for his progeny's misuse. "I invented it for protection of the motherland. I have no regrets and bear no responsibility for how politicians have used it."

The utilitarian AK-47, which stands for Avtomat Kalashnikova 1947, the year it was adopted, came along too late to end World War II, but its creation was perfectly timed to spread death and destruction throughout the world, and it will continue to do so well into this century.

I

PROTECTING THE
MOTHERLAND

I N BOOKS ABOUT THE SECOND WORLD WAR, the battle of
Bryansk is a minor conflict, barely deserving of a footnote.
But this battle, so inconsequential that most historians skim
over it without a second thought, has another place in history. It
was here that a then unknown tank commander named Mikhail
Kalashnikov decided that his Russian comrades would never
again be defeated by a foreign army. In the years following the
Great Patriotic War, as Soviet propagandists dubbed it, he was to
conceive and fabricate a weapon so simple and yet so revolutionary, it would change the way wars were fought and won.

When the German army invaded the Soviet Union, it employed
a new and frightening style of warfare. Blitzkrieg, or "lightning
war," was a fast and open doctrine of assault that relied on pound-
ing the enemy with massive air bombardments and long-range
artillery attacks. Concentrated legions of tanks and infantrymen
followed. They fired at almost point-blank range, leaving the
enemy stunned, terrified, and unable to respond.

Blitzkrieg's success hinged on concentrating forces at a single point in an enemy's defensive line, breaking a hole in that line, then thrusting deep into enemy territory, catching the opposition off guard and subjecting them to wave after wave of well-organized and brutally efficient invaders. It would all happen so quickly and on such a massive scale that armies were decisively beaten almost before they knew what hit them. The effects were psychologically devastating.

The Nazi regime employed blitzkrieg brilliantly in its swift and fierce defeat of Poland in September 1939. The tactic served Germany the following year when it invaded the so-called Low Countries—the Netherlands, Belgium, and Luxembourg—each victory allowing the Germans to build momentum and confidence. Soon after, Germany invaded France. In one instance, small and determined groups of Panzer tanks broke through French lines and reached the coast before a counterattack could even be launched.

In many ways, blitzkrieg was a logical reaction to the way war had previously been waged. During most of World War I, armies hunkered down in trenches, sometimes for months at time. Nations spread defensive lines thinly along national borders and around crucial cities. Troops armed with stationary machine guns in bunkers could repel enemy advances. Snipers poked their heads above trench tops in the hopes of picking off an opposing soldier barely visible in the distance. It was largely static warfare.

Hitler's army employed tanks and trucks—an outgrowth of the greater reliability of the internal combustion engine—and two-way radios in a concerted effort to strike the enemy at one specific point on the ground with a fast and furious show of power. Field officers were given greater responsibility in advancing their troops as fast as they could without specific orders from central command. In its simplest form, this method of waging war relied on a centrally coordinated strategy, well-trained soldiers, and a large quantity of technologically advanced matériel and the logistical infrastructure to support it. The army with these ingredients was almost guaranteed success.

So it was no surprise that blitzkrieg became Germany's main strategy during its invasion of the Soviet Union in June 1941, and soldiers, including Kalashnikov, suffered its brutal effects.

Because the two countries were supposedly allies, and had even carved up Poland between themselves several years earlier, the unexpected nature of the attack and its lightning force crushed Soviet ground forces immediately. Through city after city, town after town, superbly trained and highly disciplined German units advanced, quickly annihilating Soviet armies and civilians in their path. German infantrymen killed hundreds of thousands with fire from their automatic Maschinenpistoles (MPs), or submachine guns, spewing hundreds of rounds into knots of Soviet defenders a few yards away. They cut down soldiers and civilians en masse.

The Germans were unstoppable as they pressed on to the ultimate prize, Moscow, destroying everything in their way.

In late September 1941 the German juggernaut reached the outskirts of Bryansk, located deep in the forest and hard against the Desna River southwest of Moscow. The Luftwaffe had bombed Bryansk and its surrounding area in July in preparation for a ground attack. Thousands of Soviets evacuated the area. Factories were moved to more secure eastern locations. The inhabitants dug antitank trenches around the town.

All of these preparations proved useless. The Nazis destroyed about 90 percent of the town's housing and killed more than eighty thousand people. About two hundred thousand were forced into slave camps where most of them later died from starvation or torture.

During the battle of Bryansk, Kalashnikov's tank was maneuvering around an enemy flank when it was hit by artillery. His ears rang; a fragment of the tank's armor pierced his left shoulder and knocked him unconscious. Shell-shocked and bleeding, he and twelve others, including an attending physician, were transported to a hospital. As they entered a nearby village, Kalashnikov and the driver left the truck to check for enemy soldiers. The town was empty and dark. As they made their way through deserted streets,

German soldiers armed with submachine guns overtook the truck, riddling it with bullets. When Kalashnikov and the driver heard the automatic fire they ducked into some bushes, then crawled back to the men they had left behind. When they arrived, they saw German motorcycles with sidecars just disappearing around a turn.

The scene was horrifying. Soldiers were lying zigzagged in the truck bed where they had been shot. Others, who had tried to escape, lay in the dirt road. Some of them, seconds from death, screamed in agony as they expired. Kalashnikov vomited at the sight of the mutilated men.

For the next few days, the two survivors traveled on foot, desperate to avoid the deadly German patrols. Tired, fearful, and wounded, they finally reached a hospital. Though Kalashnikov was now safe in his hospital bed, receiving treatment for his infected wounds, he couldn't relax, especially at night.

He endured nightmares about the truck and the Germans with their superior submachine guns slaughtering his comrades. In great pain, he lay in bed and thought about his life, about the peril of his homeland, about his parents and the little town where he lived.

MIKHAIL TIMOFEEVICH KALASHNIKOV was born on November 10, 1919, into a world that had just seen the end of World War I—"The War to End All Wars"—and hoped for a lasting peace. His family had been exiled to the cold, desolate Altai village of Kurya during political purges, something that the sickly boy did not comprehend. In this harsh environment, only eight of the family's nineteen children survived.

Always one to tinker—Mikhail had taken apart every lock in his village—he and his friend obtained a U.S.-made Browning pistol. Mikhail cleaned it, shined it, took it apart and reassembled it over and over again. He burned with desire to fire it, to watch it work. He was frightened yet fascinated by the firearm and hid it in a pile of junk from the authorities, because it was illegal to possess such a weapon.

Somehow, the militia learned of the gun, and the teen was arrested but later released. He had vehemently insisted he did not own a pistol, and the authorities were unable to find it.

Fearing that he would be found out eventually, Kalashnikov and his friend fled, scattering pieces of the Browning in the snow along the way. He later wrote of this prophetic experience, "That was it. The perpetrator of my hardships, my first acquaintance with arms."

After making his way to Kazakhstan and finding a job with the railroad, Kalashnikov was drafted in 1938. Because of his mechanical acumen, he was assigned to a tank company, where he invented several improvements to gauges that checked engine operating hours. He was never able to fully test his inventions, however, because Germany attacked in June 1941, and he was sent to the front. Before he left, he heard stories of the Germans' superior tactics and savagery, but he had no idea he would be a victim or how it would change his life.

Only a few weeks after shipping out, Sergeant Kalashnikov was out of the war for good. His injuries were substantial enough to keep him from serving again. Convalescing in the hospital, he naively promised himself to build a weapon that would drive the Germans out of his homeland. This promise turned into obsession. "I thought about it when I woke up at night, and tried to imagine what kind of submachine gun I would make. In the morning, I took a notebook from the night table and made various drawings. Later, I redid them many times."

In an effort to keep his mind diverted from pain, he read everything he could find at the hospital library about submachine guns—which many military planners saw as the ultimate infantry weapon and the key to winning land battles. Combatant nations had quickly put into production their own submachine guns, but the Soviet Union was late to the game and few soldiers had access to these rapid-fire weapons.

What frightened Kalashnikov and other Soviet soldiers was the German Maschinenpistole (MP40), also known as the Schmeisser after weapons designer Hugo Schmeisser. Hugo Schmeisser did not actually design the MP40, but he worked on the MP41, which was an MP40 outfitted with an old-fashioned wooden rifle stock. Like all submachine guns, it fired pistol-sized bullets—nine millimeters in diameter, the familiar 9mm of many contemporary pistols—instead of the larger, more powerful ammunition used in rifles. (Sometimes the distinctions between pistol and rifle rounds are not always clear cut because pistols can use large-sized rounds and rifles sometimes can use small-sized rounds. With some exceptions, however, rifle rounds are generally longer and heavier and contain more propellant, thus offering more "killing power.") This necessitated firing at close range to be effective, but the MP40 made up for this drawback by being lightweight, easy to handle, and able to stream bullets at an astonishing rate of 500 rounds per minute. The magazine, a device that automatically feeds ammunition into the gun, carried thirty-two bullets, or rounds in military parlance. The MP40 (with most small weapons, the number designates the year it was introduced or produced, 1940 in this case) also was shorter than a rifle and could be easily carried by airborne and tank soldiers. It was the first firearm of its kind to be made entirely of metal, with no wooden stock or handle grips, which made it almost indestructible. By 1945, the Germans had produced over a million of these, and it became so popular that even Allied soldiers preferred using these captured weapons instead of their own submachine guns, which were variations of the Thompson submachine gun, or "Tommy Gun," of 1920s gangster fame.

Indeed, the Soviet Union had a submachine gun, the PPD34/38, but it was poorly designed. Although it fired 800 rounds per minute, it was heavy and unreliable in combat. It was also too difficult to mass-produce. A much simpler weapon followed, the PPSh41, which was put into limited production in 1941 but not approved until the following year. The gun was popular with troops. However, it was not as well made as its German counterpart, because the Soviet Union's riveting and welding technology lagged far behind that of the Germans.

Upon his release from the hospital, Kalashnikov convinced friends at the railroad to allow him to work in their metal shop. With his left arm stiff and not fully recovered, he set about improving his motherland's submachine gun, because the war on the eastern front was still raging with no end in sight.

Hitler had made a strategic error that offered the Soviets some breathing room to develop weapons. Instead of sending all his troops directly to Moscow, an overconfident Führer rejected the advice of his generals and diverted one of his three armies south to occupy the Ukraine, which was rich in oil and gas resources. After more than a month on this distraction, Hitler was running out of time; the harsh Soviet winter was coming fast. Mud roads were becoming frozen slabs and his troops were not prepared for the frigid weather. By November, the Germans had reached within seventeen miles of the Kremlin, but could advance no further due to a Soviet counterattack aided by temperatures dropping to minus twenty-nine degrees Fahrenheit. German soldiers were not acclimated or dressed for the cold; many froze to death, and the survivors were exhausted. The Germans found themselves on the defensive for the first time.

With neither side able to extract a clear victory, the war continued, and so did Kalashnikov's work. Along with several others, he toiled for several months in the railroad shop, producing a submachine gun that he hoped would level the battlefield. His single goal was to protect the motherland. With the prototype under his arm, he made his way to Alma-Ata, where he attracted the attention of Communist Party and military officials who saw promise in this self-taught designer. Although they rejected his submachine gun, Kalashnikov garnered some important lessons. He learned that his weapon was too complex to perform under rigorous combat conditions. For example, the firing mechanism employed too many moving parts. The gun overall had many small parts, increasing the chance that if any single piece were to fail, the gun would be rendered inoperable. However, seeing a spark of genius in this young man, the authorities offered Kalashnikov the opportunity to hone his skills at a technical school, where he invented a carbine, a weapon that was popular because of its versatility.

A CARBINE IS SIMILAR to an ordinary rifle but with a shorter barrel and stock. It was originally developed for cavalry soldiers because they could not fire a full-sized rifle from horseback. Later, carbines were the logical choice for paratroopers and tank soldiers, because they were light and fit in tight quarters. Unlike submachine guns, which use pistol-sized rounds, carbines employ larger, rifle-type ammunition.

Many regular rifles, like the M1 Garand, the mainstay of U.S. troops during World War II, came in both full-length and carbine versions. In fact, Kalashnikov borrowed and modified for his own carbine the M1's method of feeding bullets from the magazine into the chamber for firing as well as the spent cartridge ejection system.

By this time, however, it was becoming clear to the German military, the Wehrmacht, that warfare was changing again and neither the submachine gun nor the carbine were the best infantry weapons. Submachine-gun ranges were too short and their bullets too light for combat that was now being fought at ranges between three hundred and one thousand feet, the result of battles taking place mainly in urban environments. Machine guns had the range and the killing power of larger bullets but were too heavy to carry in fast-moving combat situations. In addition, the massive recoil from machine guns jerked the weapon around, which made them difficult to keep on target. A new kind of weapon was needed that combined the light weight of the submachine gun with the range and killing power of a machine gun.

Unbeknownst to Kalashnikov and Soviet arms designers, the Germans were already working on just such a weapon, and the key to its success was not the gun but a new kind of ammunition.

In many instances, the arcane and minute design elements of ammunition are much more complex and controversial among ballistic engineers than the weapons that fire them. Changing a bullet's weight by a few grams, altering its shape from sharp-pointed to blunt, or using a few grains more or less of powder in the cartridge case can offer a soldier a vastly different fighting tool irrespective of the gun.

Ammunition is composed of several parts. The first is the bullet, the actual projectile. Bullets are usually made from a mixture of lead and tin, and most military bullets are jacketed with copper or steel to make them harder, the so-called full metal jacket round.

The bullet sits atop and within the cartridge case, held tightly in place by a crimp in the case. Brass is the metal of choice for the case because it is soft enough to crimp yet hard enough to keep its shape during the rapid firing and ejection process. The case actually stretches slightly as soon as it is subjected to pressure, sealing the breech, a process known as obturation. It retracts as soon as the pressure drops. Brass is also lightweight for its strength. Inside the case sits powder that ignites when the firing pin in the gun strikes the primer bottom at the center of the case—much like hitting an old-style match head—which then lights the powder. When the powder ignites, it propels the bullet out of the cartridge and through the barrel at supersonic speed.

German armament engineers in the 1930s began experimenting with an intermediate cartridge (often the word "cartridge" is used to signify the entire round—bullet plus cartridge case), sized between a pistol round and a rifle round, and they came up with a compromise in the PP Kurz (kurz means "short"), which was "7.92 × 33"—the bullet was 7.92 millimeters in diameter and the case holding it was 33 millimeters long.

Sometimes, ammunition is measured in America and Britain (which continue to resist the metric system) in inches instead of millimeters, and referred to as calibers. A caliber is one inch or 25.4 millimeters. To further complicate the nomenclature, caliber sizes are not always exact; a so-called .38 Police Special bullet is actually .357 inches, and a .44 Magnum of *Dirty Harry* fame is really .429 inches in diameter.

The new German round, thinner than a rifle round and thicker than a pistol round, was a vast departure from previous submachine-gun ammunition and opened up a world of new possibilities in rapid-firing guns that were light enough for an infantryman to carry, along with a large amount of ammunition, and easy to keep on target. As a bonus to designers, the less powerful rounds offered decreased wear and tear on rifle barrels and other components.

While the Soviets were still working on perfecting a submachine gun, German designers Hugo Schmeisser and Carl Walther, whose company produced James Bond's pistol of choice, the Walther PPK, were busy building competing prototype rifles employing the intermediate Kurz round. By 1942, they were testing the Maschinenkarabiner, or Mkb for short. As the name implied, it was a hybrid of a machine gun and a carbine, but Hitler did not like this idea at all. He was wedded to submachine guns despite their shortcomings, so in an effort to circumvent him the designers and their military supporters decided to rename it Maschinenpistole (MP), or submachine gun, which *was* on the Führer's "approved list" of weapons.

The Mkb42, or MP42, was field-tested against Soviet troops in the battle of Cholm in 1942. Cut off from conventional supply routes, a German army corps found itself encircled by the Soviets in Cholm on the Lovat River south of Leningrad. From February to April, German troops died daily from malnutrition and cold, until a cache of prototype Mkbs was airdropped. Using these new weapons, the Germans were able to blast their way through the Soviet lines and escape.

It is not recorded if the Soviets were able to capture one of these breakthrough weapons, but they were impressed by its performance, and so was Hitler, who finally admitted that these rifles outperformed submachine guns. Two years later, in 1944, in a face-saving move, he dramatically renamed the Mkb the Sturmgewehr, or assault rifle, offering the world a new class of automatic weapon and a name that endured. Had World War II continued, all German soldiers would have received this weapon as regular issue.

While this was transpiring, the Soviets had been working on their own medium-sized cartridge, the 7.62 × 39, also known as the M43 for the year it was approved by Josef Stalin, who, unlike Hitler, saw the need for a new type of ammunition and weapon to fire it. In the quest for a rifle to fire the new round, the government established a contest among designers. A who's who of venerable Soviet designers entered, including Alexei Sudayev and Sergei Simonov, people virtually unknown in the West but who were household names among Soviets, on a par with legends Samuel Colt and Smith & Wesson. There was also an unknown designer who humbly threw his hat in the ring, Mikhail Kalashnikov, now only in his twenties.

By the time Kalashnikov began work on a rifle to use the new cartridge, the war was winding down and his dream of being the one to produce a weapon to drive out the Germans was dashed. In addition, Sudayev, who won the contest, designed an automatic rifle with too many production shortcomings to be considered practical.

MANY MILITARY HISTORIANS miss the cruel irony of the automatic rifle story, in which the Soviets were their own worst enemy. Although the German Sturmgewehr was considered the world's first assault rifle, the concept had inadvertently been invented in Russia in 1916 by Vladimir Federov, an arms maker for the tsar. Federov's Avtomat ("automatic") employed an intermediate round favored by Japanese soldiers, whose smaller frames preferred the recoil of the less powerful ammunition. Federov's genius was to place the 6.5 × 50.5mm Arisaka round in his automatic rifle, but he did so because the commonly used larger rounds were too hard on the Avtomats and required heavier bolts, pistons, and other components. He and his contemporaries knew little of the battle-field imperatives that would later necessitate the intermediate round. He was simply trying to make his guns last longer.

Federov's brilliance was lost with the Russian Revolution of 1917, when his political beliefs landed him on the wrong side of the changing government. He even spent time in prison. More importantly, the officers in the field did not understand that this new weapon and round combination was the wave of the future. They still clung to the idea of a more powerful, longer-range ammunition and the mistaken belief that soldiers would always fight battles at long range. As the new regime cleaned house, it swept his work away and the Soviets went back to the old, larger round, which remained standard until 1943. Indeed, some arms historians argue that the Germans were familiar with Federov's early work and built their Kurz cartridge on his experience. Whatever the true story, the Soviets were now playing technologi-cal catch-up. But the ending of the war afforded them the luxury of more time. With the Third Reich beaten by the Allies and the U.S. military showing no interest in assault rifles, the postwar Soviets had a clear road ahead.

The U.S. military was oblivious to the weapons revolution playing out in Europe. As World War II was winding down, American ordnance experts sent back samples of the German Sturmgewehr for study by the Springfield Armory that produced the M1 Garand semiautomatic rifle, considered one of the finest weapons of its type. Unlike an automatic, which sprays bullets with one continuous pull of the trigger, the semiautomatic requires one trigger squeeze per round. Although U.S. forces had heard about the power of Germany's light automatic weapon, and now had them under the microscope, the upper echelon refused to acknowledge the innovation. Like the early Soviets, they believed in the higher-powered round shot long distances by a soldier/marksman. They continued to believe that the key to war was strategy, training, and high-tech weaponry. When they studied the Sturmgewehr, they could not get past the fact that these weapons were machine-stamped and welded, which in the United States was considered a second-class production method compared to machine milling and forging. They did not understand that Germany had taken stamping and welding to a high art, and that the weapons were lighter and just as rugged as guns with machined and forged parts. Armory personnel dismissed the weapons as flimsy and cheap-looking.

Although Kalashnikov had great natural instincts about weaponry, his lack of formal education put him at a disadvantage, so authorities teamed him with a small "collective" to help refine his ideas. In addition, he believed in what we would call today a "focus" group, listening to soldiers who actually fired the weapons and then offered their opinions. Using soldiers' feedback, the weapon was changed and refined.

The young man's success also lay in his ability to take the best ideas available from other gun makers, then combine and refine them. For example, submachine guns of the day relied on a "blow-back" system that used the power of gases shooting backward from the bullet to push back a bolt that ejected the spent cartridge and allowed a fresh one from the magazine to emerge into the chamber for firing. This system worked fine for pistol-sized bullets but not for the intermediate bullet. These new rounds were too powerful, requiring a massive bolt to control them, making for a much heavier gun. Kalashnikov realized this and opted for a gas-activated automatic weapon that used a "short stroke" piston to push back the bolt and eject and load another round. The piston offered the extra power necessary to move the heavier bolt. Although it may sound complicated, the system was actually simple in the world of arms makers.

When a cartridge's primer is struck with a firing pin, the exploding powder creates gases that propel the bullet out at speeds greater than twenty-three hundred feet per second. As the bullet travels through the barrel, gases build up behind it but cannot escape because the spent cartridge is sealing one end and the bullet, traveling tight against the barrel walls, is blocking the other end.

The M-1 does _MY_ talking!

...with _your_ cartridges

U.S. ARMY OFFICIAL POSTER

The M1, or Garand, as it was known for its designer, John Garand, performed flawlessly during World War II, prompting General George Patton to call it "the greatest battle implement ever devised." It was simple and reliable and the first self-loading rifle to be adopted by any army as standard issue. Unfortunately, the rifle was heavy, clunky, and only held eight rounds in its magazine. While Germany and the Soviet Union were moving toward automatic weapons, U.S. military planners clung to old ideas that put GIs in greater jeopardy with their outmoded rifles. *U.S. Department of Defense*

As the bullet nears the mouth of the barrel, a vent in the barrel diverts some of these gases into a tube that sits parallel above or below it. The gases hit a piston inside the tube, which pushes a connecting rod into the bolt carrier, forcing it backward. The bolt carrier extracts the spent cartridge from the breech and ejects it, allowing the next round to enter the chamber from the magazine, where ammunition is pushed upward by constant pressure from a spring. The signature banana-shaped magazine is a function of how the cartridges lie when placed side by side. Because they are narrower at one end, the natural and most economical shape of a thirty-round stack of 7.92mm rounds is a curve.

Every time the trigger is pulled, the firing pin strikes the primer in the center of a cartridge, firing a bullet, and the cycle continues. This happens at a rate of more than 600 rounds per minute when the selector lever is in the automatic position.

Because their fast-moving parts are confined in such a small space, automatic rifles have a tendency to jam. All it takes is a speck of dirt to clog the various movements or keep a round from being positioned properly in the firing chamber. This is where Kalashnikov shined. The bolt rotated widely, making it easy for the round to find its proper place in the chamber. Think of trying to poke a pencil into a hole drilled in a piece of wood. It would be much easier if, when you got the pencil tip near the hole, even slightly askew, you rotated it. This turning action would slide the pencil in much easier than if you just poked it straight. This is one of the best parts of Kalashnikov's design.

In addition, rather than build components that fit tightly into each other, often a signature of professional gun makers, Kalash-nikov went the other way, designing components with looser tol-erances, more space between parts. Instead of dirt or sand clogging the gun, debris was thrown off in the firing process. During one test, soldiers dragged the gun through what was called the "sand baths." Each rifle groove and slot was clogged with sand. "I began to doubt that further shooting would proceed without failures," Kalashnikov recalled. An engineer watching the test voiced similar concerns. But the gun fired flawlessly. "The sand is flying in all directions, like a dog shaking off water," a team member shouted.

AK PROTOTYPES WERE constantly honed and field-tested, each part altered based on soldier feedback. Unlike with many inventions, there were no Aha! moments in Kalashnikov's work, only constant incremental improvement until it was soldier-proof. For example, the safety switch, which prevented the gun from accidentally firing, was combined into a single lever that also acts as a dust cover for the ejection port. In other words, a soldier who put his weapon on "safe" to slog through mud without inadvertently firing the weapon, did not also have to remember to close an additional latch to keep dirt out. Again, this was not a new idea—it existed on the Remington Model 8, one of the earliest American semiautomatic rifles, first produced in 1906—but it was Kalashnikov's cleverness and humbleness that allowed it to be employed in a Soviet weapon. Kalashnikov did not subscribe to the "it wasn't invented here" syndrome that plagued many other gun makers, and he wasn't interested in producing a unique or profound piece of machinery. His only goal was to build a weapon that would work every time. He cared even less how it looked. While other designers sought to make their guns sleek and contemporary-looking, Kalashnikov dismissed this as window dressing and very anti-Soviet, which promoted utility over style.

During these testing years, Kalashnikov often found himself guided by the words of arms designer Georgy Shpagin, who developed the successful PPSh41 submachine gun: "Complexity is easy; simplicity is difficult."

Kalashnikov's gun also had to be easy and inexpensive to manufacture with current technology and capabilities. Again, he learned from the mistakes of Federov's Avtomat, which could not be built rapidly or easily, drawbacks that sank it. Although milled or forged components were generally stronger, they were also more time-consuming and expensive to make. Kalashnikov's prototype weapon would have a stamped receiver, the gun's main frame.

After scores of modifications and adjustments, the new weapon was approved for production in 1947 with the name AK-47 (Avtomat Kalashnikova 1947), but work continued for several more years to improve the weapon before it would be officially issued to the Soviet army.

The AK-47 underwent more than a hundred modifications between 1947 and 1949. During that time, Kalashnikov had moved to Izhevsk Motor Plant 524, partially to get out of the shadow of more prominent designers who looked down upon the lowly sergeant who had moved up too fast and had not paid his dues with the obligatory decades of work. Izhevsk Motor Plant 524 was not an automotive plant but a front for an arms factory, the name designed to keep away Western spies now that the Communist satellite countries were established. Stalin's blockade of Berlin had begun and the cold war was in full swing.

By the end of 1949, arms plants had turned out about eighty thousand AK-47s, but one major modification was necessary before it could be issued to all Soviet troops and their allies. Soviet metals technology still lagged and assembly plants could not manufacture stamped receivers in large numbers. Because Kalashnikov was not versed in production techniques, the job fell to other engineers, who changed the AK assembly lines to produce forged receivers. This made the gun heavier and more expensive to produce, but there was no choice. In gearing up for the cold war, these weapons had to be made quickly.

The AK was the ideal weapon for the Soviet Union, and the nation's leaders built military and political doctrine around it. In the early days of the cold war, Soviet military planners believed that large land battles would take place between East and West on Russia's western border similar to those of World War II. Soviet authorities envisioned the so-called encounter battle in which Soviet troops would meet the enemy head-on at various pinch points. Believing that they had the more maneuverable tanks and

This AKM ("AK Modernized") introduced in the 1950s is a simplified, lighter version of the original AK-47, the world's most devastating weapon. Its banana-shaped magazine gives this gun a familiar silhouette that makes it the symbol of what an assault weapon should look like. It is the undisputed firearm of choice for at least 50 legitimate standing armies, along with untold numbers of disenfranchised fighting forces ranging from international insurgents and terrorists to domestic drug dealers and street gangs. Between 75 and 100 million have been produced. The vast majority of AK-47s in service around the world are actually AKM models. *U.S. Department of Defense.*

armored vehicles, the Soviets would attack the oncoming columns from the flanks, with infantrymen delivering thousands of rounds per minute. They would penetrate into enemy lines and overwhelm them similar to the blitzkrieg strategy. This type of close-quarter, massive infantry assault was the AK's forte, especially in the hands of a typical Soviet soldier.

The Soviet Union had a huge conscript army of poorly trained soldiers, many of whom could not read or write, and those that could often spoke diverse languages from the various Soviet states. This made standardized training difficult. Again, the AK suited the Soviet army because it was easy to fire, did not require a written manual or training, and rarely broke down.

In contrast to the U.S. military, which prided itself on having a pool of well-trained troops taught to make every shot count through intensive training and practice, the AK allowed the Soviets to put thousands of men into service quickly and with a respectable chance of killing the enemy. Because the AK employed an intermediate round, with less recoil than larger rounds, it allowed even inexperienced soldiers to control its accuracy during multiple bursts.

The Soviet military worked hard to keep the existence of the AK hidden from the West. Soldiers issued AKs carried them in special pouches that hid their shape. They were also instructed to pick up spent cartridges after maneuvers to keep the new ammunition secret.

Military and other official accounts differ on when the West learned of this deadly new weapon. Although the Soviets supplied arms to North Korea during the Korean conflict, it is not clear if they offered any AKs. U.S. Army historians make no mention of GIs seeing the weapon, and many Soviet records from the time are unavailable. Certainly, the Chinese, who supported the North Koreans with weapons and funds, would have welcomed the gun. Stalin was pleased to see China turn Communist in 1949 under Mao Tse-tung, and Mao's brutal vision of war was eerily made to order for the AK. The Maoist strategy called for massive numbers of citizen soldiers armed with simple weapons to engage a technologically superior army in guerrilla and large-scale attacks. Sheer numbers, Mao believed, could win against any army no matter how sophisticated its weaponry. Even though the Soviet Union and Communist China chose different military tactics, they both benefited from the AK's characteristics. China's tactics were put into practice in Korea when U.S. and UN–sanctioned forces faced hordes of Chinese soldiers in many battles, leaving both sides with massive casualties. In 1953, after three years of brutal fighting and millions of dead, the hostilities ceased with a shaky armistice on the 38th parallel that continues today.

In 1956, events in Eastern Europe forced the Soviet Union to unveil the AK in public. The tumult began on October 23 with a peaceful demonstration by students in Budapest, Hungary, who demanded an end to Soviet occupation and the implementation of "true socialism." The police made some arrests and tried to disperse the demonstrators with tear gas, but the crowds grew larger and more vocal. When the students attempted to free people who had been arrested, the police opened fire on the crowd. Within days, soldiers, government workers, and even police officials had joined the students.

Nikita Khrushchev, now leader of the Soviet Union, grew increasingly concerned about the situation and dispatched the Red Army to Hungary. They rode in tanks and in trucks, carrying their AKs. The demonstrators fought with whatever weaponry they could find, including Russian submachine guns, carbines, single-shot rifles, and grenades, much of it taken from liberated military depots. This was the Soviets' first large-scale use of the AK, and it performed flawlessly in an urban environment where tanks became bogged down in narrow streets against crowds wielding Molotov cocktails. The revolt was squelched, with as many as fifty thousand Hungarians and about seven thousand Soviet soldiers killed.

According to U.S. Army archives, American intelligence officers took note of the AK but appeared not to be concerned. When the Springfield Armory, the U.S. military's weapons maker since 1794, tested the Soviet weapon that year, they too appeared indifferent. It would not be until a decade later during the Vietnam War that American GIs would face the AK in action for the first time. These soldiers would pay dearly for their government's abject failure to recognize the far-reaching significance of Kalashnikov's simple weapon.

A Reputation Born
in the Rice Paddies

B Y THE LATE 1950s, the Soviet Union was employing the AK
as a key component of its strategy to spread Communism
throughout the world. In these early years of the cold war,
both the Soviet Union and the United States tried to curry favor
with undeveloped and uncommitted countries through sales and
gifts of arms. Compared to the United States' offerings of the M1
and later the M-14, the AK proved vastly superior.

Because of the AK's ruggedness, it was well suited to severe
environmental conditions and the lack of local gun repair facilities
in poorer countries. In addition, because the AK was designed
with a lot of play and looser tolerances—in the piston head, for
example—it could fire ammunition with wide variations, including cheap knockoff cartridges produced locally or ammunition
that had deteriorated in humid, jungle-like conditions, without
misfiring or jamming.

The AK quickly became the weapon of choice among ragtag
Communist-inspired rebel groups, especially in Africa and East
Asia, where a backdoor route often was used. These groups were

supplied by Soviet bloc countries instead of the Soviet Union to avoid direct confrontation between the world's superpowers. The weapons also were affordable enough for money-strapped third world nations who could save face by paying for the arms themselves.

To further distribute the rifle, the Soviets offered technical expertise to build the AK as a so-called Gift to Fraternal Countries. These "fraternal countries" included Soviet bloc nations such as Bulgaria and East Germany, which began producing their own AKs in 1959, and Hungary, which had begun a year earlier. China and Poland got an early start with production in 1956, North Korea started in 1958, and Yugoslavia in 1964. The Soviets allowed wholesale production of AK without payments or licensing fees. The guns were easy and cheap to produce in large numbers, further extending its distribution.

For the most part, the Soviet Union and Soviet bloc countries were now producing an improved version of the AK called the AKM, which stood for AK Modernized. This rifle and subsequent improvements continued to be known by many people by the original AK-47 moniker. Most firearms experts today call the rifle and its many iterations the AK no matter what model they're talking about.

The Soviet Union had finally geared itself for up-to-date sheet metal production technology, and the AKM was able to shed almost three pounds from the earlier milled version. This weight loss gave the gun an even greater cachet. Kalashnikov and his team also added a new trigger assembly component that increased the "cyclic rate" during automatic fire, meaning that less time elapsed between rounds, offering greater accuracy to inexperienced shooters.

Unlike the Germans and the Soviets, U.S. ordnance experts did not embrace the superiority of the intermediate round for modern combat. The bureaucracy was still wedded to the larger round, in this case the standard .30-06 cartridge (usually pronounced "thirty-aught-six") that was used in the M1 Garand, the army's standard issue. This view was not universally accepted, and there were intermediate-round boosters within the military establishment, but these voices were crushed by those with a vested interest in maintaining the status quo, partially because of inertia and partly because of a cozy relationship between the government and the Springfield Armory, which had held a near-monopoly position on production of the M1 since the 1930s.

Historians looking back on this often are struck by the irony that the Soviet system, so bogged down in bureaucracy, was able to move ahead in the weapons area while the United States, with its history of technological innovation, lagged behind because of entrenched financial arrangements.

The M1, or Garand, as it was known for its designer John Garand, performed flawlessly during World War II, prompting General George Patton to call it "the greatest battle implement ever devised." The M1 was simple and reliable and the first self-loading rifle to be adopted by any army as standard issue. Warfare was changing, however, and the M1 was falling behind. The rifle was heavy, clunky, and held only eight rounds in its magazine. Most important, it was not an automatic weapon.

Despite the growing evidence against the .30-caliber round, the Springfield Armory's position and that of the army remained steadfast. This was seen most dramatically during the waning years of World War II when the army had begun working, albeit halfheartedly, on an automatic weapon. But the project was doomed before it got off the ground, because instead of seeking new designs and new ammunition as the Germans had done with the Sturmgewehr or the Soviets with their AK, the Ordnance Department insisted that it employ .30-caliber ammunition, which was too heavy for automatic firing by a lightweight gun. They insisted on a design criteria that disregarded the laws of mechanics. Other resistance to an automatic weapon came from military corners that saw automatic weapons as a waste of ammunition, insisting that U.S. soldiers firing large-caliber single shots carefully from long distances was in the best tradition of the U.S. military.

Still others refused a radical new design because they wanted a weapon that could be built using M1 machinery. In reality, they wanted an improved and automatic version of the M1, an impossible task.

One of the champions of the .30 caliber was Colonel Rene Studler, who had worked his way up the military ladder to chief of the Small Arms Research and Development Division of the U.S. Ordnance Department. Studler had enjoyed an exemplary career, with a string of successes including the M1 steel helmet, the M3 submachine gun, and the Williams M1 Carbine. If anyone could get the bureaucracy moving on an automatic weapon, Studler was the man.

While work was under way, international politics entered. With the formation of the North Atlantic Treaty Organization (NATO) after World War II, there was a desire for a uniform weapon and ammunition that could be used by all signatories, including the United States. The European NATO nations believed that the day of intermediate rounds had come, and their struggle with the United States for a smaller standardized round left the world of reason and entered the realm of nationalism. With the United States being the most powerful nation in the world, and the force that had defeated the Axis powers, the Europeans faced an uphill fight. The large round became the cause célebrè for the Americans and a point upon which they seemed unwilling to yield.

British thinking on the subject of cartridge design, however, was very advanced. British designers had been experimenting with a still smaller round, the .276 caliber, as far back as 1924. Because of their light weight, small bullets like the .276 and even the .22 caliber—the kind used by weekend critter hunters—could be propelled at such high speeds that they extensively destroyed body tissue through a process known as hydrostatic shock. The argument seemed counterintuitive to many who just assumed that a larger bullet would do more damage, but in fact a smaller, higher-velocity bullet contains so much kinetic energy—because less energy is spent propelling its small weight through the air—that once stopped inside an enemy's body, all its pent-up energy is immediately discharged to destroy surrounding tissue and vital organs. These were not just ballistic theories. So-called Pig Boards, tests in which pigs, whose anatomy resembles that of humans, were shot with small-caliber bullets propelled by high-powered cartridges, proved the devastating power of small-caliber weapons.

If the U.S. military was unwilling to budge from the .30-caliber cartridge, the chances of accepting an even smaller round, let alone an intermediate round, were nil. The fight that followed almost split NATO apart only a year after the pact was signed. After witnessing comparative test firings of a Belgian FAL rifle, their own EM-2—both using a .280 cartridge—and the T-25, a modified M1 firing half-inch-shorter .30-caliber bullets, the British contingent returned home from the United States and announced they were going with a .280 round and their EM-2. To hell with the Americans and their .30-caliber weapon. To hell with NATO. The United States held fast to the obsolete .30-caliber round and, in effect, offered no concessions to its European counterparts as far as ammunition was concerned. Purists noted that although the caliber was called .30, it was not a .30-06 but a 7.62 × 51mm, also known as the .308 Winchester round. The .30-06 was in actuality 7.62 × 63mm.

You might think that the public would not have cared about these seemingly small differences, but the argument captured the attention and ire of the British public, who, somewhat remarkably, understood enough of the fine points of the ammunition fiasco to be peeved. Passionate arguments in Parliament split the country. One side wanted Britain to go it alone without the United States or NATO and produce their rifle with the small round. The other side believed that a unified NATO was the country's best defense against a growing Soviet threat and that giving in to U.S. demands was the best course.

The fight lingered for years with neither the Americans nor the British giving way. Finally, further tests in 1952 showed that the T-44, the latest incarnation of the M1, and the FAL were both viable NATO weapons, a conclusion that satisfied both parties' egos. With the Canadians as intermediaries, an agreement in 1953 between Prime Minster Winston Churchill and President Truman meant that the British would accept the U.S. 30-caliber cartridge (7.62 × 51mm) if the United States would accept the Belgian FAL as the NATO standard. U.S. bullets and Belgian guns. Even the popular press noted this important moment, as *Newsweek* declared in its July 20, 1953, edition that that FN-FAL (the full name was Fabrique Nationale–Fusil Automatique Léger, or Light Automatic Rifle) would be the new NATO assault rifle and therefore the one to be used by U.S. troops.

But the Americans did not keep their promise. Colonel Studler, who was willing to admit defeat of the American-made weapon, retired from the army. He was replaced by his subordinate, Fred Carten, a former major in the Ordnance Corps, who was unwilling to allow the non-U.S. entry to become the rifle of the American army. Under his watch, a last-ditch effort to discredit the FAL took place. With little notice, both weapons were sent to Alaska for testing under frigid conditions. Carten and others hoped that the FAL would fail, and they did everything to move results in that direction.

The Springfield Armory staffers went into overdrive, winterizing T44 components to survive the cold conditions. They even developed a winter trigger that could be pulled by soldiers wearing army-issued mittens. In early tests, the T-44 beat the FN-FAL in subzero temperatures, but neither performed as well as the AK. During sand and mud trials, where the AK shone, the FAL failed miserably because of its tight tolerances. The T-44 performed marginally better. By this time, however, pressure from Britain, West Germany, and, of course, Belgium, was mounting for the United States to keep its agreement and make the FAL the chosen NATO weapon. Arms makers in these countries had already modified the rifle to accept the outmoded .30-caliber round as agreed, and they wanted closure.

Officially, further tests showed that both weapons performed equally well, although the Europeans claimed that the tests were skewed in favor of the American rifle. They could not prove it, and accusations were lodged by both sides. A final decision was delayed several more times as it was passed around like a hot potato by various U.S. military departments. Finally, Chief of Staff General Matthew B. Ridgway reneged on the agreement with NATO allies and gave the order that the T-44, soon to be renamed the M-14, would be the official rifle of the U.S. Army. Considering Ridgway's past actions, this should not have come as a surprise to anyone, especially the Europeans.

Ridgway was a World War II hero who had helped to plan the airborne operation of D-Day, even jumping with his troops of the 82nd Airborne. In 1952, he had replaced General Dwight D. Eisenhower as the Supreme Allied Commander of Europe, but instead of building relationships with other NATO nations, he had decided to surround himself with American staff instead of a mix of European and U.S. personnel. This upset European military leaders, and Ridgway was called back to the States to replace General Joe L. Collins as chief of staff of the U.S. Army.

The final decision was based on money, nationalism, and the belief that the government's relationship with the Springfield Armory, which dated back to 1795 when it first produced flintlock muskets, should be maintained despite its detrimental effect on America's credibility with its European allies.

The FAL and its successors went on to be adopted by Britain, Belgium, Canada, and other NATO nations—all except the United States—which added an unnecessary layer of difficulty to joint maneuvers. The rifle had been adopted by the armies of more than ninety non-Communist nations, more countries than even the AK, although only about three million FALs have been produced compared to almost one hundred million Kalashnikovs. Because of its widespread use among democracies, the FAL is often dubbed the "free world's rifle" or "free world's right arm."

After more than twenty years and $100 million, the army in

1957 ended up with a rifle vastly inferior to the AK and one that was just only incrementally better than the M1. Although the goal was to produce an automatic rifle, the M-14 and its large cartridge were uncontrollable in automatic mode. It could only be used in the semiautomatic position. In fact, some opponents complained that the army used ringers to fire the M-14 during testing. These specially trained marksmen could keep the gun on target although ordinary soldiers could not.

During this protracted battle, another was taking place on the other side of the world, setting the stage for the first confrontation between the AK and the M-14, a showdown that would pit against each other the best infantry weapons of the world's superpowers.

IN MAY 1954, THE FRENCH army surrendered at the battle of Dien Bien Phu, ending almost eight years of fighting between France, which was trying to retain control of French Indochina, and the Viet Minh, led by Communist leader Ho Chi Minh. After fifty-six days of brutal fighting, the French defenders, low on ammunition, food, and medical supplies, gave up to the guerrillas, who had received direct military help from China and other Communist groups from Laos and Cambodia (now Kampuchea). Under an international agreement, the Viet Minh established the Democratic Republic of Vietnam (North Vietnam) north of the 17th parallel, and the Republic of Vietnam (South Vietnam) was established in the south.

The United States had financially and politically supported the French presence (although it refused direct intervention at Dien Bien Phu) and was gearing up to support the South Vietnamese directly with money and arms to keep it from falling into Communist hands. It was believed by many in the West that if the nations of Southeast Asia turned Communist, the Soviet doctrine would spread country by country throughout the region, even to Australia and New Zealand, until the United States would be fighting Communism on its doorstep. This became known as the domino theory, posited in a 1954 press conference by President Eisenhower in which he stated, "You have a row of dominoes set up; you knock over the first one, and what will happen to the last one is that it will go over very quickly."

Pentagon planners knew they soon would be called on to participate in a proxy war with the Soviets. A direct confrontation between the superpowers could lead to nuclear annihilation, so the only alternative was for the two sides to fight through third-party nations. That nation would be Vietnam. The fighting would use only conventional weapons in an effort to win the hearts and minds of the population into choosing democracy over Communism. Some military historians view the cold war period as one in which warfare changed from the act of beating the enemy, grabbing territory, or taking over a government to one in which arms were employed as an instrument of ideological change. If the West could win militarily in smaller countries, like Vietnam, the populace would choose democracy over Communism once they were allowed to vote in free elections shielded from outside influences such as Communist guerrillas. Other countries would follow, and the domino theory would be reversed.

The main problem with this plan was that the United States did not have an infantry weapon that could stand up to the AK, especially in close-proximity jungle combat. During the French Indochina War (the First Indochina War in some circles), the Viet Minh fought with Soviet SKS rifles and the PPSh41 submachine gun. If they were to fight anew against the West, which now was becoming a certainty, they surely would be armed with newer AKs supplied by China and other Soviet bloc nations.

The U.S. military was stuck. The M-14 was inferior to the AK, but for all practical purposes nothing else was in the hopper— nothing except for a proposed but discredited rifle so radical and sleek in its design that it resembled a child's shiny plastic toy gun. Military testers even called it the "Mattel toy." Unlike the seemingly clumsily made but deadly AK or the solid, you-can-use-it-as-a-club M1 rifle, this new entry sported a 1940s art deco–like sleek profile, a science fictionesque black body, and it weighed two pounds less than the AK or M1.

Aside from its radical appearance, this new rifle was built by a firm outside the closed circle of government-connected small-arms developers—a company with no small-arms experience to boot.

The genius behind this bizarre infantry weapon was Eugene M. Stoner. He was born on November 22, 1922, in Gasport, Indiana, and, like Kalashnikov, had no formal engineering education. He never graduated college. During World War II, Stoner served as an aerial ordnance specialist with the Marine Corps, mainly in the South Pacific and northern China.

Also like Kalashnikov, Stoner had an innate sense about firearm design and mechanics and considered guns and shooting a hobby. He too was a curious tinkerer. His vocation was aircraft, however, and he had worked at several aircraft companies, including Vega Aircraft, which was later absorbed by Lockheed. In 1954, Stoner found a job at aircraft maker Fairchild, headquartered in Hagerstown, Maryland, about sixty miles north of Washington, D.C. A year earlier, the company's president, Richard S. Boutelle, had decided that Fairchild should diversify from its core aircraft business. The 1950s were a time when many tough and lightweight materials had become newly available to the market, and he wanted to exploit them. Nonferrous materials such as aluminum were being used in aircraft because of their high strength and low weight, in addition to a new crop of plastic products and fiberglass that were also very strong for their weight. The company had gained expertise in working with these new materials and believed there was money to be made outside of aircraft fabrication.

The company decided to target small arms. Studying the terrain, they realized that the small-arms business in the United States was woefully behind the times. After all, the army had not introduced a new weapon since the M1 in the 1930s. Company engineer George Sullivan was convinced that space-age materials, especially plastics and fiberglass, could be incorporated into rifles instead of the traditional wood and steel, offering battlefield toughness with light weight. As he discussed this with Boutelle, they became more excited about the possibility of producing a thoroughly modern weapon using the latest materials technology. The two men were convinced they had a winning idea, and this is where Stoner came in. As chief engineer, his job was to design such a rifle under the company's newly established division known as ArmaLite, an appropriate name considering the company's mission.

Working in the company's Costa Mesa, California, laboratory, Stoner produced the AR-10, a lightweight rifle that surprised yet intrigued military personnel because it was like nothing they had ever seen. It fired the 7.62 × 51mm round that the army had insisted upon, but, being outsiders, ArmaLite overall received a frosty reception by Ordnance. Their timing also was poor, as the Ordnance bureaucracy was knee-deep protecting the M-14 against the foreign-made FAL and had little time for another rifle entry, especially one with such an outlandish design. Boutelle and his team persevered, however, and resistance among a few military leaders melted as they continued to test and modify the weapon. One person in particular, General Willard G. Wyman, commander of Continental Army Command, was particularly impressed. Wyman, who had been the commanding general of IX Corps in Korea, understood the lessons of that war and knew that U.S. infantrymen needed an automatic weapon that would not kick like a mule. Clearly, he was not a fan of the Ordnance Department, the M-14, or the 7.62 × 51mm bullet. If he and Stoner worked together, they could help each other.

Wyman asked Stoner to redesign the AR-10 to accept a smaller bullet that could be shot at high velocity. Both men knew they were up against the AK, which had set the standard for assault rifles. They were also up against the Ordnance bureaucracy, which had already fought successfully against an intermediate round and would surely contest an even smaller round.

Undeterred, Wyman gave Stoner his requirements. He wanted

a rifle that could fire in automatic or semiautomatic mode, a magazine that could contain twenty rounds, and a weapon that would
be lightweight, about six pounds. The bullet had to maintain a flat
trajectory like the .30-caliber round. The small projectile had to
pierce body armor as well as both sides of a standard army helmet
and a .135-inch steel plate at five hundred meters. This was a wise
move by Wyman both militarily and politically. The distance
requirements he set were beyond those suggested by reports out of
Korea about the more compact theater of combat. In this way, he
probably hoped to make the new gun more palatable to those who
opposed the smaller round on the basis of range.

Stoner had his work cut out for him. Like Kalashnikov, he
designed his weapon to fire a specific bullet, but unlike his Soviet
counterpart, he had to build his special bullet first. A .22-caliber
military round simply did not exist, so Stoner modified a commercial .222-caliber cartridge from the Remington Arms Company,
which they made to order in large numbers for his experiments.
The AR-15, as the improved weapon was named, had the same
space-age look of the AR-10, and with twenty-five rounds it
weighed a little over six pounds. Military testers at Fort Benning,
the home of the infantry, liked the AR-15's light weight and high
power. It was a truly innovative weapon, and in test firings the rate
of malfunctions clocked in at 6.1 per thousand rounds, compared
to 16 per thousand for the M-14. The Ordnance people, however,
whose stock was getting lower by the minute among military
brass, were embarrassed by the AR-15's stellar performance. They
had spent decades coming up with a new infantry rifle, and this
outside group, working only a few years, offered a better weapon
than the M-14 on all counts.

Stoner's weapon had a gas tube above the barrel similar to the
AK, but with a major difference. Instead of the gases pushing back
a piston attached to a long rod, they traveled the length of the tube
into the bolt carrier mechanism, forcing the bolt carrier to the rear,
which rotated the bolt via a cam, unlocking the breech mechanism
and forcing the bolt and bolt carrier back. This eliminated the gas

piston, and getting rid of a part is always a plus for a weapon. However, this gas system had a major flaw. Because it blew gas back into the receiver, it was prone to fouling, a trait that would not become apparent until the Vietnam War. Fouling occurs when the sticky residue of hot gases, burned powder, and microscopic particles of cartridge cases get stuck in rifle parts, literally "gumming up the works" and jamming the weapon.

Also like Kalashnikov, Stoner took ideas from previously built guns, like the FN-FAL and even the MP44 Sturmgewehr, from which he borrowed the hinged dust cover over the cartridge ejection port.

The AR-15 still needed work, especially in dealing with barrel ruptures due to water intrusion. Stoner claimed the problem was not as bad as the Ordnance people had suggested, even going so far as to imply that the tests had been rigged to eliminate the weapon. Because ArmaLite had a very small engineering staff, the weapon was at the mercy of Ordnance personnel and their technical recommendations, and they had every reason to discredit the weapon and offer Stoner bad advice.

As tensions continued to rise between Stoner and Carten, Ordnance sent three of the fifteen AR-15s they had been testing to Alaska for firing under extremely cold conditions. Without notifying Stoner, they sent rifles to Fort Greeley. This move was particularly provocative, because Stoner said he had an agreement with Ordnance that he be called on site whenever testing took place so he could answer questions and make sure that the gun was being used correctly. This was standard procedure for most new weapons, especially for a radically designed weapon like the AR-15, a gun with which shooters were not familiar.

Stoner would not have known about the Arctic tests except that he had received an unexpected request for spare parts. He flew to Alaska and was shocked by the conditions of his guns. The front sights on some had been removed and others were loosened, which prevented accurate firing. Some weapons had jerry-rigged parts welded or otherwise loosely attached to them. Stoner fixed the rifles but was furious. He believed that Ordnance was trying to discredit the AR-15 to make the M-14 look better. Many years later, he said publicly, "My opinion is that they had to get the M-14 into production to feed the Springfield Armory. They touted the M-14 as the answer to the M-1, the M-1 carbine, the grease gun [M3 submachine gun], the Browning Automatic Rifle [machine gun], but everyone in the business knew that it would only take the place of the M1." He continued, "Hardly anyone could handle it. . . . The commanding officer [in Alaska] said to me 'I can't wait to get your ass off this base. Please leave.'"

Stoner filed a grievance demanding that his repaired rifles be retested, but no retest took place.

By this time, even some of the army brass were catching on to Ordnance's egregious behavior, but they also were in need of an officially tested weapon, and the M-14, on the record at least, was still in the lead. Also, Ordnance still enjoyed political and bureaucratic clout and maintained a coterie of high-level military backers. Carten dug in his heels even deeper. After all, if he were to admit that the small-caliber AR-15 was superior to the M-14, not only would he be losing the rifle argument but also the large-caliber argument upon which he had based his career. In a last-ditch effort to sink the AR-15 Carten suggested that the AR-15 barrel be changed to accommodate a .258 round, reasoning that a round slightly larger than a .22 caliber might solve the rainwater problem in the barrel by giving it a greater diameter.

One problem: a .258-caliber bullet did not exist. So Stoner, naively, waited for Ordnance to ship him some prototypes so he could redesign the AR-15 for it. After several months of waiting, he traveled to Washington only to learn that Ordnance had dropped the .258-caliber program but had not told him or anyone at ArmaLite. By that time, Carten had issued contracts for M-14 production.

In 1959, full-scale production of the M-14 began, backed by the power of General Maxwell Taylor, army chief of staff, a die-hard large-caliber supporter who did not like the idea of the infantry using smaller-caliber bullets. Moreover, he, like other U.S. generals, would lose face with NATO allies if they were to switch to a smaller caliber after rejecting NATO's smaller bullet and shoving the larger one down their throats. Stoner and ArmaLite looked beaten. Even though they had the superior weapon, they were no match for cutthroat moves by the Ordnance Corps. The company was out $1.45 million and their only hope was to find private sales for the AR-15. First, they had to stave off bankruptcy. Eventually they found an angel in Colt's Patent Firearms Manufacturing, which agreed to buy the rights to the AR-15, with ArmaLite retaining some royalties.

COLT HAD A LARGE PROFILE in the world of small arms, with a strong global reputation. Stoner and salesperson Bobby Macdonald joined forces and took the AR-15 on the road, focusing on Southeast Asia, a territory that Macdonald knew well. They learned that the smaller-stature Asian military preferred the lighter weapon with little recoil, but sales still eluded them. It appeared to Macdonald and Stoner that the fix was in again, as foreign military leaders said they had signed agreements with the United States to buy only officially issued weapons and the AR-15 was not an acceptable purchase.

Their luck turned, however, during an Independence Day picnic at Boutelle's farm outside Hagerstown. He invited an old friend, General Curtis LeMay, air force chief of staff, who was widely known and revered as the father of the Strategic Air Command. He had also taken charge of the Berlin Airlift after the Soviet Union had isolated the city, a move that signaled the beginning of the cold war. Known for his extreme right-wing political views, "Bombs Away" LeMay, as he was dubbed, made no secret of his desire to drop atomic bombs anywhere to achieve a political goal. Years later, during a 1968 press conference, while running for vice president along with self-proclaimed segregationist former Alabama governor George Wallace, he stated to the shock and horror of many around the world, "We seem to have a phobia about nuclear weapons. . . . If I found it necessary, I would use anything we could dream up—anything that we could dream up—including nuclear weapons, if it was necessary." So excessive was his warmongering persona that filmmaker Stanley Kubrick satirized him in the 1964 hit film *Dr. Strangelove* as General Buck Turgidson (played by George C. Scott), the trigger-happy, nuclear bomb–loving top gun who nonchalantly advocated blowing the Soviet Union to smithereens despite the human cost.

It was this outrageous figure who would grab the AR-15 from the scrap heap to become the army's legendary M-16, the AK's main rival in the Vietnam War.

Boutelle's farm was a shooter's paradise, with skeet and trap fields, pistol ranges, and archery lanes. He had set up three watermelons at 50, 100, and 150 yards and gave LeMay an AR-15. LeMay hit the melons at 50 and 150 yards, and they exploded as if someone had inserted cherry bombs. (He and the others ate the third watermelon.) The AR-15's performance so impressed LeMay that he invited Colt officials to the Air Force Academy to discuss buying the rifles, and he ordered them to replace the M1 carbine for use by base security personnel. LeMay had cleverly circumvented the system by replacing not the M-14 but a different rifle, and Ordnance could not do a thing about it. At the same time, Colt executives were raising awareness on Capitol Hill about how poorly Ordnance had treated their weapon during testing and what a mess they had made with the M-14. Newspapers were beginning to publish stories about the debacle.

Now, for the first time, Ordnance's activities were out in the open, and further test firing of the AR-15 took place, with high-ranking brass, including the cigar-chomping LeMay, observing. The AR-15 put in a superb performance against the M-14, including shots fired during rain and extreme cold, which had sunk it two years earlier. Because the results were so much better, allegations of previous test-firing shenanigans had legs.

Colt was still in trouble, however. LeMay's order was personally turned down by newly elected president John F. Kennedy, who had fired the gun during a military demonstration. It wasn't that Kennedy disliked the weapon; the president and his military advisors were troubled by the notion of different branches of the military using different rifles. With the United States becoming increasingly involved in the Vietnam conflict, the compatibility issue came to the forefront.

While older military leaders focused on the compatibility issue, they still missed the big picture. Warfare had changed, and U.S. forces still did not have the right weapon. Despite the lessons of Korea, entrenched military brass were still thinking in terms of World War II infantry weapons.

The person most disturbed by the potential inefficiency of having several different rifles was Robert S. McNamara, the new secretary of defense and former president of Ford Motor Company, the first person outside of the Henry Ford family to achieve that post. McNamara had assembled a team, commonly known as the Whiz Kids, who wanted to run government by the numbers as was done at Ford. Now that computers were becoming a part of American industry, this group scrutinized every military expenditure and asked probing questions about how materials were purchased. The M-14/AR-15 conflict fell within their sights when they saw LeMay's purchase of 8,500 AR-15 rifles, making it the standard arm for air force personnel. Although LeMay was often thought of as a loose cannon, McNamara and his team respected his military expertise and hard-line approach against Communism. In fact, although McNamara had been a captain in the army, he had served under LeMay and taught air force officers analytical approaches used in business. In particular, he had offered methods to analyze the efficiency of using bombers to kill the enemy. One of McNamara's present goals was to fix the bureaucracy, which had dithered for more than a decade producing a rifle, the M-14, that nobody seemed to want except those in Ordnance.

His interest was more than academic. If the United States was to engage the North Vietnamese, it would need a single rifle that could be quickly mass-produced at low cost.

With Colt still in financial trouble—Boutelle had already been blamed and fired—Macdonald was desperate. He knew that the AR's future would be in Vietnam, so he traveled there with demonstration models. His bold move was designed to circumvent the standard military procurement process by going directly to battlefield commanders and having them put pressure on higher-ups to purchase the weapons.

Ordinarily, this kind of end-run tactic would not work, but these were unique times. The United States did not officially have troops in South Vietnam, only "advisors," nomenclature designed to make the growing commitment more palatable to the American public. As such, the job of a special unit known as the Combat Development Test Center, located in Saigon, was to evaluate the military needs of the South Vietnamese army. It was already clear that the smaller-stature Vietnamese—the average recruit was five feet tall and weighed ninety pounds—could not handle the M-14's recoil and weight. In addition, the average soldier could carry about three times more AR-15 ammunition than M-14 ammunition because of the lower weight of both the cartridges and rifle. This would be a decided advantage to jungle fighters out on long patrols.

The AR-15 was well received, and reports reached Washington about the lethality of the new weapon and smaller ammunition. American commanders and their South Vietnamese counterparts were especially impressed by the gunshot signatures seen in dead enemy soldiers, with reports of limbs being blown apart and chest cavities exploding after being hit by the high-velocity bullets.

Macdonald felt hopeful when Colt received an order for twenty thousand AR-15s, and he was further buoyed by the assistant secretary of defense's report stating that the AR-15 was up to five times effective as the M-14 rifle as well as being cheaper to manufacture. Most startling, the report stated that the M-14 was inferior to the old M1.

McNamara and his Whiz Kids were surprised and confused by the discrepancy between this report and the Ordnance Department's position supporting the M-14, so he ordered Secretary of the Army Cyrus Vance to reevaluate the M-14, the AR-15, and the AK. Even President Kennedy got involved, demanding that the situation be cleared up once and for all. Time was of the essence. By October 1962, the United States had committed more than ten thousand advisors to Vietnam without the best available weapon and it was clear that many more troops would be on their way to fight the Communist threat from the north.

Ensuing tests did not prove the anecdotal stories received from the battlefield about the AR-15's superiority, and charges flew around the highest levels of government about rigged tests designed to make the new weapon look inferior. Ironically, one test showed that the AK had significantly fewer malfunctions than *all* other weapons (there were some disagreements here, too), but several findings were irrefutable: the AR-15 was lighter, infantry-men could carry more of its ammunition, it was cheaper than the M-14, and it could be produced quickly.

McNamara decided to kill production of the M-14 by 1963 and begin production of the AR-15. He ordered eighty-five thousand AR-15s for the army and nineteen thousand for the air force. Opponents argued that his decision was based on bottom-line numbers—cheaper per unit costs and fast production—but his word was final nonetheless.

Whatever his reason, McNamara was clearly angry at the way Ordnance had handled the entire matter; several years earlier he had called the M-14 project a "disgrace" during public hearings. In congressional testimony he said, "It is a relatively simple job to build a rifle, compared to building a satellite." In McNamara's shakeup of the Ordnance bureaucracy, the name was changed to the U.S. Army Materiel Command, and Carten found himself transferred from the Springfield Armory to the army's Rock Island Arsenal in Illinois.

The Springfield Armory also took heat for its complicity in the M-14 affair. For the first time, an outside vendor, Colt, was going to be the lead supplier of the army's main weapon, now officially designated as the M-16. It used a .223-caliber cartridge with the military-metric designation of 5.56 × 45mm.

McNamara got even tougher and demanded that all branches of the military work together on modifying the M-16 for full-scale production and battle-readiness. Again, however, he found himself frustrated by the military bureaucracy's inability to move quickly and decisively. McNamara was used to giving orders at Ford and having them followed immediately and exactly, and he soon found himself at odds with career military personnel as well as civil servants who resisted the new businesslike regime. Government, especially the military establishment, did not work that way. The process was slow, arduous, and contentious. Turf battles continued as various departments micromanaged the project to protect their interests and support their beliefs.

SEVERAL EVENTS IN 1963 PUSHED McNamara for an even faster resolution. In January, the South Vietnamese army, equipped with M-14s, was defeated at Ap Bac by Vietcong carrying AKs. The reports of this automatic weapon's devastating effects worried U.S. commanders. It was becoming clear that an automatic weapon was crucial for winning in Vietnam because of a new pattern of warfare starting to emerge. Confrontations often consisted of what were termed "meeting engagements," in which jungle patrols from both sides found themselves unexpectedly face-to-face, and the side that could pump out the most rounds in the shortest amount of time won the skirmish. The M-14 was no match for the AK in these close-quarter encounters.

Again, U.S. military planners were caught unprepared for a different kind of warfare that took place in dense jungles against an enemy that you could not track in advance. Superior airpower was often ineffective, so battles would come down to the infantryman carrying the best weapon for the environment. The United States lagged.

On November 2, 1963, South Vietnamese generals assassinated

The standard U.S. battle rifle, which first saw action during the Vietnam War, was prone to jams and malfunctions when it was introduced. Although these problems were corrected, many GIs believed that the AK-47s used by the North Vietnamese and Vietcong were superior to M-16s during close-proximity jungle fighting. In the aftermath of the U.S. Invasion of Iraq in 2003, many U.S. soldiers preferred the AK-47 to their M16A2 rifles. *U.S. Department of Defense*

President Ngo Dinh Diem and his brother and advisor, Ngo Dinh Nhu. Diem was a heavy-handed dictator whose regime so enraged the majority Buddhist population that monks set themselves on fire in the street to protest their oppression. The Kennedy administration expressed shock at the public immolations and dismay at the assassinations, but did nothing to discourage the generals' actions. At the time of Diem's death, the United States had about sixteen thousand advisors in South Vietnam. Now, with Diem gone, and American casualties beginning to mount, the nation was getting sucked into a larger combat role as the South Vietnamese government foundered and a string of corrupt generals ruled the country.

Only three weeks after Diem's death, President John F. Kennedy was assassinated in Dallas, and Vice President Lyndon B. Johnson soon escalated his predecessor's policies. In August 1964, Pentagon officials said that U.S. warships had been attacked in the Gulf of Tonkin by North Vietnamese patrol boats. These attacks prompted Congress to give President Johnson a free hand in Vietnam, through the Gulf of Tonkin Resolution. This incident was later revealed to be a fabrication of the administration. No matter. The war was now in full swing and Special Forces, CIA operatives, and other elite units received the AR-15 to help counterbalance the AK.

Still, most U.S. forces were issued the M-14, and General William Westmoreland, who took command in Vietnam in June 1964, replacing General Paul Harkins, held a meeting of his commanders in Saigon in November 1965 to discuss how poorly the weapons fared against the AK. Congressional hearings held years later noted that GIs were buying black-market AR-15s for $600, compared to a list price of $100.

Back home, more testing of the M-16 continued, but McNamara was in a rush and so was Westmoreland. More than a hundred thousand M-16s were ordered by summer 1966. By October, however, some unexpected reports came in.

M-16s were jamming in combat.

American soldiers were found dead with their rifles in midbreakdown. They were trying to undo the cause of the misfire while under attack.

Morale plunged as many soldiers felt they could not trust their weapon. Some anecdotal reports indicated that as many as half of M-16s were prone to jamming, but this number was probably too high. The real number was irrelevant, because soldiers never knew if their own weapon would perform as expected, and so every rifle was suspect. As the Vietcong learned of these problems, they were less in awe of the weapon. The sight of the "black rifle," as the Vietcong had dubbed it in the early days, was now less threatening, and it empowered them. Reports indicated that Vietcong stripped dead GIs of their AR-15s and other equipment but were purposely leaving behind the M-16s.

Although the army tried to minimize the public relations fallout, reports reached Congress through the parents of men serving in Vietnam as well as from soldiers themselves who felt they had been betrayed. Small-town newspapers ran letters from local soldiers about the failing new rifle. National media also covered the story. Soldiers and their parents inundated congressional representatives with letters and phone calls, and they wanted answers. With more and more Americans uneasy about the nation's growing role in Vietnam, Congress began an investigation in May 1967. Under Democrat Richard Ichord from Missouri, a subcommittee of the House Armed Services Committee shed public light for the first time on the inner workings of the Ordnance Department and its archaic method of developing small arms.

The subcommittee called hundreds of witnesses, including Macdonald, Stoner, and other representatives of Colt, who testified about their shabby treatment by the army. Military personnel described how the Ordnance Department tested rifles, although many stated they did not recall the fine technical details of the M-16 program. One of the most dramatic moments in the hearings came when a letter from a soldier was entered into the record. This poignant letter read in part, "Before we left Okinawa, we were all issued this new rifle, the M-16. Practically every one of our dead was found with his rifle torn down next to him where he had been trying to fix it."

The subcommittee visited Vietnam to interview soldiers firsthand. They heard stories about how men routinely took AKs off of enemy dead and used them instead of their M-16s. This practice had became so commonplace that soldiers in the field officially were banned from using AKs, because those rifles' distinctive sound attracted friendly fire. In the heat of a close-quarters jungle firefight, American soldiers had little to go on to identify enemy positions other than the sound of their weapons. The other reason the AK was banned was that carrying it further stigmatized the M-16. In defiance, many soldiers still carried AKs. Indeed, special covert units of the military and CIA were sanctioned to carry AKs on their secret missions because of the weapon's reliability.

In his best-selling book *Steel My Soldiers' Hearts*, Colonel David H. Hackworth told the story of bulldozers during a base construction project uncovering a buried Vietcong soldier and his AK. Hackworth yanked the weapon out of the mud and pulled back the bolt. "Watch this," he said. "I'll show you how a real infantry weapon works." With that he fired off thirty rounds as if the rifle had been cleaned that morning instead of being buried for a year. "This was the kind of weapon our soldiers needed and deserved, not the M-16 that had to be hospital cleaned or it would jam," he wrote.

The Ichord hearings continued through the summer. In October 1967 the Special Subcommittee on the M-16 Rifle Program issued a six-hundred-page report highly critical of the Ordnance Department in general and its handling of the development of the M-16 program in particular.

The culprit, it turns out, wasn't the gun but the ammunition, and it was the result of a bad decision by Ordnance. The report concluded that the M-16s jammed because the Ordnance Department insisted on changing the cartridge propellant from extruded or stick-type powder to ball-type powder, which tended to leave a residue in the rifle after repeated firing. Although both powders are made of the same components, stick powders are shaped like tiny cylinders, extruded, and cut to length. Ball powders are extremely small spheres of propellant. One major difference is that stick powders rely primarily on the grain size and surface area to control the burn rate. Ball powders rely more on a slow-burning covering and need a hotter primer to ignite.

Stoner specified that stick powder be used in his weapon, and it is not fully understood why Ordnance insisted on changing his recommendation. The subcommittee noted that the army had a cozy relationship with Olin Mathieson, the ball-powder manufacturer, which may have influenced the decision to change powders. The subcommittee also noted that because of the powder change, mechanical modifications had to be made to the M-16, and these last-minute changes may also have hurt its performance.

These revelations finally killed the Springfield Armory. After almost two hundred years of operation, it was closed by McNamara at year's end.

The M-16 controversy was not over, however. Although Congress cited the change in powder as the reason for jamming, not everyone was satisfied. Some ballistics experts contended that the jamming was due to barrel corrosion from humid jungle conditions. This may well have been true, and would have indicted the Ordnance Department even more, because it understood the detrimental affects of barrel corrosion on M1 rifles from fighting in the Pacific during World War II. Ordnance knew that the cure was to chrome-plate the barrel, standard procedure for the AK.

Another contributing factor to jamming was that the army did not issue gun cleaning kits to troops, which gave the impression that the weapon never needed cleaning. Why the kits were not issued also was never made clear. Only speculation exists. One explanation was that McNamara's Whiz Kids wanted to save money; another is that the Ordnance Department wanted the M-16 to fail; other speculation hinged on an overconfidence in the weapon itself.

Perhaps all three reasons played a role, but the reputation of the M-16 was irrevocably sullied. Even after these issues were addressed and the M-16 proved itself a formidable weapon, it was too late. Its main rival the AK was perceived by many as the world's best infantry weapon, and the one that could beat the West's best offering. It was low-tech Soviet style versus high-tech U.S. style, and the Communists won the war of perception, especially among third world nations whose leaders were carefully watching the conflict.

By 1973, the U.S. presence in Vietnam was winding down, with soldiers officially withdrawing in March after reaching a peak of 535,000 in 1966. Without a decisive Western victory, U.S. combatants left Southeast Asia, including Cambodia and Laos. Vietnam fell to North Vietnamese troops in 1975 as the last Americans and many Vietnamese evacuated the country. Stunning television shots of desperate people clinging to helicopters taking off from Saigon building roofs only served to raise the stock of Communist fighters and their AKs.

To this day, one of the most contentious arguments in military circles is, "Which is the better weapon, the M-16 or the AK?" The argument will never be resolved, and it is moot. The AK's reputation as the underdog's weapon was born in the rice paddies of Vietnam, given a boost by an unwitting U.S. military.

The lesson of Vietnam is that determined soldiers with simple, reliable arms can beat a well-trained military force despite its sophisticated weapons, like the M-16. In the years that followed the Vietnam War, the larger-than-life AK spread around the globe, giving power and prestige to ad hoc armies, thugs, and terrorists who would change the face of the world forever.

3

PANDORA'S BOX

B Y THE LATE 1970s, the Soviet Union was ramping up for
what its leaders mistakenly thought would be a quick war
in Afghanistan. At first the AK seemed to be one of the
superpower's main military assets, but the rifle later proved to be
in part responsible for its defeat. The catastrophic Soviet defeat
following a ten-year guerrilla war eventually led to the breakup of
the Soviet Union and the proliferation of cheap AKs throughout
the Middle East.

The Vietnam War gave the AK its credibility, and the
Afghanistan war would spread it around the region, placing it in
the hands of terrorists and insurgents who embraced it as the budding icon of anti-imperialism.

The war that Soviet president Mikhail Gorbachev later called
"our country's Vietnam" had roots as far back as the 1920s, when
Afghanistan became the first nation to recognize the newly minted
Soviet Communist regime after the Bolshevik Revolution. The
two nations shared a common border and maintained friendly
relations. Soviet aid and advisors were a constant feature in

Afghanistan for the next fifty years. During the cold war, both East and West curried favor with the Afghans. The Soviets, for example, built a large irrigation project south of Jalalabad, and the United States constructed roads and an airfield at Kandahar.

By the 1970s, Communism was growing worldwide, boosted by the U.S. defeat in Vietnam. Other countries such as Cambodia, Laos, Angola, Mozambique, and Ethiopia turned Communist. In Cuba, the Communist revolution under Fidel Castro was stronger than ever despite CIA efforts to shake his hold. The Soviet Union was spreading its Marxist doctrine to the Congo, Egypt, Syria, and Latin America.

In April 1978, members of the Marxist People's Democratic Party of Afghanistan (DRA) assassinated Prime Minister Sardar Mohammed Daoud Khan during a coup supported by the Soviet Union. Although the new government enjoyed popular support, it was poorly organized and run. The following year, unknown assassins (presumably encouraged by Prime Minister Hafizullah Amin) smothered President Nur Muhammad Taraki in his sleep and Amin became president. Amin was warm to Soviet help but not as willing as his predecessor to be the superpower's puppet.

By the fall of 1979, the Soviet Union had set its sights on taking over Afghanistan by military force. Although many reasons have been suggested for an invasion, ranging from helping a neighboring Communist regime to a closer military presence in the Persian Gulf area where the world's oil tankers traveled, the situation in nearby Iran was also a factor. The country was in the midst of an Islamic revolution, throwing out the corrupt U.S.-backed government of Mohammed Reza Shah Pahlavi, the Shah of Iran, and installing the Islamic hard-liner Ayatollah Ruhollah Khomeini. Although the new regime was an enemy of the United States, it was not friendly to the Soviet Union either and presented another loss of influence to the Soviets and little hope of Communist inroads.

On Christmas Eve 1979, the Soviet army, with planning help from the DRA, rolled three divisions across the border and quickly took control of airfields around Kabul as well as the telecommunications infrastructure. In a set of clever ploys, Soviet advisors hosted a party for Afghan government leaders at the InterContinental Hotel in Kabul, and Soviet military advisors held a similar fete for upper-level Afghan military officers. At the conclusion of both galas, all the Afghan guests were taken prisoner. That same day, Soviet soldiers dressed as Afghan soldiers stormed the presidential palace, killing President Amin. Within days, more than fifty thousand Soviet troops were in Afghanistan, with all the major cities under their control.

Strategically, the invasion had been brilliant, with only sixty-six Soviet soldiers killed, most of them due to non-combat-related accidents. The Soviet strategy was to maintain control of major cities with their own forces and have the Afghan army seek out and destroy rural-based opposition groups, known as mujahideen, who were scattered throughout the countryside, mainly in the mountains. Soviet planners, elated by a quick victory and little resistance, anticipated a stay of no more than three years.

The mujahideen, which literally means "strugglers" in Arabic but also translates as "holy warriors," sought U.S. assistance against the Soviet invaders. They opposed the Soviets largely on nationalistic grounds; they were not willing to be taken over by any outside force. They also garnered strong support from influential local imams for whom the Marxist ideology of atheism was abhorrent. Hundreds of small bands were formed. Even some DRA soldiers joined the mujahideen fighters.

President Jimmy Carter authorized the CIA to supply the mujahideen with weapons and funds for their fight against the Soviets. The weapons would be funneled through Pakistan, which was uneasy about having the Soviets next door in Afghanistan. Moreover, as the war continued and the Soviets bombed and destroyed rural villages, millions of Afghans found themselves living in refugee camps bordering Pakistan and Iran, which made it difficult if not impossible to maintain the borders' integrity. Both nations supported the mujahideen movement.

The Soviets with their tanks, airpower, and AKs vastly out-gunned the mujahideen, who were relegated in the early years to whatever weapons they could scrounge or take from captured Soviet convoys and army caches. Their situation changed for the better when one of the first CIA shipments arrived, less than two weeks after the Soviet invasion, containing thousands of bolt-action .303 Lee-Enfield rifles, the British counterpart of the venerable but outmoded M1. Howard Hart, who was the CIA's chief in Pakistan, believed that the old Enfield rifles were superior to the Soviet AK. Orders went out to sources in Greece, India, and wherever else they could be found for delivery to Karachi. The CIA also shipped rocket-propelled grenade launchers, portable enough for guerrillas to carry in the field, and capable of stopping a Soviet tank.

The Soviets fought using the methods expected of any large army of the day. In many respects, they mimicked the U.S. pro-gram in Vietnam. They delivered massive firepower from bombers, helicopters, fixed artillery, and tanks upon a town, com-pletely dominating the area, and then dispatched ground troops who fired their AKs at anything that moved until the town fell under their control. Mopping up was largely unnecessary because the massive shellings took care of any resistance save a few strag-glers. The Soviets' scorched-earth strategy was considered a form of "migratory genocide." By destroying villages and forcing people into exile, they hoped to sap the rural support that fed the mujahideen.

Initially, the outgunned mujahideen were shaken by the Soviet tactics and the firepower delivered by a new version of the AK that was making its way onto the battlefield. The mujahideen so feared this mysterious this new rifle and its odd-sized cartridge that they called it "poison bullet" because of its almost supernatural destruc-tive power. The new bullet was not only smaller than previous AK rounds, many of which the mujahideen had captured during raids, but it was also more deadly—even more so than the M-16 round that had prompted its development.

Soviet weapons designers had taken note of the small, high-velocity 5.56mm bullet used in the M-16 when they saw firsthand in Vietnam its destructive bone-cracking power. The truth was that Soviet military officials were not completely happy with the AK, and they were looking for a change. Although the intermediate round was a major step forward, many troops could not keep the rifle on target during full automatic fire because of the strong recoil.

Kalashnikov, well aware of the move by the United States to a smaller bullet, was ready to embrace the new order. Later, he wrote, "Our foreign colleagues [U.S. arms designers] had already been working along this line, so the Russian command decided to do so in this country. Of course, I could not stand idle in this situation and rest on my laurels. In a way, the earned reputation won't allow you to stop working. On the contrary, it makes you take up new projects as long as you have the strength."

Through the passing of time, Kalashnikov now characterizes himself as gung-ho on the new, smaller bullet, but at the time, he, like many of his Western counterparts, was still not convinced that smaller was better. Despite the forensic and anecdotal data, many conventional arms designers had trouble believing that a smaller bullet could produce greater destruction. However, Kalashnikov was a team player and threw himself into modifying his AK to accommodate the smaller round. Moreover, he wanted to make certain that the legacy of the AK design would continue.

Making a smaller-caliber weapon did not mean simply using a narrower barrel, he learned. As in the AR-15, small-diameter barrels tended to retain water, but this was overcome. Other changes were necessary, too, for the basic AK design to be used. This included changing the bolt head, improving the extractor, and changing the magazine to a steel-and-fiberglass composite.

These changes were all doable. Kalashnikov's main challenge was not technical but political. He had to convince the other teams working on the small-bullet project that the AK design, once modified, was still viable and could handle the new bullet. After all, the United States had changed to a radically new gun design in order to accommodate the 5.56mm cartridge, and the AK itself was born to shoot the new intermediate round. Maybe a change was in order now that the AK was going on twenty years old. Some Kalashnikov competitors had likened the AK design to a lemon that had been squeezed dry with nothing left to offer, and this riled the arms designer.

Kalashnikov's main challengers were engineers from another design group known as TsNIITochmash, the Central Institute for Precision Machine Building, who were also modifying an AKM to shoot the small bullet. They went a step further, however. By the mid-1960s, they had developed a way to virtually eliminate recoil in the AKM, which used the intermediate round. The AL-7, as it was called, employed a counter-recoil system that almost perfectly matched the recoil from each round with a spring balanced in the opposite direction, thereby eliminating any backward motion. The two forces nearly canceled each other.

Unfortunately, the AL-7, completed in 1972, required substantial changes to existing factory lines, and was rejected as too expensive to produce. With this group out of the running, a newly named AK-74 (again, for the year it was accepted), which fired a 5.45 × 39mm bullet, closer in size to the M-16 round, was put into service and began replacing the older intermediate-cartridge-firing rifle. Unlike previous rifles, it used all polymer in the buttstock and grip, components known as "furniture," which had previously been made of wood. This change offered a much lighter weapon.

The Soviets had another winning rifle. It was light like the M-16, used the smaller more lethal bullet, yet maintained the legendary Kalashnikov reliability. The new AK-74 with muzzle brake had about half the recoil of an M-16 and about two-thirds that of the previous AK. Reduced recoil offered less skillful soldiers the ability to keep their weapons fixed closer on target during rapid fire. The new firearm and lighter bullets also allowed soldiers to carry twice as much ammunition into battle.

Again, Western intelligence underestimated the Soviet weapon's importance. When reports about the new rifle filtered in during the late 1970s, analysts believed the new rifles (and a light machine gun known as the RPK-74) would be issued only to special squads because of the logistical headache of issuing new weapons and ammunition to all Soviet troops. This underestimation of the weapon's importance may have been due to the belief that Soviet production capacity was still low or their technical ability poor. Nevertheless, the Soviets were committed to the new weapon and the timing was fortuitous. Phased in during the Afghanistan war, this new rifle became a fixture in the conflict as stories of its destructiveness spread throughout the rebel ranks.

The new bullet consisted of a thin-jacketed point with an airspace in the middle. As the bullet entered the human body, the impact bent and deformed the tip because the airspace offered no structural strength to keep it intact. As it penetrated, the bullet usually came apart, fragmenting and inflicting extreme damage to tissues and organs. Western intelligence knew few details about the new bullet until Galen L. Geer, a correspondent for *Soldier of Fortune* magazine in Afghanistan, wrote about it in a two-part series for the September and October 1980 issues. Not only did he obtain the new rounds, but he and *Soldier of Fortune* editor and publisher Robert K. Brown delivered two rounds to an unnamed U.S. government agency ("not the CIA," noted Brown) and beat the CIA. Geer also visited many hospitals in Pakistan and reported seeing extraordinarily large wounds. He believed the injuries were the result of rounds shattering entire bone sections. He was correct. In addition, he reported wounded fighters with limb wounds only, because those with more extensive body wounds rarely survived the trip to a hospital.

Realizing that they could not win by fighting the Soviets' type of war, the mujahideen altered their tactics. At the first signs of bombing, they would leave the area and hide in the mountains, often in caves. They would return hours, days, or even weeks later to surprise the unprepared Soviet soldiers now complacent in the belief that they had complete control of the town. The mujahideen could not engage the Soviets in head-to-head combat, because their old, long-range, single-shot Enfields and even some semiautomatic

M-14s they had obtained were no match for the rapid-firing AK, but they could fight them as guerrillas.

The old way of war was officially dead.

Another tactic of the mujahideen was to exploit the Afghan topography. The country is crisscrossed by roads that wind through mountain passes, and the Soviets were bound by their vehicles to stay on these routes. In one particular instance, in October 1980, the mujahideen heard of a convoy heading north from Bagram Air Base and crossing the Panjshir valley bridge. The convoy was to return that evening. About two hundred mujahideen armed with RPGs, mortars, and heavy machine guns set up an ambush. In the late afternoon, as the sun was setting, they waited until half of the convoy had passed over the bridge. Then they attacked the entire length of the convoy. Startled Soviet soldiers abandoned their vehicles and, realizing they were close to the air base, rushed to the river to escape home. Almost at their leisure, the mujahideen fighters were able to pick the convoy clean, taking weapons and other supplies under the cover of darkness.

The mujahideen received food and other supplies from local villages despite the Soviets' continued scorched-earth policies that leveled towns believed friendly to the guerrillas. The Soviets' plan to have the Afghan army root out the mujahideen failed as these soldiers often supported the rebels. This support grew as the Soviets' treatment of villagers and those in larger towns grew more brutal.

Nevertheless, by the early 1980s, the Soviets appeared to be winning. At least it looked as if they could outlast the mujahideen, who were still short of modern weapons, especially assault rifles, save for those taken during ambushes and weapons caches raids. But the CIA began to funnel massive aid to the mujahideen through Pakistan. In 1981, the guerrilla movement received only about $30 million, but by 1984 the amount had soared to $200 million, according to later congressional testimony. President Reagan also negotiated a deal with the Saudi royal family to match the CIA's funding.

The mujahideen were still terrified of the new AK and its "poison bullet," and pleaded for these arms from the United States to achieve parity with the Soviet invaders. The CIA's Hart finally relented and ordered hundreds of thousands of AKs, mainly from China, where production of the Soviet weapon was booming. China and the Soviet Union had had an ideological falling-out during the 1960s, and the Chinese were eager to use the Soviets' own weapon against them in the Afghan conflict. (China and Afghanistan also share a forty-seven-mile border.) Not only did they sell the 7.62mm AK called the Type 56, but they had introduced in 1981 the 5.56mm Type 81, an AK model that used the same 5.56mm round as the M-16, another poke in the eye to the Soviets. A year later, China brought on the market their 5.45mm Type 81, which was a direct competitor to the new Soviet assault rifle. AKs and their variants also poured in from Poland, where dissident army officers sold Soviet weapons to the CIA. Other nations such as Egypt and Turkey sold older Soviet and other weapons to the CIA for delivery to Afghan guerrillas.

The CIA favored Soviet weapons because of their reliability, low cost, and availability. In addition, Soviet weapons in the hands of the mujahideen would not appear to be U.S.-supplied, thus giving the CIA deniability. As history would later show, Hart's decision to buy AKs for the mujahideen may have been the most important single contribution to the spread of the weapon.

So many weapons, millions by some estimates, were passing through Pakistan that no one could keep an accurate count. The same with money; nobody could keep track of all the secret deals, payoffs, and bribes that surrounded the CIA's covert operation. Years later, in congressional testimony, CIA officials estimated that by 1984, $200 million had been sent to the mujahideen and that by 1988 the amount reached $2 billion through CIA channels alone. It had turned into the largest covert shipment of arms, and supplies, and money by the CIA since the Vietnam War.

The covert pipeline managed by the CIA usually entered Pakistan through Islamabad or Karachi. From there, arms went to staging areas in the towns of Quetta and Peshawar near the Afghan border, then into Afghanistan.

Islamabad, the center of CIA activity in Pakistan, became an arms bazaar, a wide-open and sometimes lawless town awash in weapons, where quick money could be made easily. While most of the funds destined for the mujahideen reached them, much money and many weapons went astray. In payment for their help, the Pakistani army and the Inter-Services Intelligence (ISI), that country's CIA counterpart, took a cut of the money and arms flowing through their country. AKs were sold to those inside Pakistan, including thugs, criminal gangs, and citizens who wanted protection in a region that was becoming dangerous. Many weapons also found their way to Islamic revolutionaries in Iran.

The mujahideen themselves sold some AKs and used the money for medical supplies and food. They also stockpiled weapons and ammunition to be used after the Soviets left. Convoys of mujahideen supplies from Pakistan needed protection from the Soviets and civilian gangs who roamed the no-man's-land in the border area of Tora Bora. Private truckers hauling for the mujahideen were given AKs to protect their loads. These drivers, who were paid by the mujahideen or the CIA to deliver weapons to Afghanistan's interior, would return to Pakistan with empty trucks. To help defray their costs, they sometimes hauled heroin and other drugs produced in Afghanistan. These convoys often paid gangs, drug kingpins, or local strongmen for protection. Their weapon of choice was the AK because of its low cost and reliability. Drug dealers and their gangs, who became an integral part of the arms pipeline, also chose the AK. The name Kalashnikov became well known in the region as people began to call their favorite gun by the inventor's name.

As more and more AKs flooded the region, street prices dropped, and even more people bought them on the black market. Indeed, one of the ways in which the CIA hoped to monitor the arms shipments and prevent wholesale weapons skimming by the Pakistanis was to keep an eye on prices. If they dropped too far and too quickly it would be a sign of dumping on the market. Later, the ISI was found to be skimming, including several instances involving sending weapons offshore and then back to Pakistan for sale, as well as selling back the CIA its own weapons.

AKs were seen on the streets of most Pakistani and Afghan towns as ordinary citizens armed themselves for personal protection in a region now abounding in small arms. The simple-to-use and easy-to-maintain AK—both older and new models—became the most ubiquitous weapon in the region, and all versions coexisted side by side. To avoid confusion, the Soviets cleverly placed a long smooth groove in the buttstock of the 5.45mm model so that even in the dark soldiers could tell which weapon they were holding and feed it the correct ammunition.

The newly delivered AKs offered the mujahideen an opportunity to better their tactics. One successful technique was to start a landslide on a mountain route to block it before a convoy arrived. To make it look like a natural occurrence and not a deliberate ploy, they used small rocks instead of huge boulders. The convoy would stop, and when Soviet soldiers got out to clear the roads, the mujahideen would pounce, AKs in hand, and open up at close range, spending hundreds of rounds in minutes. The guerrillas would pick up Soviet weapons and whatever else they could carry and scurry back into the mountains. Although the Soviets still had greater long-range firepower and air support, their troops quickly became demoralized at the mujahideen's hit-and-run tactics that turned their own assault weapons against them. To be sure, the AK was not the only weapon used successfully by the mujahideen. The CIA also supplied Stinger Human-Portable Air-Defense System, or MANPAD, missiles. These shoulder-fired guided missiles were effective against low-flying Soviet helicopters, although they were not supplied until later in 1986 during the war's peak years. The AK remained the most used weapon in the region.

Despite the graft, corruption, and skimming that occurred, the CIA-run arms pipeline was effective. During the course of the war, Afghanistan became the world's largest arms recipient in relation to the size of its population, according to the United Nations. With help from the ISI, the United States delivered perhaps as many as four hundred thousand AKs to the mujahideen. The ISI had access to an additional three million Kalashnikovs from pipeline operations, some of which made it to the rebels and some of which were sold on the black market. Hundreds of thousands more AKs entered the area from other countries now that the pipeline infrastructure had been established.

By 1985, the war was reaching a stalemate despite the large number of Soviet ground troops in Afghanistan, estimated to have peaked at 100,000 men. With other troops and support, that number probably reached 175,000.

Regardless of the large troop numbers, the Soviets could not beat the mujahideen. They found themselves spending 85 percent of their resources guarding cities, airfields, and supply depots, which left only 15 percent to chase after the mujahideen. The massive CIA/ISI arms pipeline kept the rebels well stocked, and more than half of all Soviet soldiers at some point were hospitalized for diseases such as cholera and hepatitis. In addition, although the Soviet government kept most of the casualty information hidden from the public and put a positive spin on the conflict, negative reports began to filter back. Soviet citizens grew weary of what was becoming a no-win war.

The Soviet Politburo was little help in formulating an end to the war. During the conflict, the Soviet Union lost three leaders in quick succession to illness and death—Leonid Brezhnev, who had begun the war, Konstantin Chernenko, and then Yuri Andropov—and it seemed as if no one had the energy to move the process along until Mikhail Gorbachev came to power in 1985. Wanting to end the war with a decisive victory, Gorbachev ordered massive attacks, but after several bloody battles, including one particularly brutal engagement at Jalalabad, the Soviet leader sought a negotiated way out of the morass.

A deal brokered by the United Nations allowed the Soviet Union to withdraw from Afghanistan and save face. The agreement specified that the Russians had entered Afghanistan to aid a friendly government, the DRA, but now threats to its well-being were diminished and a Soviet force was no longer necessary. Calling it "Afghanization"—Afghans deciding the best course for Afghanistan—Gorbachev insisted that the agreement call for Pakistan not to interfere in Afghan affairs and to sever aid to anti-Soviet groups.

Economically, the war's drain on the faltering Soviet financial system had been enormous, perhaps $2.7 billion annually from 1980 on. Moreover, approximately twenty-two thousand Soviets were killed and seventy-five thousand wounded. The Soviet invasion decimated Afghanistan. About ninety thousand Afghan combatants died, with an equal number wounded. More than 1.3 million Afghan citizens perished. One-third to one-half of the country's net worth was damaged or destroyed. Agricultural production dropped by 50 percent and livestock losses were 50 percent, mainly due to Soviet bombings and towns leveled with no people left to care for the animals or tend the land. As many as five thousand of the nation's fifteen thousand villages were destroyed or made unlivable. United Nations estimates suggest that 70 percent of paved roads were destroyed.

ON FEBRUARY 15, 1989, the last Soviet troops left Afghanistan. But the arms pipeline that had been operating for a decade, and was now ingrained in the economic and cultural landscape of the neighboring countries, did not disappear, nor did the drugs and weapons it conveyed throughout the region. Indeed, just before the Soviet withdrawal, the United States increased its arms shipments to Afghanistan to make certain the pullout held. Likewise, the Soviet Union left behind huge small-arms stockpiles for use by the new pro-Soviet regime headed by President Muhammad Najibullah, and it continued arms deliveries even after the troops returned home. Other nations such as China continued to sell small arms on the well-developed black market for delivery to drug dealers, gangs, private citizens, and extremist groups including factions of the mujahideen that kept fighting among themselves along tribal and ethnic lines.

Just prior to the Soviet withdrawal, Western newspapers had begun to take note of the huge supply of AKs in the region, especially in Pakistan. With hostilities winding down, it became easier for journalists to travel and report on the effects of cheap guns on the population and culture. In Khel, an hour's drive south of Peshawar, local arms dealer Haji Baz Gul told the *New York Times* about his brisk business in AKs. He carried three different models: the Soviet model for about $1,400, the Chinese model for $1,150, and a locally made knockoff for $400. Another arms dealer said that he noticed a dip in prices when the Soviets announced they were leaving Afghanistan, but prices rose again when the withdrawal became less certain.

A 1988 story in the *Los Angeles Times* relayed how cheap guns had turned some Pakistani cities into caricatures of the Wild West where everyone, it seemed, carried an AK. "Conservatively speaking, there are 8,000 Kalashnikovs in Hyderabad now," said Aftab Sheikh, the mayor of Pakistan's fifth largest city. "The people who have them rule supreme. They can kill anybody." Sheikh said he had not gone outside his house in three months because the last time he did, he was shot nine times by AK-wielding gunmen and left for dead in his driveway. His jeep showed ninety bullet holes. Judges and other government officials also became targets. Close to two hundred citizens alone were killed in a three-hour spree dubbed "Black Friday," the result of ongoing conflicts fueled by ethnic differences and readily available automatic weapons. A government official said, "The problem has gotten so bad that Kalashnikovs are being sold on the installment plan. The total price is 15,000 rupees [about $850]. You put 5,000 rupees down, take the Kalashnikov, go rob someone and use the loot to pay off the rest of the purchase price." In Peshawar itself, people reportedly could rent assault rifles by the hour.

A substantial part of Pakistan's economy—from gangs who robbed and kidnapped, to armed drug kingpins who followed established arms routes, to the small village arms maker who bought, sold, repaired, and produced their homemade versions—relied on the ubiquitous AK. In many small towns, the robust AK market was the only way to make a living. It was similar in Afghanistan. Thriving mom-and-pop (and kids) gun shops that built homegrown versions of the AK in seven to ten days remain commonplace to this day. Per capita, Afghanistan remains one of the world's most heavily armed countries in terms of small arms, the vast majority of which are AKs.

This economic and social reliance on AKs throughout parts of Pakistan and Afghanistan brought a new phrase to the region that is still used. One of the first to publicly describe the phenomenon was Hyderabad newspaper owner Sheik Ali Mohammed, who said, "What we have . . . is a Kalashnikov Culture."

The Kalashnikov Culture became even more pronounced after the Soviet Union finally collapsed in 1991—the costly Afghanistan invasion being a prime factor—and the Warsaw Pact nations, no longer receiving aid from the Soviet Union or beholden to its ideology, sold millions of AKs held in Soviet stockpiles to raise cash. As the scene inside Russia deteriorated, Soviet soldiers themselves looted arsenals and sold huge AK caches to criminals inside the country and to the world black market where they were bought by terrorist groups.

Years earlier, cash-strapped countries like Hungary, Bulgaria, and Romania, for instance, had been selling their own versions of the AK to raise cash. Now the AK's growing reputation as a cheap, reliable, effective weapon made sales to legitimate armies and rogue actors even easier. For example, during the chaos surrounding the bloodless revolution in East Germany, a few years before the Soviet Union's demise, the East German National People's Army began selling hardware to the highest bidders. Without the secret police or the strong hand of the Communist Party, arsenals were emptied and army commanders became rich. Even individual Soviet soldiers reportedly sold AKs on the black market for less than $100. Nobody knows how many weapons disappeared from stockpiles, but it could have been in the hundreds of thousands, perhaps millions. When the Albanian government fell in 1993, criminals looted state arsenals. Up to a million weapons, most of them AKs, found their way into the world's illegal arms market. Without the Soviet Union looking over their shoulder, even former Soviet states, such as Ukraine, sold off AK stockpiles and ammunition to raise cash.

Many weapons were sold to insurgent fighters and antigovernment rebels not only in the Middle East but also in Africa and South America. These groups could not afford expensive weapons like the M-16, nor could they legally obtain them from the United States or its allies. Because of its low price and availability, the reliable AK became *the* perfect weapon for guerrilla fighters and terrorists. Politics aside, the AK was the perfect item from a seller's point of view. It was cheap, easy to produce in great quantities, simple to transport, good value for the price, easily repairable, and it came with a ready market.

Now, with the Soviets gone, factional fighting continued in Afghanistan, with the country eventually divided into two main groups: the Taliban, which was backed by Pakistan, and the United Front or Northern Alliance. Pakistan used the established arms pipeline to continue arming the Taliban, which also relied on seizing weapons from overrun supply dumps. In late 1994, the group took possession of eighteen thousand Kalashnikovs from an arms dump in Pasha, a move that was considered pivotal to their success in eventually controlling the majority of the country.

This established Kalashnikov Culture, fueled by cheap and prolific weapons, helped to change the region's politics once again with the rise of Islamic fundamentalism embodied in Osama bin Laden.

WHEN THE SOVIETS ATTACKED AFGHANISTAN, the Saudi-born bin Laden fell in on the side of the mujahideen against the invaders. He used his considerable wealth—estimated at $250 million from his family and his construction business—to help raise even more money for the guerrillas. He worked with the CIA and employed his company's heavy equipment to build bridges and roads for the guerrillas.

As the war continued, bin Laden became more radical in his views about the idea of a jihad, or holy war, against the Soviet invaders and those who disagreed with his burgeoning Islamic fundamentalist views. Before the Soviet invasion, Afghanistan had been considered a moderate Islamic country, but now a more virulent strain of the faith was growing in the ravaged countryside, fueled by easily accessible weapons and a devastated economy. After the Soviets left, fighting continued among rival mujahideen groups.

In 1988, bin Laden had broken with a group he established four years earlier known as Maktab al-Khadamat (Office of Order), which collected money, weapons, and Muslim fighters for the Afghan war, and started al-Qaeda (meaning "the base" or "foundation") with the more militant members of Maktab al-Khadamat. In the mountainous border area near Pakistan, he built at least twenty training camps that specialized in handling the AK and RPGs. Proficiency in these weapons was followed by lessons in bomb making, urban assault techniques, and the use of chemical weapons. It is estimated that as many as fifty thousand people went through the training.

Despite continued internal hostilities, the United States showed little interest in Afghanistan until the attack on the World Trade Center and Pentagon on September 11, 2001. Less than a month after the attack, President George W. Bush ordered the invasion of Afghanistan. The goal was to rid the country of the Taliban, which was protecting al-Qaeda terrorists and camps, and to capture Osama bin Laden, thought to be the mastermind of the attack. Just prior to the U.S.-led invasion, bin Laden had distributed what was to be the first of several videotapes warning the West about reprisals for their transgressions. In these tapes, the al-Qaeda leader is seen with an AK either next to him or propped

As a way of flaunting his antiestablishment, anti-Western stance, Osama bin Laden, seen here on a videotape, fires his signature AK weapon. In almost all photos of him, he is accompanied by his AK, which he and al-Qaeda consider the terrorists' most important weapon. *Getty Images News/Getty Images*

against a background wall—his signature weapon and now the worldwide symbol of rebellion against imperialist ideology. (Gun enthusiasts point out that bin Laden is often seen with the AKS-74U, a shortened-barrel, folding-stock version of the AK-74, issued by the Soviet Union in 1982 to special operatives, mechanized troops, and armor and helicopter crews. It was prized as a war trophy and status symbol among the mujahideen, and U.S. AK enthusiasts gave it the name Krinkov.)

After several years of sustained bombings and attacks, U.S. forces were unable to find bin Laden, who was believed to be hiding in reinforced caves at Tora Bora near the Pakistani border before slipping into that country. Ironically, the United States had funded the fortification and weapons stocking of these caves during Ronald Reagan's presidency to help protect the mujahideen from Soviet troops.

Although at the time of this writing Taliban forces have been badly hurt, they continue to launch attacks on U.S. troops. Many tribal groups and al-Qaeda soldiers still carry the very same AKs that the CIA had purchased more than a decade earlier.

In essays from al-Qaeda writers that appeared several years later, the group reportedly has based its tactical doctrine on the activities of the mujahideen in Afghanistan who successfully drove out the Soviets. The tenets of this doctrine hinge on using weapons that are easily available, reliable, and cheap. "You must prepare weapons of all kinds" to fight the enemy, an essay notes. The most important is "the Kalashnikov and ammunition, and there must be large quantities of this because it is the substance of war."

Just after the U.S. invasion, American GIs began reporting up the chain of command a disturbing trend. Children, some as young as twelve years old, were seen carrying AKs. Rebel armies discovered that this light, easy-to-use weapon, which required less than an hour of training time, was perfectly suited for small hands and bodies. Even youngsters with poor coordination or strength could be turned into a lethal killers. The AKs required almost no maintenance or cleaning, so absentminded kids did not have to worry about forgetting to take care of their weapon. Poorly funded groups had no qualms about distributing AKs to children; if they lost the weapon or died in battle, the economic loss would be small.

None of this was known to thirty-one-year-old Green Beret sergeant first class Nathan Ross Chapman of San Antonio, Texas. On January 4, 2002, he became the first American soldier to be killed by hostile fire in Afghanistan. His unit was coordinating missions with friendly tribes in Paktria Province near Pakistan when they were ambushed.

The shooter was a fourteen-year-old Afghan boy, born and

nurtured in the Kalashnikov Culture and armed with an AK. Although facing child soldiers barely strong enough to hold an AK may have been a new and shocking experience for young GIs in Afghanistan, it had been a widespread and accepted practice in Africa for decades.

4

THE AFRICAN
CREDIT CARD

O N CHRISTMAS EVE 1989, forty-one-year-old Charles
Taylor, a former security guard, gas station mechanic,
and truck driver, invaded the African nation of Liberia
with a ragtag group of about one hundred rebels primarily armed
with cheap AKs. Crossing the border from Ivory Coast, Taylor
and his men first waged guerrilla warfare in the heavily forested
Nimba County, securing town after town as they added soldiers to
their force.

With the Soviet bloc countries selling AKs for quick cash, Taylor, with reported support from Libyan leader Colonel Muammar
Gadhafi, was able to arm his poorly trained and outfitted rebels for
little money. At the same time, Western nations paid almost no
attention to small-arms trade in Africa. They were still focused on
weapons of mass destruction and believed light weapons, those
that could be carried by soldiers, were of little consequence.

Throughout Africa, the disappearance of superpower support
in the late 1980s led to the collapse of traditional government mili-
taries. Countries fragmented into tribal groups that harbored

long-standing ethnic resentments. The demand for small arms grew and prices dropped dramatically because of the deluge of available arms from Afghanistan, Pakistan, and Eastern Europe. Although cheap AKs were not responsible for the beginning of brutal, decades-long conflicts in Africa, they were a principal factor in prolonging them. The weapons brought devastating changes to a frail continent fraught with disease, hunger, and few economic opportunities.

Adding to the problem was the lack of desire among Western nations to track arms. Even if they were interested, tracking became impossible due to the sheer volume of weapons flooding world markets. United Nations officials were unable to garner support for programs to monitor small arms or limit their sale. In fact, it was never illegal to sell arms to Africa except in later instances of UN-imposed arms sanctions, which were largely ineffective anyway.

"A few planeloads of arms going to an African country just didn't make the cut, in terms of an issue governments would want to pay attention to," Tom Ofcansky, an African affairs analyst with the State Department Bureau of Intelligence and Research, told PBS's *Frontline* in 2002. "But the impact of a few planeloads of arms, as we've seen repeatedly in Africa, had a devastating impact on fragile African societies."

Charles Taylor didn't know it at the time, but he was on the cutting edge of a trend that would result by 2000 in the deaths of seven to eight million Africans as well as the displacement of millions of people seeking refuge from prolonged, low-level conflicts fueled by cheap and indestructible AKs.

Like the mujahideen in Afghanistan, Taylor employed his small-arms firepower to ambush government forces. Systematically, he and his National Patriotic Front of Liberia (NPFL), isolated unprotected towns instead of fighting government forces head-on as he pushed south toward the capital, Monrovia, over the weeks and months following his Christmas Eve invasion. His group also took over key industrial facilities such as the country's second largest rubber plantation in the southern port of Buchanan.

In 1989, Charles Taylor and a ragtag group of a hundred men armed mainly with AKs stormed the presidential palace in Liberia and controlled the country for the next six years. By issuing AKs to anyone who swore allegiance to him, Taylor stayed in power with bands of thug soldiers who were allowed to pillage their defeated enemies as payment for their loyalty.
Pascal Guyot/AFP/Getty Images

Taylor garnered troops by exploiting their tribal allegiances and anger at the current government for poor economic conditions. This tribal anger stemmed from the modern beginnings of Liberia, when freed American slaves established a colony there in 1822. By 1847, these Americo-Liberians, as they were called, declared independent the Republic of Liberia, and named its capital Monrovia for President James Monroe. The second largest city, Buchanan, was named for President James Buchanan's brother Thomas, who later became vice president of Liberia. Buchanan was honored for hand-delivering the new Liberian constitution to the United States after it was written by Harvard University professor Simon Greenleaf. It was this document that sowed the seeds for Liberia's ensuing conflicts, because it denied rights to those other than the freed American slaves, the Americo-Liberians. The natives, the overwhelming majority, were considered second-class citizens, and the Americo-Liberians controlled the country's government and financial and industrial infrastructure.

Efforts over the years by various presidents to bring tribal Africans into the economic and political fold failed, and the majority of the population considered the government as corrupt. This was exacerbated by generous concessions to U.S.-owned firms like the Firestone Plantation Company, which exerted great influence on the country's internal politics, to the resentment of many Liberians.

Descended from Americo-Liberians on his father's side and the indigenous Gola tribe on his mother's, Liberian-born Taylor was fascinated by the history of his country and its relationship with the United States. In 1972, he emigrated to the United States, where he graduated in 1977 with a bachelor of arts degree in economics from Bentley College near Boston. While in college, he became the national chairman of the Union of Liberian Associations in the Americas, a group founded in 1974 "to advance the just causes of Liberians and Liberia at home and abroad." While he chaired the group, Taylor politically matured, even forming a protest demonstration against then Liberian president William Tolbert in 1979 when the leader visited the United States.

Instead of ignoring Taylor, Tolbert debated him, and by some accounts he lost the verbal joust. Taylor was arrested when he declared that he would take over the Liberian mission, but was later released when Tolbert refused to press charges. In fact, Tolbert invited Taylor to return home to Liberia, and in 1980 he did.

On April 12, 1980, army sergeant Samuel K. Doe killed Tolbert during a military coup. Doe, the first indigenous Liberian to became president, and a member of the Krahn tribe, ruled the country with an iron fist. He tortured and killed Americo-Liberians in a reign of revenge.

From here, Taylor's story took some weird turns. Despite his connection with the previous government, Doe hired him as the government's head purchasing agent, but he was thrown out in 1983, accused of embezzling more than $900,000. Taylor fled to the United States and was arrested in Boston at the request of Doe and held for extradition. After languishing for almost a year in the Plymouth County House of Corrections, Taylor in 1985 escaped by sawing through bars and climbing down a bedsheet rope. He made his way back to Africa. American officials suspected that he spent the next four years in Libya with Gadhafi before invading Liberia with his AK-armed insurgents.

While Taylor's ultimate goal was the destructive overthrow of the corrupt Doe government, he accomplished more than that. He created a watershed event in warfare history, revealing that the accepted model for modern warfare had changed. In the past, war had been conducted as a series of armed conflicts between armies of established countries. The goal was to gain territory or force an ideology. With Taylor, the world saw a different kind of warfare emerge. It consisted of paramilitary combatants, armed with light, cheap weapons, whose long-term goal was not only to topple a government but to attack civilians en masse along the way. These soldiers were permitted, even encouraged, to engage in any atrocity, including rape and ethnic slaughter, to terrorize the population and gain control. Civilians were fair game, including children, which was a major change from previous contemporary wars in

which combatants had tried to limit "collateral" damage. Even in
the case of the German bombing of London or the U.S. dropping
of atomic bombs on Japan, the goal was capitulation; once an
enemy surrendered the conflict was considered over.

Not so with Taylor. He wanted money and power in addition to
political command. He cleverly recruited fighters by encouraging
their tribal hatred and giving them cheap automatic weapons. In
return they could plunder from those they killed. They could loot,
pillage, and arrest anyone they wanted and murder them if they
chose. In this way, Taylor could build an army, and his only
expense was an AK for each recruit at a cost of less than fifty dollars each, in some cases as low as ten dollars.

Taylor went further by putting large numbers of weapons in
the hands of youngsters, many of them war orphans, who had few
alternatives for sustenance and shelter in a country already ravaged by strife. Seeing gangs of boys with AKs slung over their
shoulders, sporting baseball caps and ripped T-shirts, terrorizing
jungle villages, Western observers likened it to the book *Lord of
the Flies*, the classic William Golding novel of brutal boys running
wild, lawless gangs playing out their sadistic fantasies.

Taylor's Small Boy Units, as he dubbed them, often were put in
charge of makeshift checkpoints where they stood menacingly, AKs
at the ready, demanding bribes for passage. Other times they were let
loose in villages that stood in the way of Taylor's march toward the
capital, Monrovia. These naive youngsters were promised cars, toys,
even computers for their service. Outsiders found the contradictions
unsettling, as one minute these boys would act tough as combat veterans and in the next they would play with their toys and games. "I met
and spoke with young child soldiers in Danane, Ivory Coast. They
had crossed the border from fighting in Liberia and acted as a 'pro-
tector' force for Taylor," wrote Jamie Menutis, an officer for the U.S.
Resettlement Office of the Department of State who took testimony
from refugees of human rights abuses in asylum cases. "During their
free moments, they put down their AK-47s and played with small
matchbox cars in the dirt. This is an image I will never forget."

In a perverted context, child soldiers fit Taylor's needs perfectly. They were easy to recruit, naive enough to stay within the fold, and armed with an AK they were just as lethal as an adult. Even the youngest boys, barely able to hold the rifle, could spray bullets and hit a human target. Psychologically, child soldiers held other advantages. Youth made them feel invulnerable. Coupled with natural teen bravado and an undeveloped conscience, children offered a deadly combination in a guerrilla fighter. As one Liberian militia commander put it, "Don't overlook them. They can fight more than we big people. . . . It is hard for them to just retreat."

For opposing forces, seeing a child holding a weapon was unnerving, and there were several instances in other African countries such as Sierra Leone, in which Western soldiers sent as peacekeepers did not have the heart to fire at children even though they were deadly combatants.

The Small Boy Units were often looked upon with favor by their adult rebel comrades. Not only did they add numbers to the ranks, but their very existence seemed to be spiritually mandated. As one adult soldier put it, "God must think that [President] Doe is oppressive, too, because he sent us all these small boys to fight."

Nobody knows how Taylor got the idea for the Small Boy Units, but it was indeed inspired. "Taylor had unleashed the most deadly combat system of the current epoch, the adolescent human male equipped with a Kalashnikov—an AK-47 assault rifle," noted Michael Klare, professor of peace and world security studies at Hampshire College in Amherst, Massachusetts.

Within seven months of his invasion, barely noticed by the outside world, Taylor and an estimated five thousand guerillas reached the outskirts of Monrovia with their sights set on the presidential mansion where Doe had hunkered down. Despite his oppressive regime, Doe's government had received more than half a billion dollars from the United States since the 1980s. In exchange, Doe pushed out the Soviets and permitted U.S. access to ports and land.

During the capital's siege, U.S. Marines offered Doe safe

passage out of Liberia in August along with U.S. citizens and other foreign nationals, but he refused. Doe's rule ended during a shootout with a breakaway faction of Taylor's NPFL group led by Prince Yormie Johnson even though the president was under the protection of a four-thousand-man peacekeeping force sent by the six-nation Economic Community of West African States (ECOWAS). Johnson seized the opportunity to capture Doe when Taylor's soldiers temporarily faltered in their forward progress just outside the city. A wounded Doe was carried away to Johnson's camp, where he later died either from his gunshot wounds or from torture and execution, depending upon who told the story. His mutilated body was put on public display.

The rift between Taylor and Johnson led to six more years of bloodshed as seven rival factions, separated mainly along tribal lines, joined the conflict and fought for control of the country's natural resources, including iron, timber, and rubber. The brutal warfare continued as more light weapons reached the combatants. One of the last and darkest moments was the April 6, 1996, siege of Monrovia, during which an estimated three thousand people were killed as five factions converged on the capital. After several unsuccessful cease-fires brokered by ECOWAS and others, major hostilities finally ended. In 1997, elections were held.

Some international observers, including former U.S. president Jimmy Carter, deemed the elections fair, and Taylor received 75 percent of the votes. Others believed that citizens were afraid to vote for anyone else. Moreover, many Liberians feared that Taylor would resume the war if he was not elected.

With the elections drawing world attention, those outside Liberia began to understand the staggering effects of the war. More than 200,000 people were killed, most of them civilians, and another 1.25 million became refugees. Through the use of his AK-based system of warfare and intimidation, Taylor became one of the richest warlords in Africa, pulling in $300 to $400 million in personal income through looting and illegal trading of commodities and arms.

Because AKs are inexpensive, easy to fire, require almost no training, need few repairs or maintenance, they are ideally suited for child soldiers. As many as 80 percent of the Revolutionary United Front (RUF) rebels in Sierra Leone, shown here, were boys and girls between seven and fourteen. *Jean-Philippe Ksiazek/AFP/Getty Images*

The impact on a generation of children was devastating. According to the United Nations Children's Fund (UNICEF), fifteen thousand to twenty thousand children participated in the Liberian civil war between 1989 and 1997; perhaps as many as 60 percent of the combatants in some factions were under eighteen, with some as young as nine years old.

Unfortunately, Liberia's violence did not end with Taylor's election. With the country's infrastructure in shambles, heavily armed gangs continued to roam the countryside, stealing food and other necessities. People were afraid to give up their AKs, which now represented a way to make a living, albeit a ruthless one, in a country with little opportunity for legitimate work.

Despite a UN embargo imposed on Liberia in 1992, small arms continued to enter the country. Indeed, the United Nations charged that Taylor was a major arms conduit in Africa, operating with impunity and giving shelter to well-known arms dealers such as Gus Kouen-Hoven, a Dutch national who ran the Hotel Africa outside Monrovia. Also prospering under Taylor's largesse was the notorious Russian trafficker Victor Bout, one of the world's most active and notorious arms dealers. Bout's specialty was handling small arms from the Soviet Union and former Soviet states. Another Taylor-connected trafficker was the Ukrainian Leonid Minin, who, UN officials said, supplied arms to Taylor for money but also to win timber export contracts for his company, Exotic Tropical Timber Enterprise. These men made repeated appearances throughout Africa, selling small arms, mainly AKs and RPGs, to insurgents, rebels, and even legitimate armies.

In 1999, Taylor's regime faced opposition from a group better organized and more effective than the others he had encountered. Liberians United for Reconciliation and Democracy, commonly known as LURD, reportedly backed by U.S. ally Guinea, was consolidating control in the northern part of Liberia using many of the same tactics and engaging in similar atrocities as Taylor. Several other anti-Taylor groups emerged, including the Movement for Democracy in Liberia (MODEL), allegedly backed by neighboring Ivory Coast, which maintained a stronghold in the southern part of the country. Slowly and amid continued bloodshed, Taylor's grip on the nation was slipping away. In desperation, Taylor launched Operation No Living Thing, a campaign of atrocities designed to deter civilians from supporting and aiding LURD, whose ranks had swelled with Sierra Leonean militia wanting to destroy Taylor's regime. Taylor's terror program failed, and by the end of 2003 he controlled less than a third of Liberia.

A UN tribunal issued a warrant in June 2003 for Taylor, charging that he had exported his brand of AK-based carnage to neighboring Sierra Leone. His instrument there was the Revolutionary United Front (RUF), a group that he surreptitiously funded through the sale of weapons and timber. Again, unlike traditional conflicts, neither territory nor ideology were goals. Taylor's interest in Sierra Leone was its diamond mines, one of the largest deposits in the world. In March 1991, the RUF, under the command of former army corporal Foday Sankoh, gained control of mines in the Kone district. A small band of men, mainly armed with AKs, pushed the government army back toward the capital city of Freetown. Widespread civil war ensued, but this time it was more brutal than anyone had envisioned, even eclipsing Liberia in its depravity.

To maintain control of these diamond mines, the Taylor-backed RUF fighters engaged in atrocities against workers and others never before witnessed in Africa. Using AKs and wholesale rape, torture, mutilations, and amputations of arms and legs of those who opposed them, the RUF terrorized Sierra Leone. Within several years, the group controlled 90 percent of the country's diamond-producing areas.

Taylor repeatedly denied any involvement, but the statistics on diamond exports belied his claims. Liberia's annual mining capacity had been 100,000 to 150,000 carats annually from 1995 through 2000, but the Diamond High Council in Antwerp, Belgium, recorded imports into that country from Liberia of more than 31 million carats. According to U.S. ambassador Richard Holbrooke's testimony before the UN Security Council on July 31, 2000, the RUF gained $30 to $50 million annually, maybe as much as $125 million, from the illicit sale of diamonds. At the same time, exports from Sierra Leone slowed to a trickle, from $30.2 million in 1994 to $1.2 million in 1999.

The originating point of diamonds is pegged to their country of export, not the country of origin, so tracing is virtually impossible; however, Liberia's diamonds could *only* have come from Sierra

Leone. Taylor sold these "blood diamonds," or "conflict diamonds," as they became known, or traded them for small arms directly or through countries like Burkina Faso, Guinea, Ivory Coast, and Togo, whose exports of diamonds on the world scene also showed unexplainable increases. Arms dealer Leonid Minin also involved himself in the illegal diamond trade as a way to finance arms purchases for Taylor and others in West Africa.

As the years progressed, Taylor found many ways to escape detection for his arms transfers. In 2002, however, the United Nations officially documented a shipment of five thousand AKs from Serbia to Liberia in violation of an arms embargo. Although UN officials had been trying to obtain documented proof of illegal arms shipments to Taylor, hard evidence had always been difficult. In this one case, however, UN weapons inspector Alex Vines painstakingly traced the small arms, starting on the battlefield. He began his investigation in a no-man's-land in the middle of the Mano River Union bridge between Sierra Leone and Liberia. "A rebel child soldier showed me his AK-47 assault rifle which was stamped with M-70 2002 and a serial number. I knew immediately that this weapon had been made in Serbia," Vines said. The M-70 is the Yugoslav version of the AK. The child relayed that the weapon had recently been captured from a Liberian government soldier he killed. Discussions with officials in Belgrade showed a certificate on file for a sale to Nigeria, but close inspection revealed the document as a forgery. Further investigation showed that about five thousand AKs had traveled by plane to Libya where the plane was supposed to refuel en route to Nigeria. But instead of terminating in Nigeria as intended, the plane had continued on to Liberia.

ONE OF THE PROBLEMS ENCOUNTERED by officials trying to trace weapons was the almost indestructible nature of the AK. As AKs traveled from country to country, from war zone to war zone, their serial numbers often were obliterated through heavy usage or purposely erased, but the rifles remained usable and sellable. In one case, UN experts documented a cache of AKs that had seen action in Angola, Mozambique, and Sudan, recycled from conflict to conflict.

The shame of blood diamonds focused the world's attention on the atrocities in Sierra Leone, and the United Nations in 1999 established a mission in that country with an initial force of six thousand soldiers. Horrific violence still continued, however, with incidents like the brazen capture of hundreds of these peacekeepers by RUF guerrillas, who reportedly skinned alive some of the hostages.

One incident, not publicized at the time, but known to political leaders, altered Western military protocol forever. Although child soldiers had been used in Liberia and even more commonly in Sierra Leone, they mainly engaged other rebel forces or government soldiers. On August 25, 2000, this changed.

Eleven soldiers from the Royal Irish Regiment (and their Sierra Leone liaison), part of a larger UN presence that had previously secured the capital city and assisted in the capture of Sankoh, were taken hostage by the West Side Boys, a group of rogue boy soldiers armed with AKs. The British cadre was surrounded and unwilling to fire on children. It was one of the first engagements by Western soldiers against child soldiers, and it challenged for the first time the way Western military leaders viewed underage enemy combatants.

According to later reports, the West Side Boys were a band of AK-armed youths, perpetually drugged and drunk, who looted villages as they roamed the countryside. They demanded the release of their leader, General Papa, from prison as well as food and medicine in exchange for the captured British troops.

British forces immediately launched a search but could not find their comrades. Over the coming weeks, five soldiers were released in exchange for a satellite phone and other supplies, but the West Side Boys held fast to their other demands. On September 5, more than a hundred elite paratroopers from the 1st Battalion

Parachute Regiment landed in Senegal to stage a rescue operation. Special Air Service operatives cased the West Side Boys' camp and saw the rebels laugh as they carried out mock executions of the British soldiers.

Eavesdropping indicated that the rebels were planning to move their hostages to more dense jungle areas, so any rescue attempt had to be made soon. Prime Minister Tony Blair and the cabinet gave the go-ahead, and at dawn on September 11, 2000, three Chinook helicopters and two Westland Lynx gunships took off from Freetown airport and headed for Rokel Creek, the location of the rebel camp.

The Lynx gunships strafed the area, providing cover for the Chinooks, which landed about three hundred feet away to let off troops. Fierce firefights ensued, and in twelve minutes British troops overtook the Boys' position on the south side of the creek at Magbeni. On the north side of the creek, British troops reached the hostages held in the village of Geri Bana, but as they ran to waiting Chinooks, the West Side Boys sprayed the area with AK and machine-gun fire, hitting one paratrooper, who later died. Other British troops suffered nonlethal injuries during their escape. The rebel group lost twenty-five fighters, and eighteen were captured. Hundreds more were captured in operations during the following days; others escaped into the dense jungle. Their leader, Foday Kallay, was taken prisoner and turned over to Sierra Leonean officials.

This operation has been studied by many Western military officials not only because of its surgical precision but because of the child soldiers involved. The incident set a new standard for Western military behavior. Now soldiers are trained and indoctrinated to consider children as legitimate targets during combat situations.

Although many countries have employed child soldiers, Sierra Leone is often the center of discussion because of its prominence during the civil war that officially lasted from 1991 to 2001. As many as 80 percent of all combatants were between seven and fourteen. In addition, unlike other conflicts, children were recruited—often by abduction and forcible service—early on, rather than being brought in later to bolster dwindling adult forces. The number of child soldiers used by all sides, including government forces, was close to ten thousand, making them the majority of fighters.

Nobody knows the actual number of people killed in Sierra Leone—the violence continues—but the United Nations estimates the number at between fifty thousand and seventy-five thousand, with as many as one hundred thousand people mutilated. More than a million people, a third of the population, became refugees. The economy is still in ruins. The country's already feeble infrastructure has been destroyed, and the United Nations now considers Sierra Leone one of the poorest nations in the world.

The extent of the damage still is unfolding, made public through testimony during a war crimes trial, which began in March 2004 in Sierra Leone. The court is looking only at crimes committed after the November 30, 1996, Abidjan Accord between the government and rebels. So far, more than a dozen people have been indicted. RUF leader Sankoh died of a stroke in 2003, while Taylor, also indicted, sought safe haven in Nigeria and in early 2006 was extradited to Liberia to face war-crime charges. Gadhafi has been charged as a coconspirator.

Court testimony has stunned the world. One witness, a middle-aged woman identified only as TF-1196, said rebels used machetes to hack her husband's limbs off before he died. Then a rebel "young enough to be her child" raped her. She showed the court the hacked-off ends of her arms to illustrate why she could not sign court documents.

Child soldiers relayed how they called rebel leader Foday Sankoh "Pappy," and how he gave them AKs, marijuana, cocaine, and amphetamines to bolster their courage and spur them to kill and maim in the most brutal ways their young minds could imagine.

One child, identified as TF-1199, was twelve when rebels abducted him in 1998. He testified that he was taught how to fire an AK, smoke marijuana, and rape. He raped a fifteen-year-old girl presented to him after his commander threatened to kill him if he did not do what he was told.

REPORTS FROM THE WAR CRIMES court showed how wrong the Western world had been to focus on larger weapons and dismiss the importance to world security of small arms, especially the AK. During the proceedings, court documents revealed that Taylor sold conflict diamonds to al-Qaeda operatives that may have been used to finance the 9/11 attacks on the World Trade Center and Pentagon.

Diamonds and other gemstones are perfect for moving wealth around; they are small, hold their value, are universally acceptable as barter, don't set off airport metal detectors, and can easily be converted to cash. Al-Qaeda, the Taliban, and the Northern Alliance have a history of exploiting gemstones, such as those found in Afghanistan's emerald fields.

They transferred this gem-selling acumen to Africa. Al-Qaeda reportedly operated in West Africa from 1998 and maintained a continuous presence through 2002, according to the office of war crimes prosecutor Dave Crane. Weak and corrupt governments made West Africa an ideal choice for terrorist bases. In the case of Liberia, Taylor ran the country as his own criminal enterprise. Because of his status as a legitimate government leader, he issued visas and passports, and offered protection to anyone within his country's borders—for a fee. For example, he issued airplane registrations to arms dealer Victor Bout, who often took payment in diamonds for weapons.

Beginning in January 2001, al-Qaeda increased their purchases of diamonds, and continued until just before the September 11 attacks. According to a Belgian police report, the terrorist group purchased about $20 million worth of RUF diamonds during the fourteen months prior to 9/11. "The evidence suggests a rapid, large scale value transfer operation that allowed the terrorist group to move money out of traceable financial structures into untraceable commodities," Douglas Farah, author of *Blood from Stones*, told Congress during his February 2005 testimony.

During the upheavals in Liberia and Sierra Leone, the United States and other Western nations dismissed Taylor's activities—

especially his dealings in diamonds and small arms—because they were not considered a direct threat to their security. With the attacks of 9/11, this has proven a dangerous assumption.

Just as Afghanistan and Pakistan were the arms bazaar of the Middle East, Liberia and Sierra Leone became the nexus of small-arms smuggling in Africa from the mid-1980s to the present day. But the scourge of AKs did not stop in these West African nations. Cheap and plentiful small arms plagued the people of Mozambique, Rwanda, Somalia, Congo, and South Africa, among others. Indeed, from 1990 through 2000, Africa experienced more than a hundred conflicts, twice the number of previous decades, fueled mainly by AKs. In a continent where the price of an AK was often less than ten dollars, it became not only a weapon, but a way to make a living through criminal behavior and barter as in Liberia and Sierra Leone.

In Somalia, the AK played a pivotal role in that country's civil war and was at the root of unsuccessful efforts by the United Nations and U.S. forces to bring peace there.

IN 1992, SOMALIA WAS in the midst of a civil war that, coupled with a drought, brought widespread famine and disease. With the country in chaos and no single government emerging to take charge, a multinational military force under control of the United Nations in 1993 began humanitarian efforts to relieve hunger and aid displaced people. These troops' efforts met with mixed results. Assaults directed against them often prevented food and water from reaching those in need.

As violence escalated, several areas of the country seceded and formed their own independent states. One warlord in particular, General Mohammed Farrah Aidid, was not afraid to engage UN troops, killing soldiers from Pakistan, the United States, and elsewhere with bombs and small-arms fire.

On October 3, 1993, in the hope of capturing leaders of Aidid's rebel forces, U.S. Army Special Forces were deploying troops in

Mogadishu when the assault force was fired upon. Two UH-60 Black Hawk helicopters were shot down by rocket-propelled grenades and three others were disabled.

Most of the original assault force went to the first crash site, where about ninety Rangers found themselves under siege, mainly from massive small-arms fire, which kept them pinned down in the urban setting. They were stuck for the night while rebels and even Somali citizens angry at the United States and armed with AKs kept the GIs trapped. At the second crash site, two soldiers, dropped by helicopter to protect downed pilot Mike Durant from a street mob, were killed. Durant was taken hostage. By the next morning, the battle ended as reinforcements from the 10th Mountain Division and troops from Pakistan and Malaysia fought their way in and evacuated the remaining U.S. soldiers amid heavy gunfire and mobs firing AKs.

In the end, eighteen American soldiers were killed in action and seventy-nine sustained injuries. One Malaysian soldier was killed and seven injured. The Pakistanis suffered two injuries. Anywhere from three hundred to a thousand Somalis died, according to Pentagon estimates.

The incident, one of the most dramatic urban encounters endured by U.S. military forces, was chronicled in the popular book and movie entitled *Black Hawk Down*. The event's significance went far beyond Hollywood, however. Although U.S. forces won the battle, they did not complete their mission: to provide continued food and medical supplies to Somalians. To be sure, the efforts did save lives, perhaps as many as two hundred thousand people, but after seeing dead American soldiers dragged through the streets of Mogadishu, as well as footage from the battle itself, the Clinton administration lost its will for the peacekeeping action in Somalia. In March 1994, U.S. public opinion turned against keeping troops in the war-torn nation, and they were brought home. The United Nations, no longer able to count on the more than twenty thousand American troops, also pulled out as the situation deteriorated. Current conditions remain unsettled as Somalia has since split into several countries seeking international recognition. Warlords and their militias continue to engage in low-level wars fueled by cheap small arms, mainly AKs.

Small-arms attacks often thwarted UN humanitarian efforts. In one incident in 2000, a small single-engine plane was fired upon by AKs, leading to the curtailment of aid to Kismayo in Southwest Somalia. This scene has been repeated in other areas since then.

Not only did the experience in Somalia fuel the debate over using U.S. forces in areas in which U.S. security was not directly threatened, but it also spurred Pentagon planners to think more about how well-trained American troops outfitted with the latest high-tech weaponry can win against poorly trained militia armed with simple, low-tech automatic rifles, especially in urban settings.

The battle of Mogadishu brought to the foreground the growing debate about "asymmetric warfare." Although no single definition of the phrase exists, most military planners describe it as war between two dissimilar forces using vastly differing weapons and employing vastly different doctrines. On the surface, it would seem that the force with the best technology and best weapons would win quickly and decisively, but this is not always the case.

This was clearly the situation in Mogadishu. Commenting on *Black Hawk Down*, veteran BBC correspondent Yusuf Hassan noted, "It was sort of portraying the Americans as heroes, when in fact they had *all* the technology. It was a high-tech war—against people who only had AK-47 rifles." (They also had RPGs.) Since Mogadishu, the Marine Corps has instituted its Urban Warrior Program, one facet being the familiarization of troops with the AK. This is the weapon they will face most in future conflicts.

In Somalia, as in many areas of the world, the price of an AK can be an indication of social stability. In a sign of optimism, the price in Mogadishu of an AK dropped from $700 to between $300 and $400 after the Somali parliament in October 2004 elected Abdullahi Yusuf Ahmed president. Although fighting continued among the other self-proclaimed independent areas of Puntland and Somaliland over disputed territories, and in Somalia itself, there was hope that the new president would bring stability to the region. In response, the perceived need for people to arm themselves dropped, bringing a subsequent drop in price of the AK.

Unfortunately, the price steadily rose as Ahmed and his prime minister, Ali Mohammed Ghedi, remained in Nairobi, Kenya, where they were inaugurated under the security of that country's military and have lived ever since, running the government from exile.

THE SCOURGE OF LOW-COST AKS also spread to Rwanda as weapons poured in, fueling that country's genocide in 1994, a systematic horror that had not been seen since the "Killing Fields" of Cambodia in the 1970s.

The animosity between the Hutu majority and the Tutsis had been ongoing since before the country was a German colony, which was ceded to Belgium after World War I. A Tutsi monarchy ruled the country until 1959, when a Hutu uprising forced the Tutsis from power. In the process, thousands of Tutsis were killed and many foreigners, especially Belgians, were driven from the country. The Hutus, now in power, with sponsorship from France, engaged in large-scale murders of Tutsis from 1959 to 1966, during which time between 20,000 and 100,000 Tutsi were killed and about 150,000 fled to neighboring countries including Burundi, Uganda, Zaire, and Tanzania. In these other countries, Hutu and Tutsi conflicts spilled over. For example, in 1972, Hutus attacked Tutsis in southern Burundi and in counterattacks more than 80,000 Hutus were killed.

Kalashnikovs poured into Rwanda from Russia, Romania, Bulgaria, and other Warsaw Pact countries whose cash-strapped governments were eager to sell weapons to both sides. The Rwandan Popular Front (RFP), which operated from camps in Uganda and Tanzania and was predominately composed of Tutsis, mainly carried AKs from Romania. The Rwandan Armed Forces (FAR) also carried AKs as their weapon of choice.

Although large-scale genocide had already occurred in sporadic bursts, the worst was yet to come. On April 6, 1994, a Mystère Falcon jet carrying the presidents of Rwanda and Burundi was shot down, most likely by those who wanted to stop the peace process following the signing the previous August of the Arusha Accords. Rwandan president Juvenal Habyarimana, under heavy pressure from the United States, had begun to implement the accords, which would allow for the return of Tutsi refugees and power sharing between the Hutus and Tutsis.

Within hours of the plane crash, Hutu militia began hunting down and killing Tutsis in the capital city of Kigali. The killing spread throughout the country, with Hutus ordered to kill Tutsis or be killed by the militia. Between April and July 1994, at least half a million people were killed, according to UN relief groups, but some U.S. intelligence groups put the toll at over one million. About 2 million Rwandans, split evenly between Hutu and Tutsi, fled the country, about 1.5 million to Zaire, 200,000 to Burundi, and 460,000 to Tanzania, according to the UNHCR, the United Nations refugee organization.

Most news accounts emphasized the use of farm implements such as machetes, hoes, and axes in the genocide frenzy, but these reports did not tell the full story. Before the well-planned, systematic killing began, the Hutu government distributed thousands of AKs to militia, paramilitary gangs, and citizens to facilitate the roundup of Tutsis for slaughter. Many were then killed by traditional tribal weapons, and the rest were mowed down by automatic fire.

In mid-July, RPF forces led by Major General Paul Kagame finally defeated the FAR forces and ended the genocide, and Kagame became Rwanda's president in April 2000. During a ceremony in 2004 honoring those who died in the genocide that ended ten years earlier, Kagame blamed France more than any other country for its role. "They knowingly trained and armed government soldiers who were going to commit genocide," he said during his speech. However, Kagame failed to mention the role of other countries such as China, which supplied half a million machetes, and Egypt, which supplied more than eighty-five thousand tons of AKs and hand grenades. Incidentally, with its purchase of $26 million in weapons after a large-scale RPF attack in 1990, Rwanda became Africa's third largest importer of weapons. The catalyst for some of the earliest deals was Egypt's foreign minister, Boutros Boutros-Ghali, with guarantees from a French bank. Boutros-Ghali would later become the sixth secretary-general of the United Nations in January 1992.

There was little public mention of inaction by the United States, although U.S. officials knew about the genocide and did nothing to stop it. In fact, in communiqués from the Clinton administration's State Department, officials were careful not to use the word "genocide," because that would have provoked action under the 1948 International Treaty on the Prevention of Genocide, to which the United States was a signatory. Not until July 1994 were U.S. troops sent to Rwanda, but only to help refugees. Although many reasons have been proposed for why the United States did not intervene earlier—other countries and the United Nations had their own reasons—the one most probable was that America had been hurt so badly by its failure the year before in Somalia against mobs with AKs and other light weapons that it was reticent to engage in such an asymmetric conflict again.

Other reasons were much more nefarious, based on details that have only recently been made public. Some evidence suggests that the RPF, with the cooperation of Western nations including the United States, shot down the plane carrying the two presidents in an effort to provoke a "genocide" that they could then stop by force. Why? Chris Black, lead counsel at the International Tribunal for Rwanda, suggests that the United States wanted to replace the Hutu regime with one that would be more favorable to its aggressive stance toward Zaire; that the United States wanted to reduce French influence in central Africa; and that the ultimate U.S. goal was control of the Congo Basin's natural resources. By provoking the genocide, the RPF could legitimately fight the FAR and defeat them with the world's blessing.

There is also evidence of a so-called genocide fax sent to UN headquarters in New York that outlines plans for mass killings, but this document has been discredited by many as a hoax, another attempt to bolster support for the RPF among Western nations.

One of the ironies of the genocide was that Kagame and his 12,000-strong RPF defeated the FAR and Hutu paramilitary groups with no artillery, aircraft, or armored vehicles. Their main weapon was the AK. In his best-selling book *We Wish to Inform You That Tomorrow We Will Be Killed with Our Families*, author Philip Gourevitch noted this about Kagame: "That he had pulled it off [the defeat of FAR and the end of genocide] with an arsenal composed merely of mortars, rocked propelled grenades and, primarily, what one American arms specialist described to me as 'piece of shit' secondhand Kalashnikovs, has only added to the [Kagame] legend. 'The problem isn't the equipment,' Kagame said, 'the problem is always the man behind it.'"

Whether the Rwandan war turns out to have been a true tribal conflict, a war perpetrated by Western nations, or a combination of these factors, one thing is certain: the AK was the main fuel that fed this terrible tragedy.

RWANDA AND OTHER COUNTRIES in Africa make up just a small part of a long list of devastation brought about by the AK and other small arms. In some countries, people half jokingly call the AK the "African Credit Card," because in many parts of the continent having one is necessary for everyday existence. In Angola, for example, refugees and former rebels fleeing from government forces during their civil war traded AKs to Zambian villagers for food.

In pastoral areas, traditional people such as the Karamajong in Uganda had always fought other groups using spears because of traditional and spiritual imperatives. Introduction of the AK, however, spewing hundreds of bullets a minute, turned their societies topsy-turvy. The weapon not only raised the level of destruction among warring groups but also ratcheted up hostilities against repressive governments with whom the tribesmen formerly held no advantage. On a tribal level, AKs immediately endowed power to warlords over the authority traditionally held by tribal elders. Age and wisdom no longer determined status; Kalashnikovs did.

The AK changed cultural patterns in ways that westerners could hardly fathom. It became a standard-exchange barter amount for cattle among the group. In 1998, an AK might be worth three or four cattle. If the gun was registered with the Ugandan government, it was considered more valuable and the investment could be recouped in a few years. It also could be used to increase a person's herd through cattle rustling, which until the advent of the AK was a relatively small-scale activity.

The AK also began appearing as parts of dowries.

This day-to-day incorporation of the AK was far from unique. In South Africa, black youths considered buying an AK as a rite of manhood as well as a way to fight government-sponsored apartheid. The rifle became such a strong icon of antigovernment groups like the African National Congress (ANC) that the government demonized the weapon in the media, equating it with the Soviet Union and Communism and thus justifying its legitimate suppression of such groups. In this way, the government used the ANC's interest in the AK to allege that it was supported by the Soviet Union and was not a homegrown, grassroots organization.

Many AKs in South Africa came from Mozambique in the early 1990s as that nation's twenty-year civil war was winding down. (South Africa is the only sub-Saharan nation that produces its own AK version, the Vektor R4, which is actually a copy of the Israeli Galil, itself a modified AK.) In that country, AKs were so commonplace, so easy to get, that they were used as currency.

This was a far cry from the situation when Mozambique in 1974 won its independence from Portugal. When the colonial power left, it took most of its arms with it. However, this did not deter groups contending for power from increasing their small-arms

Introduction of the AK turned pastoral people's societies upside down. It not only raised the level of destruction among warring groups, who usually fought with spears and swords for traditional and spiritual reasons, but also ratcheted up hostilities against repressive governments over whom they formerly held no advantage. Here, Hamer warriors in Ethiopia's Omo Valley patrol Lake Chew Bahir for protection against the Boranas, their worst enemies. © *Remi Benali/Corbis*

caches. According to UN estimates, armies on both sides of the ensuing civil war—the Front for the Liberation of Mozambique (FRELIMO), which had initiated the armed campaign of independence against Portugal in 1964, and the Mozambique National Resistance (RENAMO)—never amounted to more than 92,000 people, so outside authorities were shocked when they looked at the number of weapons left over after fighting ended in 1993.

One report had the Mozambican government handing out 1.5 million AKs to civilian self-defense groups. But a 1994 Interpol presentation noted that 1.5 million AKs came from the Soviet Union alone. UN reports pegged the number at between 5 and 10 million weapons.

The true number may never be known. Although the United Nations collected almost 170,000 AKs from uniformed troops, many more weapons were kept by private individuals or smuggled or sold to neighboring South Africa, which saw an unprecedented surge in AKs as evidenced by prices plummeting to as low as five to ten dollars in some instances.

As a cultural icon, the AK clearly left its mark on Mozambique. The country's flag features an AK crossed with a hoe on a field of horizontal red, green, black, gold, and white stripes. Both images are superimposed on an open book. The flag symbolizes the country's commitment to defense, labor, and education. Mozambique's coat of arms also displays the AK, hoe, and book over a map of the country and is seen every day on paper money and coins.

In 1999, the country held a contest to change the flag, ostensibly to replace the AK with a more peaceful symbol. Jose Forjaz, a widely known Mozambican architect, won the design competition, but nothing further happened. A constitutional package that would change the flag and coat of arms, and provide a new national anthem along with some other amendments, has been stalled for years. It's unclear when or if the flag will ever change.

Even if the AK image is deleted from the flag and emblem, it remains embedded in the country's consciousness, not only through the estimated one million deaths it caused, but through children, many of them now grown, who were named for the gun. "When I met the Mozambique minister of defense, he presented me with his country's national banner, which carries the image of a Kalashnikov gun," said Mikhail Kalashnikov. "He told me that when all the Liberation [FRELIMO] soldiers went home to their villages, they named their sons Kalash."

By the late 1980s, the Kalashnikov's reputation had already spread like a virus throughout the Far East, Middle East, and Africa, leaving a path of destruction and human suffering. In the

Western Hemisphere, Central and South America were not spared the AK's wrath. This ten-dollar weapon of mass destruction had already penetrated Latin America, leaving millions dead and displaced and helping to foster the world's most powerful and brutal drug cartels.

5

THE KALASHNIKOV CULTURE
REACHES LATIN AMERICA

A MID THE COLLAPSED buildings of Nicaragua's capital, Managua—many structures remain in ruins after a devastating earthquake in 1972—rises the city's largest statue, an iron figure with his outstretched arm thrusting skyward, defiantly gripping an AK.

Because of his exaggerated muscle-rippled chest, this statue of a Sandinista guerrilla was dubbed the Incredible Hulk by locals, who employ the comic-book hero's name to direct tourists, telling them to "take a right at the Incredible Hulk." At the base of this landmark, erected to honor the freedom fighters who drove out the Somoza-family dictators, are inscribed the words of General Augusto Sandino, for whom the Sandinistas are named: *In the end, only the workers and peasants will remain.*

Sandino got it partly right.

Along with the workers and peasants are tens of thousands of unaccounted-for AKs left over from the country's forty years of strife that spilled over into neighboring Honduras and El Salvador and caused Kalashnikov Cultures to spring up in Peru, Colombia,

In Nicaragua's capital of Managua, this statue of a Sandinista guerrilla thrusting an AK skyward was erected to honor the freedom fighters who drove out the Somoza-family dictators. Because of its exaggerated muscle-rippled chest, the locals dubbed it the Incredible Hulk after the comic-book hero. © *1999, James Lerager*

and Venezuela. Like Kalashnikov Cultures in the Middle East, these are just as ingrained and just as deadly.

Despite government initiatives to disarm citizens and destroy weapons, most are still around, and with new weapons pouring into the region daily from around the world, parts of some Central and South American countries remain gun-heavy and dangerous.

Unlike Africa, where AK-toting, poorly disciplined gangs mainly engaged in small-time subsistence looting, pillaging villages and supporting despots like Charles Taylor in his gun and blood-diamond trade, the Latin American scene evolved from violent civil wars between rebel groups and government forces to powerful, well-trained and disciplined drug cartels that operate under the guise of political ideology.

These groups are so rich and powerful that they mimic small countries, maintaining order in their strongholds, taxing drug farmers, and keeping government forces at bay. Their political ideologies, both right- and left-wing, exist mainly as the glue that supports a social, economic, and cultural infrastructure focused on growing, smuggling, and profiting from illegal drugs such as cocaine and heroin. (Afghanistan remains the largest producer of heroin, its exports reaching the United States through drug smuggling routes established and protected by South American drug cartels.)

As these groups grew stronger, they were able to purchase larger weapons—one Colombian drug cartel even had a submarine on the drawing board to smuggle cocaine—but their workhorse remains the AK, which is often paid for with drugs instead of money. This barter was so institutionalized that a de facto exchange rate of one kilo of cocaine sulfate per AK was established. (Cocaine sulfate is produced by mashing coca leaves with water and dilute sulfuric acid. This produces an easily transportable paste that is an intermediate step to producing cocaine hydrochloride—common street cocaine.)

As the civil wars in Nicaragua, El Salvador, and Guatemala petered out in the 1990s because of exhaustion by the combatants, tens of thousands of small arms, mainly AKs, remained in the hands of former rebels and government soldiers who used them in criminal acts ranging from robbery and homicide to protection for South American drug cartels that employed Central America as a waypoint for contraband heading north to the United States. Currently, more than 70 percent of the cocaine entering the United States comes through the Central America–Mexico border, according to the U.S. Drug Enforcement Administration, and governments weakened by civil wars and ensuing domestic violence often are powerless to stop the traffic.

These civil wars, fueled by AKs supplied by the two superpowers, have left Central America as one of the most violent regions in the world, with crime rates more than double the world average. These crime rates not only impede democratic processes but have locked the region in widespread poverty. The Inter-American Development Bank estimates that Latin America's per capita gross domestic product would be 25 percent higher if the crime rate were more in line with the world average.

LIKE AFGHANISTAN, NICARAGUA became its hemisphere's premier entry point for AKs. In almost parallel fashion, the U.S. government, wanting to fight pro-Soviet regimes, covertly armed Nicaraguan Contra fighters with AKs manufactured by Warsaw Pact countries. The Soviets did the same for their comrades.

Drugs, AKs, and political dogma are so tightly bound together in this region of the world that they may never be unwound. Unless they are, however, the three will feed on each other as Latin American nations remain mired in the chaos of government corruption, violence, and severe urban poverty.

This deadly triad in Central America can be traced to U.S. intervention in Nicaragua in the 1850s when the conservative elite of the city of León invited American adventurer William Walker to fight against their rivals, the liberal elite of Granada. Remarkably, Walker was elected president in 1856, but forces from neighboring Honduras and other countries drove him out and later executed him.

From 1912 through 1933, except for one nine-month period, U.S. Marines were stationed in Nicaragua; the U.S. administrations said they were needed to protect American citizens and property. From 1927 to 1933, Sandino led a revolt against the conservative regime and their U.S. supporters, and U.S. troops finally left in 1933, but not before they had set up the National Guard, a militia designed to look after U.S. economic interests after the marines' exit. Anastasio Somoza Garcia was put in charge of the National Guard, and he ruled the country along with Sandino and President Carlos Alberto Brenes Jarquin, a figurehead politician. Half a century later, the fragments of this National Guard would became the focal point of U.S.-supplied AKs.

With U.S. support, Somoza Garcia took full control of the country, and the National Guard assassinated Sandino in 1934. The Somoza clan held dictatorial power through torture, intimidation, and military force until 1979. During the family's reign, which was passed along to sons and brothers, they built an enormous fortune through bribery, exports of coffee, cattle, cotton, and timber, and by accepting financial and military aid from the United States—as long as they remained anti-Communist. Like Charles Taylor in Liberia, the Somozas ran Nicaragua for their own personal benefit.

Opposition was building, however. Buoyed by the success of the Communist revolution against Cuban dictator General Fulgencio Batista in 1961, Sandinista forces backed by Cuba staged raids from Honduras and Costa Rica against Somoza's National Guard troops. Although Cuba did not produce AKs, it received them from the Soviet Union and Warsaw Pact countries as well as North Korea and supplied them to rebel forces in Nicaragua. Aside from hunting rifles and other scrounged firearms, the AK became the Sandinistas' main weapon. Cuba had previously backed pro-Communist rebels in Angola with weapons, funding, and troops and was doing the same for the Sandinistas despite protests from the United States.

U.S. officials were torn. On one side was a dictatorship that was growing more brutal as the revolutionaries became more active. On the other side was the specter of the Soviet Union gaining a foothold in Nicaragua as it had done in Cuba. The United States continued to support Somoza with funds and weapons until December 1972, when an earthquake destroyed much of Managua, killing ten thousand people, leaving fifty thousand families homeless, and ruining about 80 percent of the city's commercial buildings.

Instead of keeping order, Somoza's National Guard joined much of the looting that followed the earthquake, but what happened next shocked and horrified the international community even more than the soldiers' behavior.

With millions of dollars in relief aid pouring into Nicaragua, Somoza took advantage of the situation, keeping most of the money that was intended for victims. Funds earmarked to purchase food, clothing, and water and to rebuild Managua were diverted into Somoza's personal bank account. By 1974, his wealth was estimated at more than $400 million. Even his supporters were sickened by the dictator's actions, and opposition within the business community, one of his strongest allies, was rising.

The Sandinista National Liberation Front (FSLN) grew during this time as anti-Somoza sentiment grew throughout the country. Somoza responded with even more repression, prompting President Jimmy Carter to make military assistance contingent upon human rights improvements. Somoza stepped up his oppression. Street protests continued, and the country was in a state of siege. Strikes were commonplace and the economy was in ruins. Somoza relied on foreign loans, mainly from the United States, to prop up the country's finances.

Somoza's eventual downfall was precipitated by the assassination in January 10, 1978, of Pedro Joaquin Chamorro Cardenal, outspoken publisher of the newspaper *La Prensa* and leader of the

Democratic Liberation Union (UDEL). A massive nationwide strike paralyzed the country for ten days, and Sandinista attacks on government forces continued—but Somoza clung to power.

In 1978, the United States stopped military assistance to Somoza, forcing him to buy weapons on the world market. In one instance, no longer able to purchase M-16s from the United States, Somoza's National Guard bought Israeli Uzi submachine guns and the Galil, that country's version of the AK, first introduced in 1973. Because of his outlaw behavior, many countries refused to sell arms to Somoza. Israel was among them, at first, but the Israelis succumbed to pressure from pro-Somoza entities within the U.S. military, fearing that refusal would cut off their own U.S. funding.

The Israelis had built the Galil, named for its inventor, Israel Galili, in response to the poor performance of their standard-issue FN-FAL during the 1967 Six-Day War. (Israel Galili is often confused with Uziel "Uzi" Gal, the inventor of the Uzi submachine gun.) Having seen the reliability of the AKs used by Arab nations in battle, the Israelis realized that their rifles were not tough enough for desert conditions. In addition, the Israeli army was overwhelmingly a conscript force with most troops considered reservists available for a call-up during emergencies only. With little ongoing training, these soldiers could be hard on their weapons—leaving them in the dirt during bivouac, for example, something a professional soldier would never do—and the AK-type rifle could withstand abuse. (In an odd but practical concession to these unprofessional, part-time fighters, the bipod stand included with the weapon sported a bottle-cap opener. This would keep Israeli soldiers from damaging the flanges on their magazines by opening bottles with them.)

For Somoza, a major draw of the Galil was that it fired the 5.56mm round, the same as the M-16, so his army could use the tons of U.S.-supplied ammunition it still had on hand. The rifle was also inexpensive, less than $150 each.

As Somoza's popularity waned, the National Guard became

even more brutal in their attacks, including widespread bombing of León after the Sandinistas had taken control of that city. Still, Somoza would not yield to pressure for inclusion of the Sandinistas in the government.

The country continued to deteriorate. High unemployment, violence, inflation, food and water shortages, and massive debts racked the nation. In February 1979, the Sandinistas formed a junta combining several anti-Somoza groups that garnered a broad following. By March, the FSLN, now better equipped with small arms, launched a final assault on many areas, and by June these AK-wielding soldiers had secured most of the country.

In July, Somoza finally resigned, and with U.S. help fled to Miami and then to Paraguay, where he was murdered the following year, reportedly by leftist Argentine guerrillas.

Faced with a debt of $1.6 billion, an estimated 50,000 citizens dead and 120,000 homeless, the Sandinista administration was doomed from the start despite an optimistic citizenry. But even with widespread disease and lack of food and water, for many people the situation was still better than under the brutal Somoza regime.

With no cohesive government in charge, FSLN leaders formed coalitions, and finally in 1980 a government incorporating large numbers of Nicaraguans was formed. Not everyone embraced the new regime, however. President Jimmy Carter tried to work with the FSLN, but his successor Ronald Reagan, who took office in January 1981, immediately began to isolate and vilify the new government, claiming it was arming pro-Soviet guerrillas in El Salvador.

Nicaraguan problems aside, Carter had lost the election in part because Americans blamed him for not securing the release of fifty-two U.S. hostages held by Islamic fundamentalists at the American embassy in Tehran. The hostages were released twenty minutes after Reagan's inauguration, leading to speculation that a secret deal now known as the "October Surprise" had been reached between Reagan's campaign officials, notably William

Casey, and Iranian officials to hold the hostages until after the election, thus ensuring that Carter would not win. In return, Iran would receive military and funding support to help fight their war with Iraq that had been ratcheting up for years and fully commenced on September 22, 1980, when Iraqi troops invaded Iran. This covert involvement of the United States in the Iran-Iraq war would later become a crucial element in the spreading of AKs a half a world away in Nicaragua.

As the Sandinistas took hold, the Reagan administration supported opponents with funds and military aid. The core of these were remnants of Somoza's original National Guard, who operated hit-and-run raids from camps in Honduras where many of them had fled after the dictator's fall from power. These Contras (from *contrarevolucianarios*) grew in strength as Nicaraguans became less enamored with the slow economic progress of the Sandinista government. Because they had to spend more and more of their budget on fighting the Contras, the Sandinistas were left with less for social reform. In addition, they grew less tolerant of legitimate opposition groups and began employing intimidation tactics against those who did not believe in the revolutionary movement. Even *La Prensa*, once ardently anti-Somoza, voiced its concern over the tactics of the Sandinistas, who, during a state of emergency declared in 1982, censored the newspaper.

As hostilities grew, small arms rushed into Nicaragua. The Sandinistas received support from the Soviet Union, mainly through Cuba and the Warsaw Pact nations. The Sandinista army at first was poorly equipped and ill managed. Their weapons consisted of some AKs from Cuba and whatever was left behind when Somoza's National Guard fled the country. This hodgepodge was gradually replaced by AKs only. The Contras had very few weapons save some hunting rifles, shotguns, and pistols. This changed immediately after they began to be funded by the United States beginning in 1981 when William Casey, newly appointed CIA director, suggested to Reagan that he support $19 million for the agency, which Congress later approved, to establish opposition to the Sandinistas. In 1982, the CIA created Contra bases in Honduras. In southern Nicaragua and northern Costa Rica, CIA-supported Contra camps were established under the leadership of a former Sandinista commander with the colorful moniker of "Commandante Zero."

Congress was becoming increasingly uneasy about the conflict, however, and the situation came to a head when the CIA illegally mined one of Nicaragua's harbors, sinking a Soviet freighter. In December, Congress unanimously passed the Boland Amendment to the 1983 military budget bill, which made it illegal for the CIA to continue funding the Contras. This did not stop the Reagan administration. They continued to fund the Contras through third parties, other countries, and through other U.S. government agencies that, the White House maintained, were legally outside the Boland Amendment's edict.

In August 1985, the Contras received a shipment from Poland of ten thousand Polish-made AKs worth about $6 million. Polish officials denied they would ever directly sell weapons to a group opposed to the Marxist Sandinistas. Polish embassy official Andrzej Dobrynski said publicly, "It is so preposterous, it is undignified even to deny it." Indeed, Nicaraguan president and Sandinista leader Daniel Ortega was a guest of honor at ceremonies in Warsaw commemorating the fortieth anniversary of the end of World War II.

U.S. officials claimed that the Contras had hijacked the Polish shipment, intended for an unspecified Latin American country, but government critics suggested that the United States had bought the AKs for the Contras despite the congressional prohibition. They said that although it did seem preposterous, Poland needed the money so badly that it was willing to go against its political ideology for cold cash.

Neither side budged from their accusatory position until late 1986 when Sandinista soldiers monitored a camouflaged Vietnam-era C-123 cargo plane that had taken off from a field outside of San Salvador and was nearing the Nicaraguan town of San Carlos.

As the plane flew down to twenty-five hundred feet, preparing to drop its load, a nineteen-year-old soldier fired his shoulder-mounted surface-to-air missile. Direct hit. The plane spiraled, trailed smoke, and crashed, but not before a single parachute opened, safely lowering Gene Hasenfus of Marinette, Wisconsin, to the ground.

When soldiers reached the wrecked plane, they discovered seventy AKs, 100,000 rounds of ammunition, rocket grenades, jungle fatigues, boots, and two dead Americans. One of the dead crew members, William J. Cooper, carried an ID card from Southern Air Transport, a Miami company once owned by the CIA and still thought to have ties to the agency. The plane had previously been used in 1984 as part of a government sting, filmed by the CIA, showing the Nicaraguan interior minister involved in selling cocaine. Reagan had publicly displayed a still photograph from the film months earlier to bolster the administration's position that the Contras should be supported to fight the Sandinistas, who were now drug dealers. He could not have known that the photo later would provide solid evidence of his illegal connection to the Contras.

Any doubt about the CIA's involvement in funding the Contras, including the AK shipment from Poland, disappeared as the captured Hasenfus spilled the beans on the entire operation, telling about flying missions for the CIA, bringing weapons and supplies to the Contras. Even Reagan supporters felt betrayed at the disconnect between the administration's public rhetoric denying aid to the Contras in violation of law and the mounting evidence to the contrary. The fact that the plane carried Soviet-style AKs added a more sinister veneer to a situation that was growing more disturbing every day.

In November 1986, the scandal grew even larger when the Lebanese magazine *Ash Shiraa* reported that the United States had been selling weapons to Iran. Profits from the arms deals were being used to buy weapons and for direct funding of the Contras. These weapons sales to Iran reportedly funded Hasenfus's ill-fated flight.

During congressional testimony about the Iran-Contra affair—
which only covered activities from October 1984 to 1986—investigators uncovered more details about arms shipments. For
example, investigators learned that White House aide Lieutenant
Colonel Oliver L. North had shredded documents pertaining to
the arms sales shortly after Hasenfus's plane was shot down. Contra leader Adolfo Calero offered documents showing that he had
established a financial structure to funnel aid to the Contras.
North, who was at the National Security Council, had set up
dummy corporations and bank accounts to transfer money to
Calero's organization. Two former military officers, Major General Richard V. Secord and Major General John K. Singlaub, were
also involved in the ruse.

Calero testified that Secord and Singlaub were particularly
pleased at the bargain prices the group had received. The Contras
paid half of the going rate for ammunition, about nine to twelve
cents a round, and $145 for AKs, which normally cost $230 on the
open market. He went into great detail about the $6 million
Poland deal, handled by Singlaub, that netted several thousand
AKs and millions of rounds of ammunition.

Calero also testified that Secord said that he had not profited
from the total $11.4 million arms deals, but he later learned that
Secord had lied and doubled the price of the AKs that he sold to
the Contras.

Further media investigations revealed that the CIA maintained
stateside warehouses of Soviet bloc weapons, mainly AKs, as did
the Defense Department. In several instances, records showed that
these AKs entered the United States from Eastern Europe and
landed at the port of Wilmington, North Carolina. Many had their
serial numbers removed so they could not be traced to their country of origin.

The televised hearings from May to August 1987 captured the
attention of Americans as they watched North and others endure
hours of probing questions. When Congress issued its findings on
the Iran-Contra scandal, they said that North had been the main

negotiator of the deals despite his pleas that he was only following orders from superiors. In May 1989, he was convicted of obstructing Congress and destroying government documents. His conviction was later overturned.

The results of the Iran-Contra probe—the full report was issued in January 1994, seven years after it began—never uncovered the entire story, because CIA officials refused to disclose the full extent of their involvement with the Contras. North, the principal dealmaker, also refused to answer many questions put to him, invoking his Fifth Amendment right against self-incrimination. The report concluded, "The underlying facts of Iran/contra are that, regardless of criminality, President Reagan, the secretary of state, the secretary of defense, and the director of central intelligence and their necessary assistants committed themselves, however reluctantly, to two programs contrary to congressional policy and contrary to national policy. They skirted the law, some of them broke the law, and almost all of them tried to cover up the President's willful activities."

While this was a low point in U.S. history, the real legacy of the Iran-Contra scandal was that it brought tens of thousands of AKs to Nicaragua. These arms have spread throughout Central and South America, wreaking havoc and devastation not only in these countries but also in the United States, which has become a final destination for drugs produced there.

BY 1989, EXHAUSTION WAS SETTING in among the Nicaraguan combatants, but as happens in many postwar situations, like Afghanistan and in Sierra Leone, the large number of cheap leftover arms gave people a way to survive amid the chaos. As in Pakistan, Afghanistan, and other Middle Eastern countries, the weapons became a way to make a living. As the war wound down, there were widespread reports of soldiers and former soldiers armed with AKs hijacking government trucks for food. Citizens bought rifles for protection against such gangs, while others set up firing ranges so well-to-do people could fire these plentiful weapons safely, for a fee, in a convivial setting. Still others, seeking to obtain hard currency, sold caches of leftover AKs to rebels in other countries such as El Salvador.

By 1989, the civil war in El Salvador was already a decade old. The country had been ruled by a string of dictatorships since the 1930s, but the seventies saw the growth of more active guerrilla movements, most notably Farabundo Martí National Liberation Front (FMLN), which opposed the oppressive right-wing government. Between 1979 and 1981 about thirty thousand people were killed by government death squads, and the moderate presidency of José Napoleon Duarte from 1984 to 1989 failed to end the war. Instead, it grew even more violent.

During this time, the FMLN had received large shipments of AKs to bolster their struggle against the U.S.-backed right-wing regime. President George H. W. Bush publicly stated that the weapons were coming from Soviet-backed groups in Cuba and Nicaragua, mainly the Sandinistas. These were not trivial shipments. According to U.S. ambassador William Walker, the entire guerrilla force of six thousand to eight thousand was now reequipped with AKs and ready to renew its efforts against the government.

Walker claimed that these weapons came from Cuba, which turned out to be wrong. The White House later amended his statement, saying that the weapons were from Soviet bloc nations but the ammunition came from Cuba through Nicaragua.

As the days progressed, the story changed again. The U.S.-backed government in El Salvador never blamed the Nicaraguans, and the White House offered scant evidence to back its own claim of a Nicaraguan connection.

As it turned out, the weapons came from an unexpected source. Honduran military officials, hoping to cash in on the debris of Nicaragua's civil war, had raided weapons caches left over by the CIA in their country. These arms originally were intended for the Contras as Congress was preparing to cut off funding. When the Contras faded from the scene, the weapons lay unused but secured. With the assistance of professional arms dealers, they found their way to left-wing rebels in El Salvador.

This influx of AKs bolstered the rebels' morale and offered them greater firepower over the Salvadoran army, which was outfitted with M-16s from the United States. The FMLN even changed their battle tactics to take advantage of the AK's intermediate round—7.62 × 39mm models were and are still manufactured in many Warsaw Pact countries like Romania, as well as China—which was heavier and traveled farther than the smaller M-16 round. On election day in March 1989, for example, one battle of a coordinated nationwide push by AK-armed rebel forces held government helicopters at a distance in the village of San Isidro, keeping them just out of range from supplying air support to their ground troops. This tactic was repeated throughout the country.

This and subsequent guerrilla attacks were so successful that the government had no choice but to accept a peace accord that included the FMLN and was brokered by the United Nations in 1991. A nine-month cease-fire took effect on February 1, 1992, and has held since. The last remnants of the FMLN's military structure were dismantled as it became a legitimate political party and integrated into the government. Unfortunately, El Salvador, like its Central American neighbors, still suffers from domestic violence, gangs, street crime, and high homicide rates as AKs and other weapons remain plentiful despite arms collection and destruction programs.

In a ceremony intended to symbolize a more peaceful era for the region, Nicaraguan president Violeta Chamorro in September 1990 gave President George H. W. Bush an AK cut in half by a blowtorch. The weapon had been taken from a citizen as part of the country's efforts to destroy the large numbers of small arms that still existed. (Many of these weapons were distributed wholesale by Sandinista leaders when Chamorro in 1990 beat their candidate, Daniel Ortega.)

Other countries, including Guatemala and Honduras, had similar programs to de-arm their nations, but they, like Nicaragua, met with less than stellar results. Small arms possess too much utility to be turned in. Not only can they be used for hunting and self-protection against domestic crime, but also as a hedge in case of renewed civil war or an oppressive regime taking power. The tradition of people holding small arms and the prestige associated with it was just so strong in the region; government decommissioning programs could not overcome it.

To Chamorro, a disabled AK was the perfect icon of the country's efforts to stem violence, but despite this gesture, the cold war had left Central America awash in weapons, which were now heading southward to countries like Venezuela, Peru, and Colombia where they were slowly replacing the Belgian FN-FALs that had for decades been popular among rebel groups because of their availability. In addition, because of the now weakened and lawless condition of Central American nations, illegal arms shipments from Europe were streaming through these countries on their way to South America.

Just as it had done in the Middle East and Africa, the indestructible and cheap AK worked its way from country to country, turning small conflicts into large wars.

THESE NEWLY IMPORTED AKS were ending up in the hands of groups like the antigovernment Revolutionary Armed Forces of Colombia (FARC), the Western Hemisphere's largest guerrilla group; the left-wing National Liberation Army (ELN); and the United Self-Defense Forces of Colombia (AUC), the largest federation of right-wing paramilitaries. These groups have been accused of human rights abuses, kidnappings, bombings, assassinations, drug trafficking, airline hijackings, and extortion.

FARC is by far Colombia's largest and best-equipped guerrilla group, with almost twenty thousand members. It was formed in 1966 by survivors of a U.S.-supported raid on a Communist

Party–inspired cooperative calling itself the Independent Republic of Marquetalia. It controls of about half of the country, mainly in the southeastern jungle areas and plains surrounding the Andes. FARC reached a peak of power in 1999, and the president of Colombia, Andres Pastrana, had offered to give the group a huge tract of land twice the size of New Jersey if it would end its violent activities. These negotiations broke down and fighting between government forces and FARC continued. Although FARC originally received assistance from the Soviet Union and its satellite countries, it now finances itself through kidnapping, drug dealing, and extortion. FARC often uses child soldiers, many impressed against their will, armed with AKs.

ELN was founded in 1964 by Cuban-trained Colombian students inspired by the Cuban revolution. Currently the group has fewer than four thousand members and has been dealt military setbacks by right-wing paramilitary groups such as AUC. ELN finances itself by kidnapping and holding for ransom wealthy Colombians. It has also extorted from oil companies by threatening to bomb their pipelines and facilities. It is estimated that FARC and ELN take in $200 to $400 million annually, at least half of it from drug dealing, including protection money paid by growers and other dealers.

The last major group, AUC, grew from the consolidation of other right-wing paramilitary groups in 1997, expanded rapidly to about eight thousand members, and is still growing. The group has a stronghold in northern Colombia, where it receives funding from wealthy landowners and drug traffickers, but operates throughout the country. The AUC engages in drug smuggling itself. It attacks leftist guerrilla groups as well as trade activists and human rights organizations. It often recruits from citizens who have been victims of attack from left-wing groups. Although Colombia's army does not officially support AUC, various human rights groups have documented ties between them.

The one thing that all these groups have in common is their need for more inexpensive weapons, mainly AKs, which now are the preferred firearm because of their low cost and durability in jungle conditions. Unlike the mujahideen in Afghanistan, South American fighters and their counterparts in Central America have favored the heavier 7.62mm bullet instead of the lightweight 5.56mm or 5.45mm rounds because it tends to penetrate jungle foliage better and has a longer range to fend off government helicopters. Culturally, these fighters have been "brought up" on the larger round and are used to it.

The illegal trade in AKs and ammunition in Latin America offers intriguing views of how difficult it is to stop small-arms smuggling because of the layers of middlemen and corrupt government officials. The deals are further obfuscated by the inclusion of legal elements of arms purchases that turn illegal at some point in the transaction. By then, however, it often is too late to stop the deal. While the vast majority of illegal arms deals go unnoticed by authorities, some well-documented cases have been made public, and they offer a glimpse into the shady world of gun-running.

One incident in October 1999 began simply and legally enough but evolved into the illegal transfer of three thousand AKs and two and a half million rounds of ammunition from official Nicaraguan government warehouses to the AUC guerrilla group in Colombia. Originally a deal was cut for the legitimate transfer between the Nicaraguan National Police and a private Guatemalan arms dealer, Grupo de Representaciones Internacionales S.A., known as GIR S.A. GIR S.A. offered to trade new Israeli pistols and Uzi submachine guns for five thousand surplus AKs and two and a half million rounds of ammunition. This was a good deal for the Nicaraguan police, because they wanted the pistols and Uzis, which were more useful for police work than the AKs.

GIR S.A. found Shimon Yelinek, an Israeli arms dealer based in Panama, to buy the AKs. Yelinek said he was representing the Panamanian National Police, but his papers later turned out to be forgeries. After inspecting the weapons, Yelinek decided that the weapons were not satisfactory and threatened to scuttle the deal.

After some negotiation, Yelinek and Nicaraguan army officials decided to exchange the 5,000 weapons that Yelinek deemed unsatisfactory for 3,117 AKs. Yelinek arranged for a Panamanian cargo company to pick up the weapons in Nicaragua on their ship the *Otterloo*, whose manifest stated it was sailing to Panama.

Instead of sailing to Panama, the ship landed in Turbo, Colombia, in November 2001—customs officials conveniently disappeared for several days while it was unloaded—and the arms ended up in the hands of the AUC, which controlled the area. The ship's captain disappeared, and the company was dissolved several months later. The ship was later sold to a Colombian citizen.

Not knowing about this diversion, GIR S.A. started another deal with Yelinek using the same purchase order, but when authorities discovered that the first shipment had gone astray they organized a sting operation to find those responsible. GIR S.A. officials learned about the first shipment and canceled the deal before any sting could take place.

Panamanian authorities arrested Yelinek and tried him for arms diversion. His case was thrown out, though, because the court determined that his actions did not harm Panama; they took place in Nicaragua, outside of their jurisdiction.

This is a classic example of what is known as the "gray market" in small-arms trading, which rests, as you might expect, between white- and black-market arms sales. White-market trading is the legal and transparent sale of small arms. Documentation is honest and official and includes state-to-state sales as well as private sales to individuals. Black-market trading is the extreme opposite. These are completely illegal sales with no accountability or documentation and often with individuals or groups who are prohibited from buying arms under local laws or government or UN sanctions. In gray-market trading, two legitimate parties may arrange what they think is a legitimate sale—in this case the Nicaraguan National Police and GIR S.A.—but the weapons were diverted through forged documents and a series of confusing but seemingly benign tangent deals.

What makes the above example even more intriguing is that the whole operation would have remained hidden except that Carlos Castano, head of the AUC, boasted in April 2002 to a reporter from the Colombian newspaper *El Tiempo* that he bought the guns carried by the *Otterloo* from Nicaragua. In fact, he said he bought even more weapons. "This is the greatest achievement by the AUC so far," he bragged. "Through Central America, five shipments, 13,000 rifles." The other shipments were never discovered.

This incident of arms smuggling signaled a new, more terrible era for South America that continues today. Previously, arms imported to Colombia had been arriving in small shipments, tens or hundreds of rifles at a time, often on board private fishing vessels, speedboats traveling through swamps and rivers, or by light planes landing on dirt fields or dropping containers filled with arms. This bulk shipment proved that the combatants were becoming more sophisticated in their gun procurement, intent on rearming current members and adding recruits.

Many of these new recruits were children. More than eleven thousand child soldiers have been fighting in Colombia's conflicts, one of the highest totals in the world, according to Human Rights Watch. At least one of every four was under eighteen, and thousands were younger than fifteen, the minimum age permitted for armed forces recruitment under the Geneva Conventions (still below the minimum age for many countries). About 80 percent of child soldiers belong to FARC or ELN, with AUC using fewer children. Most children join voluntarily, although many were recruited by force, drugged into enlistment, or saw no other opportunities for safety, food, and shelter.

A major difference between African guerrilla forces that used children and those in Colombia was the high number of girl combatants, comprising as many as one-quarter to one-half of guerrilla units, especially in FARC. Some were as young as eight years old. The reasons they joined were similar to those of boys, with sexual abuse at home being an additional factor. (A guerrilla group with an even higher girl population is the Liberation Tigers of Tamil

Eelam of Sri Lanka.) One reason why girls were acceptable in combat was that Marxist ideology (as practiced in South America) embraced equality of the sexes and female liberation, which extended to the armed revolutionary struggle.

These left-wing groups, children and all, became the seeds of large-scale narcoterrorists that today control large swaths of South America, especially in Colombia, Peru, Ecuador, and Brazil, and threaten the stability of the Western Hemisphere.

One impetus for the increased interest among these groups in larger arms shipments during this particular time frame may have been Plan Colombia, a multibillion-dollar U.S. initiative begun in the spring of 2000. The plan had been in the works for some time and everyone knew it would be instituted. Its intention was to help Colombian authorities eradicate drug cultivation and smuggling. Insurgents considered this as a threat to their trade and began seeking larger AK purchases and increasing recruitment.

Despite its size, this instance was relatively simple compared to another case that occurred around the same time and had further-reaching implications. This involved the CIA's top asset in Peru—that country's chief intelligence officer—who planned to funnel AKs to FARC rebels in Colombia with the help of one of the world's largest arms dealers. This broker was the same man who supplied weapons to Saddam Hussein during his war with Iran at the behest of the Reagan administration. The incident involved the sale of ten thousand AKs—a huge shipment for the time—and eventually led to the downfall of Peru's government and the exile of its president to Japan.

GROWING IN SIZE AND SCOPE, FARC wanted to standardize their rifles. The group owned a mixture of weapons including different versions of AKs and FN-FALs. By outfitting most of their eighteen thousand fighters with one type of weapon, they hoped to save money by buying only one type of ammunition. Even a few pennies per round translated to big savings.

FARC had no experience handling such large shipments, so they sought help through intermediaries from Vladimiro Montesinos, commonly known as "Peru's Rasputin" for his puppetmaster control of President Alberto Fujimori. Montesinos began his career in the army in 1965 as a cadet and studied at the U.S. Army's School of the Americas (now Western Hemisphere Institute for Security Cooperation) at Fort Benning, Georgia. The school, dubbed the "School of Assassins" by its opponents, had long been criticized as a training ground for military officers of repressive right-wing Latin American nations who used techniques they learned from U.S. instructors to torture and kill political foes.

In September 1976, Montesinos stole a blank army travel form and visited the U.S. embassy in Lima, where he received a free flight to the United States. Saying that he was an aide to Prime Minister General Guillermo Arbulú, he met with State Department and CIA officials. A Peruvian general saw him give a talk at the Inter-American Defense College and reported him. Upon his return to Peru, authorities immediately arrested Montesinos, and he was placed in prison for one year for desertion and lying.

Shortly after his release in February 1978, Montesinos enrolled at San Marcos University to study law. Only a few months later, using a forged degree, he registered as a lawyer with the Superior Court of Lima and became a member of the Colegio de Abrogados de Lima, an organization similar to a bar association. His clients were Colombian drug dealers, and he became involved in the trade himself through ownership of warehouses and manufacturing facilities used by drug dealers. He also sold classified documents in 1984 to Ecuador about Peru's weapons purchases from the Soviet Union.

Montesinos achieved a reputation as the "go-to lawyer" for anyone involved in high-level crime and corruption, and this is how he met Alberto Fujimori, a candidate in the 1990 elections accused of underpaying his taxes by undervaluing real estate sales. The accusations were so massive that the attorney general was preparing criminal charges against him. Through Montesinos's contacts and influence, at least one witness was persuaded to change his testimony, and files that would have indicted Fujimori were altered. Montesinos also helped Fujimori produce a birth certificate proving that he was born in Peru and not Japan so he could run for president.

When Fujimori was elected president, Montesinos became his right-hand man and was secretly put in charge of the Servicio de Inteligencia Nacional (SIN), Peru's intelligence service. By convincing Fujimori that his life was in continual danger from enemies of the state, Montesinos fed the president's paranoia and did away with opponents who stood in their way. Through a death squad known as Grupo Colina, he solidified his position, eventually controlling Peru's military. He undoubtedly became the most powerful person in Peru and arguably all of South America.

Montesinos went into business with the country's drug dealers, offering them protection. At the same time, the CIA put him on their payroll at $1 million a year for ten years to fight drug trafficking. Curiously, a 1996 U.S. Drug Enforcement Administration document showed that the administration knew that Montesinos took protection money from Peruvian drug dealers, but the CIA continued to deal with him.

FARC officials figured that if anyone in the region could handle their AK purchase, it was Montesinos. Through a Miami contact, he got in touch with Jordanian officials who could fill such a large order. Montesinos showed them purchase documents signed by Peruvian army officials giving the deal the appearance of a white-market transaction. Jordanian authorities chose Lebanese-born arms broker Sarkis Soghanalian, who had worked with the CIA during the cold war, to handle the details. At the request of the Reagan administration, Soghanalian had helped Saddam Hussein purchase weapons for his war with Iran, the same weapons that were later turned against American GIs during the Gulf wars.

Jordanian authorities contacted the CIA's chief in Amman to make sure this sale was vetted because of the close military relationship between the two countries. Soghanalian, too, who considered the United States a major customer, made certain that the CIA signed off on the sale. They did.

Even though FARC requested ten thousand AKs, the purchase order was for fifty thousand. The price came to about $75 a rifle—$55 for the weapon, $10 for shipping, and $10 for packing and handling. Soghanalian readied the first shipment of ten thousand AKs but thought it odd that the Peruvians wanted the cargo airdropped to troops near the Colombian border. Nevertheless, since Montesinos had suggested further weapons sales, for a lot more money, he went along. Later, he denied knowing that the weapons would end up in the hands of Colombian rebels, but as he was an experienced arms dealer, and a follower of world hostilities, it's difficult to believe that he didn't have an inkling about their final destination.

From December 1998 through April 1999, five Hungarian-registered cargo planes carried ten thousand AKs from Amman, through Algeria, Mauritania, and Cape Verde to the Caribbean islands of Trinidad and Tobago or Grenada. From there, the rifles were flown to Iquitos, Peru. The airdrops occurred in full view of U.S. radar systems and spy satellites, which were always scanning for drug traffickers. U.S. and Colombian authorities never hindered these shipments.

The plan was discovered in July 1999, when Colombian troops found AKs with East German markings. They traced them to Jordanian stockpiles, and the scheme unraveled. Soghanalian claimed that he learned from his U.S. contacts that the rifles had been sold to FARC after Montesinos missed a payment, and the arms dealer had stopped further shipments pending his inquiry.

As more details emerged about Montesinos's arming of Colombian rebels, Fujimori's administration began to fall apart. In public statements, Montesinos said he did not know how the weapons ended up in Colombia, and even boasted that his office had arrested Peruvian army officers involved in the airlifts. But by then it was too late. Two days after videos emerged showing Montesinos bribing a congressman to support the president, Fujimori announced his intention to resign, and Montesinos fled to Venezuela. He was later extradited to Peru, where he was convicted and sentenced to fifteen years on various charges including bribing TV executives to support Fujimori. Authorities charged him in connection with the AKs sale, but he has not yet been tried. Fujimori escaped to Japan, faxed his resignation, and vowed to return someday to run again for president.

Why would Montesinos, a staunch anti-Communist, sell AKs to left-wing Colombian rebels? In public, he and Fujimori often complained that the Colombian government was too soft on rebel groups.

Several theories have been suggested, with the simplest being greed. Although Montesinos had already amassed a fortune estimated at more than $260 million, he could probably make a decent profit selling fifty thousand AKs. The other possibility, put forth by critics of the CIA, is that a well-armed FARC presented an increased danger to U.S. interests. Seeing this new threat, Congress would be obliged to pass the budget for the controversial Plan Colombia. These funds would benefit CIA and CIA-connected private contractors who would be used for some of the work. Montesinos had been on the CIA payroll for some time and was a cooperative operative.

A more intriguing possibility, one that embraces all the others, hinges on the configuration of these particular East German AKs and the rounds they fired. The surplus rifles were an AK version known as MpiKM that used the 7.62 × 39mm ammunition as opposed to the 7.62 × 51mm, which was more common in South America and therefore less expensive. At the time, a 7.62 × 39mm bullet cost about 5,000 Colombian pesos ($2 U.S.) and the 7.62 × 51mm cost about 1,000 pesos (42 cents). Some people suggested that Montesinos had perpetrated the perfect deal. Not only would he have made a personal profit, he would have curried favor with his CIA handlers, and as a bonus he would have weakened FARC's financial and strategic position by forcing them to buy more expensive and hard-to-get ammunition in the future.

The fact that the Colombian army began finding these weapons only a few months after the last drop bolsters this scenario, as they knew through their surveillance, perhaps supplied by Montesinos and U.S. intelligence sources, where and when the packages were dropped. With Montesinos involved in domestic scandals now made public, the CIA was perfectly willing to turn him out. This clandestine scheme injured FARC, but it also helped to destroy Fujimori's administration.

Without ever being used in battle, these AKs brought down a government and changed the face of South America.

With Montesinos and Fujimori gone, Peru is undergoing democratization. The executive branch is becoming more transparent and the Congress is acting as a counterbalance. Both branches are working to weed out corruption and hold accountable the judicial branch of government. Unfortunately, the rebels are also getting stronger and more efficient in their drug smuggling, as evidenced by the price of cocaine, which wholesaled in the United States for $38 a gram in 2003, down from $48 in 2000 and $100 in 1986.

The only bright spot for the Colombian government is that the rebels are running low on $7.62 \times 39mm$ ammunition. In June 2004 former political commandante of FARC Carlos Ploter spoke before the Heritage Foundation in Washington, D.C., and noted, "FARC brought great quantities of AK-47s for which there is no ammunition." He also testified before a congressional committee that week about FARC's narcoterrorist activities, saying that drug money was distracting many in the group from pursuing their fight for social justice. In other words, politics was taking a backseat to profits.

THE AK WILL ONCE MORE CHANGE the face of South America. In February 2005, Venezuela's Marxist president Hugo Chávez confirmed the largest small-arms purchase in South American history. Having survived a 2002 coup, which he claimed was supported and instigated by the United States, Chávez said his government would buy one hundred thousand AKs and ammunition from Russia.

While U.S. officials expressed immediate concern when the deal was announced—Venezuela's standing army was only thirty-two thousand troops and about thirty thousand national guard—it wasn't until they learned the exact type of AK that they became truly alarmed. Once again, the technical aspects of the weapon played an important role in changing the political landscape.

Venezuela's military planned to purchase AK-103s and AK-104s, which were manufactured as part of Russia's plan after the breakup of the Soviet Union to export small arms to raise hard currency. Desperately in need of money, the Russians wanted to capitalize on their expertise and brand recognition. The AK-100 series, as it was known, featured only minor improvements on the AKM, but it offered several benefits. The Russians had hoped that by producing about a half dozen models with different ammunition choices, Rosoboronexport, Russia's state exporter, could penetrate new markets worldwide, including NATO nations, with its AK-108, for example, which shoots the 5.56mm NATO round, the same as the M-16. The marketing plan was largely a failure, however, because the Warsaw Pact countries, which were once the largest customers of Soviet arms, had already upgraded their plants and were producing their own AKs. In addition, because of the AK's almost indestructible nature, and the recent unleashing on the world of Warsaw Pact and Soviet Union arsenals, the market was flooded, at least for the time being. Most of the 100-series models were relegated to storage.

This situation produced a windfall for Chávez, because the Russians had stockpiled thousands of these weapons that they could not get rid of and were willing to sell cheap. Chávez's interest in the 103s and 104s, which used 7.62 × 39mm ammunition, was at first a surprise to military observers, because the country had a history of using FN-FALs, which shoot the more easily obtained and cheaper 7.62 × 51mm round, the so-called full-sized

NATO round. With this large a purchase, he obviously planned to replace the country's entire arsenal.

But why?

It only took a few days for small-arms experts to suggest that Chávez also was planning to supply FARC, which was desperately seeking this specific ammunition for their AKs. Not only was Chávez sympathetic to FARC's Marxist ideology, but relations between his country and the Colombian government had been at an all-time low since December 2004, when Colombian troops snatched FARC leader Rodrigo Granda from inside Venezuela. Chávez was incensed that neighboring Colombia would violate his country's sovereignty.

The 7.62×51mm ammunition was used by NATO rifles such as the FN-FAL and often was easier to acquire in regional black markets, but it also was a proxy for Western nations and ideology. By moving FARC toward a bona fide Soviet-style round, the 7.62×39mm, Chávez was helping FARC make a true anti-Western statement, a nuance not lost on U.S. military analysts.

Relations between the United States and Venezuela were becoming strained as well, with Secretary of Defense Donald Rumsfeld saying that he thought the purchases would destabilize South America and lead to a regional arms race. Chávez insisted that the weapons would be used by the regular army and planned "citizen militias" to defend the nation against its enemies. As tempers flared, Chávez's government unexpectedly ended a long-standing military exchange program with the United States. U.S. military advisors were told to leave the country. Chávez also said that he would cut off oil to the United States—which imported 15 percent of its supply from Venezuela—if the U.S. government attempted to force him out of office.

U.S. officials paid less attention to other items on Chávez's shopping list, including fifty MiG29 jets from Russia and Tucano jets from Brazil. The Pentagon considered these legitimate purchases, because they could be used for border protection and other sovereignty-related activities. Not worried that these large armaments could be turned against the United States or its allies, one State Department official said, "We [can] shoot down MiGs."

The AKs were a different matter. After decades of underestimating the importance of AKs and focusing on larger weapons, U.S. officials appeared to be reversing their ingrained notions. The "Black Hawk Down" incident in Somalia may have been a factor. They acknowledged privately the devastating effect that AKs could bring to a region and how difficult it was for conventional armies like that of the United States to fight against soldiers armed with them. Even if Chávez intended to deploy them within Venezuela's borders, Rumsfeld and others expressed concern that they could end up in the hands of drug dealers and other criminals. Speculation also arose and was later confirmed that Chávez was planning to build a factory to produce 7.62 × 39mm ammunition.

Rumsfeld discussed the AK purchase in every public forum available, hoping to draw out specific answers from Chávez about his intentions. At a news conference in Brazil during a hastily organized visit to South America, Rumsfeld said, "I can't imagine what's going to happen to 100,000 AKs. I can't imagine why Venezuela needs 100,000 AKs. And I just personally hope [the sale] doesn't happen, and I can't imagine that if it did happen, that it would be good for the hemisphere."

Chávez did not immediately respond, but Kalashnikov felt compelled to counter Rumsfeld's official U.S. position. While attending the 2005 IDEX international arms exhibition in Abu Dhabi, an annual trade show that brings together the world's buyers and sellers of all kinds of weapons from small arms to tanks and fighter jets, Kalashnikov said, "We have been blamed and will be blamed for many things. We need to treat these accusations critically, as they are, as a rule, prompted by the Americans' desire to bar us [Russia] from entering new markets. I believe we need to continue to promote our Russian weapons on foreign markets, because they must safeguard peace and friendship between nations."

For his entire life, Kalashnikov had purposely kept his distance from politics. He disliked politicians, blaming them for the misuse of his weapon. However, the importance of this mammoth sale to the Russian economy drove the usually nonpolitical Kalashnikov to denounce American foreign policy.

What a change this was from the naive, less sophisticated Kalashnikov who had visited the United States in 1990, the first time he had ever been allowed to travel outside of Russia.

KALASHNIKOV AND HIS GUN VISIT AMERICA

I N 1990, UNDER THE GOODWILL of glasnost, Mikhail Kalashnikov, aging and poor, traveled outside the Soviet Union for the first time. He was the guest of Ed Ezell, small-arms curator at the Smithsonian Institution, who had visited Moscow two years earlier to meet the AK-47's inventor as part of the museum's program to videotape the twentieth century's most influential inventors. Also in the collection were tapes of Eugene Stoner, inventor of the M-16, the AK's rival.

Soon, the world's gun titans would meet.

Prying Kalashnikov out of the Soviet Union had not been easy. Ezell wrote him a letter in 1972 through the Soviet embassy in Washington. When Kalashnikov received the envelope with a U.S. postmark he was both astonished and frightened. No one from the United States had ever contacted him before. Despite fame and notoriety in his home country, few outside the Soviet Union knew anything about the man whose weapon had changed the face of modern warfare. At home, he was a war hero who had helped protect the motherland and spread the Communist doctrine to every corner of the globe. To the rest of the world, his name symbolized two extremes—terrorism against legitimate governments and the struggle for freedom against ruthless dictators—but few knew that he was even alive. During the deadly conflicts of the cold war years, Soviet authorities purposely kept this man hidden from outsiders.

Fearful that government agents would deem the American's note as his compliance in a subversive action, Kalashnikov contacted local Communist Party officials, who subjected him to a lengthy "consultation" during which they suggested he get in touch with the KGB. Kalashnikov's first instinct upon discussing the unsolicited letter with the local KGB agent was to throw up his hands in an ignorant gesture. "Oh, no! Why should I ever write there, to the States?" After more than a year of these back-and-forth consultations, Kalashnikov received permission to respond to the letter with Ezell's innocently requested items: a biography and a signed photograph.

The door opened.

Over the following years, Ezell mailed Kalashnikov several books he had authored, including *The AK-47 Story*, which he wrote by piecing together snippets of information about the history of Soviet firearms back to the 1800s, the AK-47, and Kalashnikov. With the softening of Soviet-U.S. relations in 1989, Ezell and a video crew met the sixty-nine-year-old Kalashnikov in Moscow for sightseeing and filming. At first apprehensive, Ezell was put at ease upon seeing an animated, congenial Kalashnikov, who greeted him with a hearty bear hug. It became clear to Ezell over the following days that Kalashnikov deemed the visit an important event for him, the first recognition of his contribution by those outside the Soviet Union. He was also flattered when Kalashnikov told him that he planned to have *The AK-47 Story* translated into Russian so he could see what Ezell and the English-speaking world knew about him.

Over the following days, the entourage visited firing ranges and museums, including Leningrad's Central Museum of the Artillery,

Engineer, and Communications Troops, which housed more than 120 types of AK rifles. Ezell soon understood that he was in the presence of a national celebrity whose name was known on the street by Soviet citizens, yet unknown elsewhere. In a private moment, away from the others, Kalashnikov confided to Ezell that he had appreciated the books he had sent over the years and his attention, but he was unable to express his appreciation during the cold war environment. Now he hoped this would change with the easing of tensions between the two superpowers.

And they were. During a later presentation before the Virginia Gun Collectors Association, Ezell spoke about his visit to Moscow and mentioned that he would like to bring Kalashnikov to the United States to meet Eugene Stoner but did not have funding in the Smithsonian budget. In concert with a hunting club called NORVA in the Washington, D.C., suburbs, the group footed the bill for the arms maker, his daughter Elena, and an interpreter to visit.

On May 15, 1990, Kalashnikov arrived at Washington's Dulles Airport, the first time he had been permitted to visit a foreign country. After decades of animosity between the two nations, Kalashnikov had worried about his treatment by the American bureaucracy, but his anxieties disappeared when Customs and Immigration officials moved him and his small group quickly through the line.

The next day was the big day. He and Stoner finally met at the Seaport Inn in the Old Town section of Alexandria, Virginia, a restaurant where President George Washington had dined and slept two centuries earlier. Both men knew each other's work intimately, but the two had never met or even corresponded, because the gulf of the cold war was too wide.

Before the gun makers met over dinner, Kalashnikov's hosts took him shopping for new clothes to replace his tattered ones. The inventor of the world's most popular firearm was so poor that his hosts gave him money for his purchases. He explained to them how the government had never patented his design, and it was licensed for free to many countries. Kalashnikov never saw a ruble

from his work beyond his small government stipend. On a shopping trip to buy a pair of shoes, Kalashnikov didn't see his size. He
became dejected, until one of his hosts told him that the salesman
could walk in the back and look for a different style in his size. His
face brightened. This was typical of Kalashnikov's Soviet perspective, where scarcity was commonplace and you made do without
life's niceties.

The irony of the situation was not lost on Stoner or Kalashnikov's hosts. They saw a man whose invention was found in virtually every country, and had made millions of dollars for
middlemen and gun dealers, yet he was a pauper who knew practically nothing of the outside world. His country had kept him
purposely isolated.

These two symbols of the cold war were cordial as they discussed their competing weapons, but when they talked about
money, Kalashnikov began to understand the stark difference
between the Communist and capitalist marketplace. Stoner said
that he made about one dollar per M-16 sold. At the time, about six
million were in circulation. Kalashnikov admitted, sheepishly, that
he made no money from his invention, which had sold ten times
the number of M-16s, but added that he did it for the motherland,
and it didn't bother him a bit. Clearly, it did. The rest of the
evening went well, but one could see Kalashnikov and his daughter engaged in lively but whispered discussions. They were talking
about how much money Stoner enjoyed from the M-16 and scores
of his other inventions. They were flabbergasted to learn that
Stoner flew around the country in his own plane.

This visit to the United States opened Kalashnikov's eyes. His
government had awarded him medals and citations but no money.
Schoolchildren knew his name and studied his contributions. He
was a hero in Russia. On the other hand, Stoner had no military
medals, and only gun enthusiasts and military historians knew his
name, but he had benefited richly from his invention.

During dinner, Elena asked her father, "Would you like to
trade places with Stoner?"

"No," he answered, honestly and sincerely. Still, there was a trace of envy in his voice.

Over the following days, the arms designers visited the Smithsonian Institution, the NRA's National Firearms Museum, and a hunting lodge owned by the gun club at Star Tannery, Virginia, near the West Virginia border. There, both men fired each other's weapons, and it was clear that each understood the other's firearm intimately. Stoner introduced Kalashnikov to skeet shooting and as the two fired in turn, Ezell noted how they had bonded, not needing an interpreter to get their thoughts across. He was fascinated at how well these two men got along. "They are self-made men," Ezell later said. "Gene Stoner has made a lot of money and Kalashnikov has a lot of social status in the Soviet Union, but neither one of them is pompous. They are both down-to-earth people. Both are relaxed and secure in knowing they are good at what they do, but don't have to bandy that about and try to impress anybody with it. I think that's one of the reasons they get along."

They also shared a sense of humor. In between skeet-shooting rounds, Kalashnikov relayed to Stoner how the AK-47 was field-tested for durability, drawn through mud, dragged over sand and brush. He asked Stoner how the M-16 stocks were tested, and Stoner replied that they were hoisted up a flagpole at Aberdeen Proving Grounds and dropped repeatedly. Kalashnikov responded, "In the Soviet Union, this is what they do to gun inventors whose guns jammed in combat." This was a somewhat cutting remark about M-16s jamming in Vietnam but it was done good-naturedly, as Kalashnikov knew that the rifle had malfunctioned because the army had insisted on using rounds that Stoner had not approved and had advised against deploying.

A high point of Kalashnikov's visit was a trip to the Marine Corps base in Quantico, about thirty-five miles south of Washington, D.C. The base is widely known in military circles as the place where amphibious warfare techniques were conceived and tested, as well as the tactics of close air support using helicopters. The base is also home to the real-life FBI's Behavioral Sciences Unit, famous for its profiling of serial killers, which most people know through fictional characters such as Hannibal Lecter in *The Silence of the Lambs.*

The openness of the military base surprised Kalashnikov, especially when he was allowed to watch marine training in action. He also witnessed new firearms testing and was fascinated at how computers processed firing data in real time, allowing on-the-spot correction of production defects and other changes. "It's very impressive here . . . the shooting ranges and the workshops," said Kalashnikov. "I liked the U.S. Marines who I saw for the first time in my life . . . a year and half ago this would have been impossible just to imagine that."

Kalashnikov received unexpected praise from Major General Matthew P. Caulfield, who was then deputy commander for training and education and the director of the Marine Air-Ground Training and Education Center. Caulfield remarked to the inventor, "I must admit that I personally would prefer to fire your gun in combat, Mr. Kalashnikov." This candid comment came from a professional soldier who, as a captain, had commanded a company in Vietnam and participated in the siege at Khe Sanh, a turning point in the Vietnam War. Caulfield's experience at Khe Sanh surely colored his remarks to Kalashnikov.

On January 21, 1968, a sudden and ferocious attack on the Khe Sanh Marine Corps base by North Vietnamese forces stunned and shocked Americans, including those in the Johnson administration who had underestimated the Communist resolve. Every night for almost two months, television news covered the siege as the North Vietnamese bombarded the base, even digging trenches and tunnels on the perimeter hoping to overrun the outpost from a close-in vantage point. Located only a few miles from the North Vietnamese border, Khe Sanh had become a symbol of U.S. determination in winning the war, and losing it was likened to the French loss at Dien Bien Phu, which, fourteen years earlier, had spelled the end of that country's occupation. The battle sparked a public debate over whether Khe Sanh was of crucial strategic importance and worth the fight or simply a line drawn by commanders' ego in the sand. Ultimately, U.S. forces prevailed, but not before 205 Americans were killed, with hundreds more wounded, and about 8,000 North Vietnamese dead. The military abandoned Khe San a few months later, which further eroded the American public's support for the war as it appeared the base had no military value from the start. As it turned out, the vicious attack on Khe Sanh was a diversionary tactic designed to siphon off U.S. resources in preparation for the upcoming Tet Offensive.

With the Khe Sanh debacle still on his mind, Caulfield told Kalashnikov, "I always wanted to have a Kalashnikov, but there was one thing that stopped me. Your gun's rate of fire was different from that of an M-16, and it had a different sound. If my soldiers had heard it, they would have opened fire on me thinking I was Vietcong." Even today, now retired Caulfield remains bitter about the malfunctioning M-16s supplied to him and his men in Vietnam. "Everyone knew it but the damn generals," he says.

KALASHNIKOV'S VISIT TO THE UNITED STATES opened a new world of travel for him and brought him notoriety beyond Russia's borders. For the first time, people outside saw the man who gave his name to the world's most popular weapon. Newspapers wrote stories about him. Filmmakers wanted to do documentaries about his life. All this attention was foreign to Kalashnikov, but he took it in stride, even enjoying the accolades once he got over the initial shock. All his adult life he had accepted the meager offerings of his country, because it was his patriotic duty. Now, no longer insulated from the rest of the world, he told his story to an interested and eager world press.

His story made great copy in the Western media because of the ironies surrounding Kalashnikov's life. Here was a national hero, in his seventies, now a budding world figure living in a small apartment under spartan conditions with a pension amounting to fifty dollars a month. He wore a large cluster of honorary medals on his chest, but the only furniture in his three-room flat was bought in 1949 with money from his first Stalin Prize. Ironically, it was Stalin who had exiled his family to Siberia.

His tragic personal life was revealed for the first time in public. His wife, Yekaterina, had died twenty years earlier after a long illness. She was a graphic artist who had helped him with his gun drawings. They married in 1943 and each brought one child from a previous marriage. His wife's daughter was named Katya, and Kalashnikov had a son, Viktor, who became an arms designer in his own right. Growing up, Viktor did not live with Kalashnikov and Yekaterina until his natural mother died. The couple had two daughters of their own: Elena, the oldest, who continues to travel with her father, and Natasha, who died in a car crash at the age of twenty-nine. With that accident, Kalashnikov lost not only a daughter but also a companion. After his wife died, Natasha had moved in with her father, helping the elderly man in his daily routine. Natasha is buried next to her mother's grave, and Kalashnikov built a fence that he designed himself around the two headstones. Like his rifle, the fence is simple, sturdy, and reliable.

With his new fame, however, Kalashnikov soon received invitations from all over, and his spirits rose. During the following years he traveled to China, Bulgaria, Argentina, and again to the United States in 1991 as the guest of Bill Ruger, president of gun maker Sturm, Ruger & Co., which produced a range of firearms, the most famous being a .22-caliber Long Rifle that started the company in 1949. During this U.S. trip, Kalashnikov made a guest appearance at the National Rifle Association's annual meeting in Salt Lake City and attended a reception for firearms magazine writers.

With all this attention, Russian president Boris Yeltsin, prodded by a high-ranking military officer, was shamed into upping Kalashnikov's pension to about $100 a month. He also received a small wooden vacation home, or dacha, and driver/companion courtesy of the government, but there was another reason why the government began treating their national treasure better.

By this time, it was clear to Russian officials that Kalashnikov was becoming a celebrity, a man whose name was instantly recognizable. He possessed a cachet that could open doors to arms buyers. Russian officials witnessed his drawing power when he visited arms shows and people rushed over for his autograph or shoved through lines to take a picture with the inventor of the famous AK-47. Kalashnikov was affable; people enjoyed talking to him, even if they were not particularly fond of Russia's ideology. Besides, Kalashnikov, now in his seventies, with a shock of white hair, seemed harmless, and the powerful Soviet Union, once a bitter enemy of the West, had dissolved. People seeing this humble, diminutive, frail man for the first time were taken aback and intrigued. They had trouble reconciling the vision of the man before them with what they imagined the inventor of the notorious AK-47 should look like. Could the kind-looking gentleman standing before them really be the creator of such a deadly weapon?

Kalashnikov retold his story many times: how he got the idea while recuperating in a wartime hospital, how he wanted to protect the motherland from the Nazis, and how he hadn't made a cent from his steel progeny. The Russian told the story at the now defunct Houston Astrodomain Complex during a trade show for sporting firearms and outdoor gear. He was there to drum up excitement for the Saiga, a version of the AK modified for hunting.

Named after an antelope that lives on the steppes of Russia, the Saiga was an act of desperation. The Soviet Union was unraveling politically, culturally, and financially. By the late 1980s, it could no longer support a robust military and had cut expenditures on weapons by 14 percent in 1989; further cuts were expected. By 1991, Izhmash, a.k.a. Izhevsk Machine Works, the country's prime armorer and home of the AK, was in deep trouble. The factory had at one time employed fifty thousand people. Now only thirty thousand worked there, and more than half of them were part-timers or what was euphemistically known as being on "forced vacation." Like others at the plant, Kalashnikov, who retained the title of chief designer, had not been paid in months. Just to feed their families, some rogue Izhmash engineers had built guns for the growing legions of Russian mobsters who took advantage of the chaotic situation as the old Soviet Union stumbled into financial meltdown.

When the USSR finally dissolved in 1992, Izhmash faced a shutdown. In a last-ditch effort to keep the factories operating, its managers looked outside their domestic markets for revenue, but with the cold war over and the world awash in indestructible AKs, selling military small arms like their 100-series AKs met largely with failure.

Looking to tap the civilian market, Izhmash designers turned out a series of semiautomatic hunting rifles and shotguns based on the Kalashnikov basic action. Not only was the AK design tried and true, but they had a plan to sell the firearms by exploiting the Kalashnikov mystique.

While in Houston shilling these hunting rifles, Kalashnikov met Stoner, who was also fronting for civilian versions of his M-16, which had been licensed out for years to several gun makers as hunting rifles. Stoner was already semiretired, living in Vero Beach, Florida.

Still friends, the two did not have much time to talk during the show. Both were busy tending their booths, trying to attract visitors and buyers. When asked by a reporter what he thought of the AK-47, Stoner said, "The Kalashnikov weapon was a good one, but his was different [than the M-16] because the requirements under which he was to build it were different. The Russians wanted a weapon simple and rugged and weight was not a factor." He was referring to the fact that the M-16 was about four pounds lighter than the AK. When asked about the M-16, Kalashnikov simply nodded with approval. Compared to Stoner, Kalashnikov was a bigger arms personality, drawing curious gawkers and determined autograph seekers.

Amid all the accolades and fascinated onlookers, the world beyond the closed Soviet Union forced Kalashnikov to confront publicly the impact of his invention. Western reporters wanted to know how he felt about his brainchild's being responsible for killing millions of people and wreaking abject destruction on several continents. Kalashnikov again said that with the Nazi invasion of his country, all he could think about was getting better weapons into the hands of Soviet soldiers. He expressed regret, however, that criminals in his own country were using the AK. "I am sorry brothers are killing each other with a rifle I made to fight the occupiers of my country."

This small, modest man who had been kept under wraps by his country for more than half a century was out in the open now and confronting a free press that demanded to know even more about his life and his invention. He took every opportunity to defend his work, blaming politicians for exploiting the AK in deadly ways. Sometimes the questions got to him, and he erupted curtly, angry that he was being held liable for his invention's legacy. "Arms builders have never been given their just deserts in this country [the Soviet Union]. If the politicians had worked as hard as we did, the guns would never have gotten into the wrong hands," he said. He expressed great sadness at Russians killing Russians with AKs during ethnic clashes that grew out of the Soviet breakup. He was horrified to learn that Soviet soldiers were stealing AKs from armories and selling or trading them for bottles of vodka. Kalashnikov kept on message, though, stressing that the AK was designed to protect his nation's borders and that it should never have been used for internal conflicts such as those occurring in Africa, Latin America, and, sadly, his own country.

Kalashnikov, now a public figure and feeling freer to offer his opinion, met with Boris Yeltsin and told him that he saw no reason to have broken up the Soviet Union. Like many other Russians, he longed for the old USSR and abhorred the domestic chaos that was becoming commonplace. The motherland that he had fought for was now dealing with civil strife and corruption.

With his seventy-fifth birthday coming up, Kalashnikov found himself further bombarded by interview requests. Western reporters, now permitted to travel about Russia more freely than before, accompanied him on hunting trips and visited him in his home in Izhevsk, which had been closed to foreigners because of the arms factories located there. Most times, they portrayed Kalashnikov as a simple person who rightfully bristled at seemingly obvious and repetitive questions about his weapon's grim legacy. He tried to keep his annoyance in check when the question was asked over and over, "How do you feel about your gun being used to kill innocent people?" Other times, another side would peek out. He seemed almost pompous, arrogant in the belief that no other weapon could ever supersede the AK's utility, proud that his country had beat back the invading Nazi hordes, and he rarely missed an opportunity to chide politicians who made decisions he deemed contrary to common sense.

Observers also took note of Kalashnikov the reluctant capitalist, a poor man attempting to make up for lost time. Arms factories in the area around Izhevsk formed the Joint Stock Company Kalashnikov to produce and market civilian weapons turned out by the old military facilities. They made Kalashnikov their honorary president, hoping that his name would draw attention as they sent him around to various trade shows. Kalashnikov signed on, albeit reluctantly. "I did not make the weapon in order to sell it, but at a time when it was needed to save the motherland," he had said when the idea of selling civilian versions of AKs was first floated several years earlier.

As Russia looked to the AK and its famous inventor for hard currency, American lawmakers put the weapon in their sights, too. As the world's most distinctive-looking assault rifle, the AK was the poster child for those who wanted these weapons banned from the United States in a movement that had started several years earlier but was now quickly building momentum.

THE FIRST AKS SEEN IN THE UNITED STATES probably were brought back by soldiers returning from the Vietnam War in the late 1960s and early 1970s. Many of these had their firing pins removed or were otherwise disabled, and were kept as souvenirs by former GIs who were fascinated by the weapon responsible for driving American forces from Southeast Asia. As the weapon's notoriety spread to the general public, more of them began to be imported.

Although their importation seemed contrary to the 1968 Gun Control Act—passed in the wake of the assassinations of Robert F. Kennedy and Martin Luther King Jr.—which prohibited the importation of any firearm unless it was "generally recognized as particularly suitable or readily adaptable to sporting purposes," the government's focus was really on handguns. The main thrust of the bill was to outlaw cheap imported handguns like the so-called Saturday night specials because they had no recreational value. Some of these handguns were so inexpensive and poorly made that they fell apart after firing and had to be discarded after only their maiden job. Nobody paid much attention to assault rifles at the time because few were being imported. In addition, when the subject arose, proponents made the case, albeit dubious to those on the other side of the issue, that these weapons had hunting and target-shooting value.

As the source of cheap handguns dried up, Uzi and AK imports grew in popularity. Timing was not the only reason. Part of this new interest in assault rifles was fueled by economic and mechanical factors related to the weapons, in addition to an emergence of street violence spurred by drugs and gang activities.

Economically, Israel enjoyed a "most favored nation" status with the United States as far as import duties were concerned. As a result, the Uzi submachine gun sold for as little as $500 when first introduced to the U.S. market in 1980. Because of its small caliber and short range, it was ideal for drive-by shootings and close-in gang fights. Although the civilian export version was sold in semi-automatic mode only, it could be converted to automatic action, albeit illegally, by using a kit. It became a favorite of drug dealers and gang members, because it could be easily hidden underneath jackets then quickly exposed to fire 9mm bullets at the rate of 600 per minute. Magazines came in 25-, 32-, or 40-round versions.

Like the submachine guns used during World War II, these Uzis had no sporting purpose. They were designed to kill people.

The same was true of the AK, which arrived on U.S. shores in the mid-1980s, mainly from China. It too enjoyed a low price because of China's favored nation trade status. The AK began to usurp the place of the Uzi because it was $200 less and possessed an aura of counterculture and rebellion that appealed to drug dealers and gang members. Like the Uzi, the import model was sold as a semiautomatic weapon only, but conversion kits for full automatic firing were sold on the black market.

As gun enthusiasts argued that these weapons could be used for hunting and recreational purposes such as target shooting and were therefore protected by the Gun Control Act, their opinions were being drowned out by a nationwide string of shootings involving "assault rifles." Even the term "assault rifle" would become a point of contention between gun enthusiasts and those who opposed them. There is no universal definition of an assault rifle. Indeed, this is one of the problems that crop up when legislators try to write laws that limit their import, sale, and use. In general, assault rifles are characterized by several salient features: they can be used in semiautomatic or automatic mode, have low weight, fire intermediate rounds, have high-capacity magazines, and are usually intended to be used as a military weapon. Gun opponents often used the term to mean anything that looked like an AK or M-16 rifle, even if it only fired in semiautomatic mode. This distinction later would play a crucial part in gun control legislation and the rhetoric surrounding it.

Semantics aside, one incident in particular garnered the attention of the nation, and indeed the world, because of its horrific nature.

On January 17, 1989, twenty-four-year-old Patrick Edward Purdy, a.k.a. Patrick West, parked his eleven-year-old Chevrolet station wagon outside a Stockton, California, elementary school. Before leaving the car, he lit a fuse stuffed into the neck of a beer bottle filled with gasoline and tossed it onto the front seat.

As two open gasoline cans sat in the backseat ready to explode, Purdy, dressed in military fatigues and flak jacket, sauntered through a hole in a fence and into the schoolyard where four hundred first- to third-graders were playing during their noon recess. On his shirt, he had written "PLO," "Libya," "Earthman," and "Death to the Great Satin," an obvious misspelling.

Lori Mackey, who taught deaf children at Cleveland Elementary School, looked out her classroom window and watched a straight-faced Purdy, standing in place, not talking or yelling, make wide sweeping motions with what turned out to be a semi-automatic AK from China. "It did not look like he was really angry," said Mackey, who led her children to the safety of a rear room. Kids and teachers ran in every direction trying to escape the bullet storm. The rampage ended about a minute later when Purdy shot himself in the head with a 9mm Taurus pistol.

When police and paramedics arrived, they found five dead children, mainly refugees from Southeast Asia, and more than thirty others wounded. Next to Purdy's body they discovered a 75-round rotary magazine, a 30-round banana magazine, and shell casings showing that he had fired 110 of the 7.62×39mm rounds. Purdy, who had purchased the AK in Portland, Oregon, carried three extra magazines marked with the words "humanoids," "evil," and the initials "SSA," which authorities believed may have meant Social Security Administration. Purdy had received Social Security benefits and apparently was not satisfied with the government's handling of his case. He also had two boxes of unused ammunition with him.

Purdy had carved into the stock of the Chinese-made AK, technically known as the SKS Type 56 (used often by Vietcong during the Vietnam War) the words "Freedom," "Victory," and "Hezbollah," the Middle Eastern terrorist group that has the AK on its flag. (The AK is also seen on the flag and emblems of other terrorist groups. The Palestinian Liberation Front, which operates in the Middle East, has an AK; a map of the West Bank, the Gaza Strip, and present-day Israel; and a Soviet-type red star in its emblem.

This AK-wielding soldier in southern Lebanon stands in front of the flag of Hezbollah (Party of God), a terrorist group founded in that country in 1982. The flag uses the imagery of an AK gripped in an outstretched arm on top of a globe, suggesting the group's violent role in worldwide affairs. © *Mike Stewart/Corbis Sygma*

The Salafist Group for Call and Combat, which operates mainly in North Africa, has a sword, Koran, and AK in its coat of arms.)

Authorities suggested that Purdy, who, ironically, shared the same November 10th birthday as Mikhail Kalashnikov, and had attended the Cleveland Elementary School as a youth, may have grown resentful of the large number of Southeast Asian refugees living in Stockton. He had expressed bitterness about his teenage life to coworkers—he had worked as a machinist—complaining about absent parents and alcoholism. In the hotel room where he had been living before the shooting, police found tiny green plastic soldiers, tanks, and jeeps set up to battle on the floor.

The incident proved to be a catalyst for action in California and later for the rest of the nation.

On February 6, 1989, less than a month after the Stockton schoolyard shootings, the Los Angeles city council passed by a twelve-to-zero vote a ban on the sale and possession of semiautomatic weapons. Owners had fifteen days to either dispose of the weapons or change them to comply with the law. The council's action followed a similar law enacted by Stockton only two days earlier.

This movement had been gaining traction for some time, but the killings in Stockton propelled it quickly. Ordinary citizens were learning the differences among automatic, semiautomatic, and single-shot weapons—information few people had needed to know before. On the East Coast, Washington, D.C., in the throes of growing gang- and drug-related deaths, had already passed a law restricting semiautomatic weapons.

Gun enthusiasts argued that the deaths in Stockton as well as other recent high-profile incidents were not, as had been portrayed in the media, caused by assault rifles but by semiautomatic rifles, but these protests only served to fuel the controversy. Opponents portrayed the technicalities as nitpicking, and with children dead and police officers outgunned, they thought the distinction petty and typical of gun enthusiasts who they believed were more interested in minor mechanical differences than in human lives.

One of the hot points was the number of rounds in the magazine. The law in Washington, D.C., banned weapons with magazines carrying more than eleven rounds; in Los Angeles, the cutoff was twenty rounds. The bullet-limiting provisions were crucial in the fight against any argument that these weapons could be used for hunting, because most hunters got only one shot off when stalking prey—partly because of the "one-shot" tradition of hunters but also because hunted animals, such as deer, bolt after hearing the first missed shot.

Even former president Ronald Reagan, a staunch supporter of gun owners' rights, had changed his mind about assault rifles. During his first public appearance after leaving office, Reagan answered questions from University of Southern California students after a speech. Asked by one student about his stance on gun control in light of the Stockton shootings, Reagan remarked, "I do not believe in taking away the right of the citizen to own guns for sporting, hunting and so forth." The seventy-eight-year-old ex-president continued, "But I do believe that an AK-47, a machine gun, is not a sporting weapon." Although Reagan was mistaken in labeling the AK as a machine gun, his remarks were of great comfort to the anti-gun lobby, which had always considered Reagan, and Republican politicians in general, as opponents of antigun legislation.

President George H. W. Bush found himself modifying his position on assault weapons, too. He acknowledged that the national discussion about semiautomatic weapons "had gotten pretty hot." He noted the public outcry about children being killed by assault rifles and said that a temporary ban by his administration—begun two days earlier on imports of the AK, Uzi carbine, and three other semiautomatic weapons—"represented a heightened concern on my part about AK-47s." The U.S. drug czar, William Bennett, had urged the suspension of more than 110,000 import permits for assault rifles, mainly AKs and Uzi carbines, to give the administration breathing room to evaluate whether these weapons were suitable for sport and recreation activities, and if a permanent ban was appropriate.

Bush, a lifelong National Rifle Association member, had always opposed bans on semiautomatic rifles, so this turnaround was indicative of the country's mood and concern about these weapons' destructive power. The Bush change of heart surprised many people, especially those in the NRA and other gun groups who had always counted him as a staunch ally.

It was a bold move by the administration considering the power of the gun lobby. Indeed, since the temporary import ban was announced, the White House was abuzz about alleged warnings from gun groups who threatened to politically destroy Bush and Bennett using their massive war chest and ability to rally members. Although NRA officials denied any strong-arm tactics, the administration was incensed that it was being portrayed as an enemy of gun owners. Publicly, Bennett acknowledged that his office had received a lot of phone calls and pressure from "third parties," although he did not name any specific people or groups.

The times were changing for many law enforcement agencies, too. Police chiefs from many large U.S. cities banded together to lobby against the spread of assault rifles. In retrospect, this move appears obvious, but at the time, many police officers, often gun enthusiasts and hunters themselves, bristled at any law that restricted gun ownership. Now, with police officers outgunned on the streets, they started to see the debate in a different light.

The administration, not wanting to pick a fight with gun groups but not wanting to back down from their position either, called for all sides to take a deep breath and consider the issue calmly. "Let's cool off," Bennett told them. He reassured gun owners that this was not the beginning of a movement to ban all guns. He noted that since the import ban took effect—and Colt had voluntarily suspended sales of AR-15s, the civilian version of the M-16—Americans had begun buying semiautomatic rifles in large numbers, which was an error on their part. "If people are doing this because they think this could mean the end of guns, that no more guns would be available, then they are mistaken." Whether the sales jump was indicative of an NRA fear campaign or simply individual initiative was unclear, but Bennett reassured people that an all-out ban on guns was not in the future. "On the other hand, he added, "the 'anything goes' idea—let's just get our hands on any kind of weapon—I think that's a view of the world that's not shared by most Americans, by most members of the National Rifle Association, but I think an awful lot of people out there are concerned about the kind of firepower that we're seeing used in our streets."

The winds of public opinion convinced President Bush to make the import ban permanent, and what many opponents had said would happen under such a ban did indeed occur. Prices of the forty-three weapons banned from importation in July 1989 rose dramatically just prior to the ban. In January, the price of an AK was $300, but just after the ban became permanent, the price spiked at more than $1,000 in some parts of the country. More important, because pre-ban weapons from company stockpiles would be allowed for sale, companies rushed to produce as many as they could and ship them to U.S. stores. In addition, U.S. gun makers ramped up production of domestic lookalike assault rifles called "copycats." Made in the United States, these were unaffected by the import ban. The homegrown weapons were made to look and shoot like the imported models. Many of the companies that make them still exist, and if it were not for the import ban, they would never have been established in the first place.

Foreign gun makers found ways around the import ban by following the letter of the law. Within a year, a half dozen foreign gun makers had applied for permission to import assault rifles that were altered to meet the criteria for export to the United States. For example, characteristics of a banned assault rifle included a fifteen- (or more) round magazine, a pistol grip (so the gun could be held by one hand and shot from the hip in a spraying fashion), bayonet holders, and grenade launchers. For many gun exporters, it was a simple matter to offer only ten-shot magazines, cut off the bayonet holders, and eliminate the pistol grip and replace it with a thumbhole in the stock. The thumbhole still allowed one-hand, spray-from-the-hip firing, Rambo style, but fell neatly within the letter of the law.

Of the approximately three million semiautomatic weapons owned by Americans at the time, about 25 percent were foreign models, according to the Bureau of Alcohol, Tobacco and Firearms. Without the ban, about 700,000 to one million more would have been imported, officials estimated. In that respect, the ban was successful. On the other hand, it spawned a new industry of copycat rifles that had not existed before the ban.

Supporters of national legislation to ban assault rifles (again, technically, semiautomatic rifles) were led by California senator Dianne Feinstein, who dramatically made her point about the dangers of these rifles by holding up AKs at news conferences. The familiar and menacing weapon with its signature banana-shaped magazine drew attention as she listed the incidents in which assault rifles had killed people. Her message hit home.

Momentum was building on a national level, propelled by still more cases of street violence and the specter of a new and horrific practice—drive-by shootings—most of it drug- and gang-related. Despite the obvious flaws of the Bush import ban, lawmakers sought similar national legislation, and they strove to eliminate the loopholes this time.

As the national debate heated up, some of the largest U.S. gun makers tried to home in on what they perceived as the hot-button issue: the large-capacity magazine. If they could get Congress to focus on this particular matter as the root of the problem, then they might escape more severe restrictions. They had been success-ful in getting the Bush administration to focus on the magazine capacity as the focal point of their import ban, and they wanted to extend this to any national legislation that was bound to follow.

Thirteen gun makers, with William Ruger as their point man, led the charge as a group called the Sporting Arms and Ammuni-tion Manufacturers' Institute (SAAMI). The group also included well-known gun makers Winchester and Smith & Wesson. "Semiautomatic firearms as such should not be the object of any legislative prohibition," SAAMI's official position noted. "It is actually the large-magazine capacity, rather than the semiautomatic operation, which is the proper focus of this debate." Ruger again hammered home the technical point that there was no such thing as a semiautomatic assault rifle, and this resonated with gun owners who felt that their weapons were unfairly portrayed. But when Ruger publicly reiterated the group's stance, that magazines should be held to fifteen rounds, he attracted the anger of these same gun owners who felt betrayed by the high-profile gun maker whom they had considered an ally in their fight against firearm restrictions.

Many in the gun community could not understand Ruger's position of giving in to *any* kind of limitations, offering *any* type of concessions. They did not understand that Ruger and his SAAMI colleagues were hoping to head off more restrictive legislation. Ruger also hoped to save his own Mini-14, a popular semiautomatic, but during the contentious months ahead he was portrayed by pro-gun groups as a Benedict Arnold. He was also compared to British prime minister Neville Chamberlain, who had appeased Adolf Hitler in the hope of avoiding World War II only to see Germany grow more emboldened and belligerent.

Congressional lawmakers spent five years trying to pass an assault rifle ban, without success, but they got the boost they needed from another high-profile case involving an AK. This time, the violence struck close to their Capitol Hill offices.

On January 22, 1993, Aimal Kansai, a twenty-nine-year-old Pakistani citizen, enraged by U.S. policy toward Muslim nations, traded in his AR-15 (bought a few days earlier) and purchased a Chinese-version AK at a Virginia gun shop. Three days later, he stopped his car on Dolley Madison Boulevard next to a line of cars waiting to turn into the Central Intelligence Agency headquarters in Langley, Virginia.

He later wrote that he wanted to kill CIA director James Woolsey or his predecessor, Robert Gates, but he knew that entry to the secure facility would be impossible. He settled for aiming his

AK point-blank at a group of commuters waiting to make a left turn. Firing through their car windows, Kansai shot and killed two CIA employees and injured three others before he sped away.

Police found shell casings at the scene and knew they were from an AK. As they canvassed local gun shops, they received a call from Kansai's roommate, who reported the man missing. He had last seen Kansai on the day of the shootings. Two days later, the roommate called police again, telling them that he thought Kansai might have been involved in the shootings.

When police searched the apartment, they found an AK and several other rifles. They also discovered clothes that matched witnesses' descriptions and what appeared to be car window glass stuck to the clothing. Subsequent ballistics tests showed that the shell casings found at the scene matched Kansai's AK. The glass matched the shot-out car windows.

The Washington, D.C., area was stunned by the randomness of the crime. Even though the victims were CIA employees, and one was in covert operations, many in the region saw them as regular people killed on their way to the office on an ordinary Monday morning. It could have been almost anybody. The CIA "hardened" its entrance (the building itself is about a quarter mile in from the entry point) with round-the-clock manned SUVs and security teams sitting in cars up and down Dolley Madison Boulevard. Rolling patrols started as construction began on a permanent security booth with bulletproof windows.

Kansai had flown to Pakistan a day after the shooting, and despite the CIA's and FBI's best efforts, they could not get their hands on him for another four and a half years. (Eventually he was extradited to Virginia, tried, and executed for murder.) During his absence, however, the assault rifle ban moved ahead in Congress, buoyed by stories on television and in newspapers about how easy it was for Kansai to purchase his AK and emphasizing that these weapons were not for sport as the gun lobby had led many to believe but were designed to kill people. Like the Stockton shooting, the incident pushed many lawmakers who had been on the fence into voting for restrictions. This, along with stories about the use of AKs in Africa and South America, pushed even ardent pro-gun lawmakers into changing their position.

On September 13, 1994, Congress passed the Violent Crime Control and Law Enforcement Act, which banned the manufacture, transfer, and possession of certain semiautomatic weapons. Many gun owners were furious at the new law and stepped up their criticism of Ruger, because this time, instead of a limit of fifteen rounds per magazine, the number was now ten. They believed that if the famous gun maker had not pushed for the fifteen-round limit for the import ban Congress would not have lowered it still further.

In a break for gun owners, though, Congress grandfathered weapons and magazines manufactured before the ban. Aside from the magazines being limited to ten rounds, semiautomatics could not have folding or telescoping stocks (to prevent secreting under clothes), a pistol grip (to prevent rapid hip firing), a bayonet mount, a flash suppressor (flash suppressors prevent the enemy from locating your position in the dark), or a grenade launcher. The ban also applied similar criteria to semiautomatic pistols and semiautomatic shotguns.

The act outlawed exact copycats and lookalike guns, but the wording still provided loopholes similar to those in the import ban. Whether the law actually prevented crimes was an issue that continues to draw debate. A report by the National Institute of Justice in March 1999, covering the years 1994 through 1996, noted that the ban had clear-cut, unintended short-term effects on the gun market. For example, not only did manufacturers step up production while the ban was being debated—giving many thousands of rifles "pre-ban" protection—but prices rose dramatically, more than 50 percent in some cases, during the year before the ban took effect and then fell afterward. This suggests that the weapons became generally more available after the ban, probably from the stockpile of pre-ban weapons and from new copycats that hit the market. Also, there was a measurable short-term drop in criminal

use of the banned weapons after the act, according to law enforcement officials who monitored so-called tracing requests of
weapons used in crimes.

Within a few months of the ban, however, it became clear to
almost everyone that the loopholes were so large that they rendered the law's intentions largely useless. Proponents said it was
better than no law, but its full intent certainly was being thwarted.
Even gun makers noted that the law did little to get banned rifles
out of the hands of criminals. Colt president Ron Whittaker said
that the ban was simply about cosmetics: "We had a crime bill that
was supposed to focus on crime, and hopefully, criminals. We
ended up with an assault weapons ban that has nothing to do with
defining assault weapons, but it had a lot to do with what something looks like." His company's Sporter rifle did not pass the ban
test until it had the flash suppressor removed and the pistol grip
altered. It was then sold under the name Match Target. "They
passed a cosmetic law, and now they're [Congress] sitting back saying, 'Oh, woe is me. . . . People are changing the cosmetics!' I don't
understand that logic."

Copycats and pre-ban stockpiles filled gun buyers' needs, and
gun makers readily advertised post-ban models alongside their
outlawed kin that were no longer for sale. The inference was obvious: these were basically the same weapon. The gun industry
called altering a firearm to legal status "sporterization," which
sometimes meant only changing a minor detail such as removing
the flash suppressor or taking away the threaded portion of the
barrel to prevent a suppressor from being mounted. Manufacturers had learned how to fit within the letter of the law from their
experience getting around the import ban. AKs, for example,
banned by the Bush import restriction, were resurrected by
China's NORINCO as the MAK-90, which stood for Modified
AK-1990—modified to go around the 1989 import ban. Not only
was the pistol grip replaced by a thumbhole in the stock, but a nut
was welded at the barrel's end to prevent a flash suppressor from
being screwed in. In addition, the bayonet lug was machined

down so a bayonet could not be mounted. More MAK-90s were imported from China than any other country, and they remain one of the most popular, because they are inexpensive and plentiful.

When the 1994 ban took affect, Russian gun makers also saw an opportunity to make money. Vyatskie Polyany Machine Building Plant, or MOLOT (which means "hammer"), produced the VEPR, their "sporterized" version of the AK. The VEPR was actually based on the RPK, the light machine gun version of the AK. The action worked the same as the AK, but the receiver (the main frame of a firearm) was a little thicker and stiffer.

Gun magazines, which had opposed the ban in editorials, understood that the act had a bigger bark than bite and reveled in its impotence. In essence, the pro-gunners had won. A story in *Gun World* bore this out: "In spite of assault rifle bans, bans on high capacity magazines, the ranting of the anti-gun media and the rifle's innate political incorrectness, the Kalashnikov in various forms and guises, has flourished. Today there are probably more models, accessories and parts to choose from than ever before."

Senator Feinstein admitted that while many gun makers were getting around the spirit of the law, its most important part, the limit on magazine size to ten rounds, still was a great step forward, but this turned out not to be the case either. Gun dealers had mountains of high-capacity pre-ban magazines on hand, enough to last ten years—when the law was set to expire. Moreover, some gun dealers became even more creative, especially with the pistol section of the law that limited the number of bullets a pistol could hold. They offered police departments an exchange of new pistols and magazines for their old ones, which they could then legally sell to the public because they were produced before the ban. Since new, large-capacity pistols were allowed for sale to law enforcement agencies, this system added to gun dealers' stocks for public consumption. Most police agencies shied away from the offer.

"If I could have gotten fifty-one votes in the Senate," Feinstein lamented, "for an outright ban, picking up every one of them, I would have done it. I could not do that. The votes weren't here."

But even such an outright ban would not have prevented the most vicious police standoff in Los Angeles history, sparking a nationwide debate about how best to arm law enforcement officers against the growing numbers of assault rifles being used against them. Police around the country were scared. They were under-armed, facing criminals carrying AKs and other high-powered assault rifles.

ON FEBRUARY 28, 1997, less than a week after the Russian Army Museum opened an exhibit celebrating the fiftieth anniversary of the AK, two men, armed with M-16s and AKs, and both wearing masks and body armor, entered the North Hollywood branch of the Bank of America. With their nerves steeled by phenobarbital, veteran bank robbers Larry Eugene Phillips Jr. and Emil Matasareanu pushed a hostage into the bank door as Los Angeles Police Department officers came upon the scene by chance. Officer Loren Farell, a nine-year veteran and his partner, Martin Perello, who had been on the job for only eighteen months, were on patrol. Perello, driving slowly, casually eyed the bank, checking the door of the division's busiest bank as he always did. Farell was making entries in his administrative log when his partner yelled, "Two-eleven!"—robbery in progress.

Perello described two men dressed like Ninja Turtles pushing someone through the front door. Both officers then saw the rifles. After the officers requested backup, they took cover just outside the bank and heard automatic fire from inside. "Witnesses report suspects are shooting AK-47s," officers at the scene radioed the dispatcher so she could warn others who were on their way. "Subjects are firing AK-47s. . . . Stay down!" Then, "Officer down!"

They warned helicopters to keep their distance as the robbers exited the bank, spraying the area with hundreds of steel-jacketed bullets. Armed as they were with only 9mm pistols, their bullets bounced off the robbers' armor. Patrol officers could do nothing but wait for reinforcements. "It was like throwing a rock at a wall," Officer John Goodman later said. They also knew that their own vests would not protect them against the AK rounds. Several more officers lay injured.

As additional officers arrived, they could do little but hide behind their cars for protection. They watched helplessly as their patrol cars' tires exploded, windows shattered, and steel side panels were riddled with holes. They soon discovered that the only parts of their vehicles that the robbers' bullets could not penetrate were the massive engine blocks, so they hid behind them. Helicopters, hovering just out of firing range, offered a brutal bird's-eye view of the surreal, close-in firefight, with the gunmen calmly changing magazines including hundred-round drums.

The city and world watched as these two heavily armed men kept L.A.'s finest at bay and the city partially paralyzed. Nine nearby elementary schools went into lockdown. Area residents were told to stay inside, or call 911 if they had to leave for an urgent trip. Police closed the bustling Hollywood Freeway in both directions, causing massive traffic tie-ups.

In what they later termed "willpower beats firepower," police officers exhibited great bravery. In one instance, they drove a car through a parking lot across the street from the bank, flung open the doors, and scooped up a wounded colleague. Taking heavy fire, they punched the car into reverse and sped out of range to a waiting ambulance.

The siege continued, and police were powerless to stop the bank robbers. The call had gone out to SWAT, but it would take twenty to thirty minutes for them to arrive. In an attempt to close the firepower gap, several officers found a nearby gun shop and borrowed two AR-15s, a shotgun, and high-powered hunting rifles with telescopic sights. "These people had body armor and they needed something that would break body armor," the store owner said. "We supplied them with slugs that would at least break bones on someone wearing body armor." One detective lamented, "They're waving AK-47s, and I have a nine-millimeter. I'm in the wrong place with the wrong gun."

In the end, Phillips shot himself in the head as officers fired upon him at close range after his AK malfunctioned. SWAT team members killed Matasareanu a few minutes later as he tried to steal a pickup truck and escape. They fired underneath their car, hitting him in his unprotected foot. Then they shot him as he folded, and he bled to death.

When the shooting was done, the area looked like a war zone, with police and civilian cars riddled with bullet holes. Miraculously, of the eleven officers and six civilians shot, none were killed.

The incident shocked police around the country, who considered it a breach of the unwritten code of conduct between police and criminals. Law enforcement had long been complaining about the gun situation, but now the public understood firsthand as they watched it unfold on their TV sets, and later through a movie entitled *44 Minutes*. That year, the *LAPD Annual Report* included a special five-page section on the shootout. In it, Lieutenant Nick Zingo, in charge of the North Hollywood Division that morning, summed up the incident's meaning: "Bank robbers are supposed to go in, get the money and leave. If they get trapped inside, they're supposed to take hostages and make SWAT come and talk them out. That's the norm. They're not supposed to come outside and take on patrol officers. . . . It's not supposed to happen that way."

Police officers around the country suffered the same "outgunned" feeling, especially when confronting drug dealers and gang members armed with AKs and Uzis. Some called for parity to protect officers, while others suggested restraint to protect the public against assault rifles becoming everyday police weapons. L.A. police chief Willie Williams found himself at the center of the controversy. His rank and file had asked months earlier for greater firepower for patrol officers. Williams sat on the proposal, unsure that placing high-powered rifles in the hands of patrol officers (as opposed to specially trained SWAT units) was in the public interest. "You can't equip our general patrol officer with an AK-47," he said at a news conference. "We're supposed to live in somewhat of a civilized society."

Several months later, the Pentagon donated six hundred M-16s to the Los Angeles Police Department. The weapons were converted from automatic to semiautomatic and were to be carried in the trunks of sergeants on patrol. All officers were also authorized to carry a .45-caliber pistol instead of their 9mm sidearm because of the better stopping power of the larger bullet against criminals wearing body armor. Ironically, the 9mm pistols were issued a year earlier because officers had complained that their .38-caliber revolvers fired too slowly and they were being outgunned by criminals using 9mm handguns.

Law enforcement agencies around the United States began equipping their officers with semiautomatic rifles, pointing to the Los Angeles incident or one in their own area that had not garnered media attention. Some departments, like the Palm Bay, Florida, police, already had been carrying AR-15s in their patrol cars after an incident in 1987 in which a gunman killed six people including two officers. They were the exception, as most police agencies allowed only SWAT officers to carry assault rifles even though in many areas it could take up to two hours for SWAT teams to arrive.

SWAT teams were not designed for fast deployment. These specially trained and outfitted officers normally responded to blockade and hostage situations in which time was not of the essence. Usually, the longer a barricade situation lasted, the better the outcome as both sides tended to negotiate a nonviolent end. Now, times were different. Criminals were wielding assault rifles to shoot out of situations instead of bargaining for a peaceful conclusion.

The roster of police departments outfitting officers with semiautomatic rifles grew rapidly over the following years. The move was given a boost by the National Defense Authorization Act of 1997 that allowed the Defense Department to release some of its seven million older M-16 models as well as other surplus material such as cars, body armor, trucks, and radios to local law enforcement agencies at little or no cost. Police agencies paid about fifty dollars each for rifles, but many police departments either could not wait for their turn or wanted civilian versions right off the bat, so they bought rifles on the open market for up to a thousand dollars each.

Some citizen groups feared that the powerful rifles would make the streets more dangerous. Police agencies found themselves explaining why the new rifles would actually be safer than the shotguns they currently carried. Because the rifle rounds were designed to inflict maximum damage on human flesh—the hydrostatic effect of a small mass fired at high velocity—they were less likely than a shotgun to penetrate drywall or cars, or hit innocent bystanders.

Police were routinely issued shotguns, but they were not designed for accuracy, as the pellets contained in the shells spread out rapidly after firing. As such, they could be useful for hitting several close-in subjects at the same time, but their effectiveness dissipated rapidly with distance. Orlando police officer Eric Clapsaddle, who ran the department's shooting range, found himself defending the police department's decision to buy 250 civilian-version M-16s. "If you're not educated on the weapon, people will think it's a dangerous military assault rifle. In reality, it's safer in an urban setting with a lot of people."

Police agencies acknowledged that although incidents of violent crime were remaining somewhat constant in the 1990s, their ferocity was rising. Police were up against better-armed criminals who were not afraid to use their superior firepower. (This was not just an American phenomenon. Police in London began equipping their officers in 2001 with Heckler & Koch G36K assault rifles as confrontations with criminals grew more volatile.) National Park Service law enforcement rangers who patrolled national parks found themselves changing with the times, too. Park officers were issued M-16s in addition to their sidearms, because they often came upon heavily armed drug dealers in remote areas. Far from immediate backup help, sometimes out of radio range, these rangers had to fend for themselves.

Even small-town police agencies without budget power gave their police more firepower. Alexandria (pop. 45,000) and neighboring Pineville, Louisiana (pop. 15,000), for example, allowed officers to carry semiautomatic rifles if they paid for them out of their own pocket. Despite their small-town profile, two Alexandria police officers were shot and killed in 2003 by a man firing an AK.

Large cities gave officers options, too. St. Petersburg, Florida, police began allowing officers to buy their own AR-15s, after police found themselves confiscating increasing numbers of semiautomatic and automatic rifles, mainly AKs.

Against this backdrop of increasing police firepower was the assault rifle ban, which was set to expire on September, 13, 2004. With police agencies ramping up to counter heavily armed criminals, opponents of extending the law said the ramp-up offered proof that the ban was not working as hoped. Criminals were still getting their hands on assault rifles, mainly pre-ban and copycats, and police continued to feel threatened.

Others defended the ban. The Brady Center to Prevent Gun Violence offered statistics showing that crimes involving assault weapons had dropped from a high of 6.15 percent the year before the ban to 2.57 percent in 2001, a 58 percent decrease in eight years. Opponents offered their own statistics, claiming that the overwhelming majority of crimes were perpetrated by handguns and not assault rifles, and any emphasis should be on criminals and not law-abiding citizens.

In the post-9/11 atmosphere, fears of terrorism helped pump up the volume. The Brady Center ran full-page ads in national newspapers stating, "Terrorists of 9-11 Can Hardly Wait For 9-13," with a picture of Osama bin Laden and his signature Krinkov along with excerpts from an al-Qaeda training manual advising, "In countries like the United States, it's perfectly legal for members of the public to own certain types of firearms. If you live in such a country, obtain an assault rifle legally, preferably an AK-47 or variations."

Even supporters admitted that the act had too many loopholes and that a tighter act should be passed. Josh Sugarmann, executive director of the Violence Policy Center, said, "For those who fear that if the ban expires there will be a flood of AKs and Uzis on our streets, the sad truth is that we're already drowning." The law necessary to truly keep assault rifles off the streets needed to be changed to close all loopholes, he added.

Some state assault rifle bans also were at stake if the federal ban faded away. In Massachusetts, for example, that state's assault rifle ban was set to expire concurrent with the national law, and supporters there erected a mammoth billboard with a huge AK, the message stating, "Coming to a Home Near You." The billboard, reported to be the largest in the United States, showed an AK that measured a hundred feet long and thirty feet tall. "We chose it because the AK-47 is a recognizable weapon in the American lexicon," said John Rosenthal, founder and chairman of Stop Handgun Violence, the group that erected the billboard. "The AK-47 has a sordid history with mass shootings in America," added Rosenthal, a gun owner and skeet shooter. The billboard itself has become an icon, appearing in movies such as *Fever Pitch*. Situated as it is next to Boston's Fenway Park, more than a quarter of a million Massachusetts Turnpike commuters see the billboard every day, now with an even larger AK and new text that reads, "Welcome to Massachusetts. You're more likely to live here," a reference to the state's assault weapons ban.

Without a very recent high-profile shooting, supporters had trouble making a dramatic case. President George W. Bush supported renewal but did not press Congress to act, prompting critics to suggest that he played it both ways. Bush said he would sign the bill if Congress presented it, but chances were slim that would happen. In addition, adept lobbying by the National Rifle Association and others secured the renewal's demise. The NRA was even able to include an amendment giving gun makers protection from lawsuits. This amendment tainted the act for advocates, who now found it impossible to vote for it.

As the act was about to expire, gun shops did not report any abnormal shopping behavior, no slowdown in anticipation of the end of restrictions, and no indications of pent-up demand. When the law finally expired, there were no reports of consumers lining up to buy rifles. It was business as usual, leading many to believe that the act was not the deterrent they had touted. Anyone, criminal or upstanding citizen, could have gotten all the firepower they wanted during the ten-year ban.

It was also business as usual in some of the country's roughest areas. On the night before the act's expiration, a twenty-six-year old Miami-Dade police officer was on routine patrol when she pulled over a white Impala to investigate reports of gunshots in the area. The driver opened the car door, pointed his AK at the officer, and fired more than two dozen rounds. Her patrol car exploded after bullets struck either the gas tank or the fuel line. The officer, a single mother of a young boy, was hit in the shoulder and the forehead. She recovered following several operations for the head wound. The shooter, a thirty-six-year-old man, had been arrested thirteen times in the previous nine years and carried convictions for drug possession, robbery, and possession of firearms by a convicted felon. He has not yet faced trial for the attempted murder of a police officer in addition to gun infractions.

The assault rifle issue also affected the presidential election held two months later. "Today, George Bush made the job of terrorists easier and made the job of America's law enforcement officers harder, and that's just plain wrong," proclaimed presidential candidate John Kerry when the ban expired. Although Kerry won the endorsement of some national police organizations for his stand against assault rifles, many pro-gun groups used his words to portray him as rabidly anti-gun. The NRA mobilized its members to vote against him, reminding them that the senator had voted nine times for the assault rifle ban. One NRA ad even called him "the most anti-gun presidential nominee in history."

Kerry lost his 2004 bid for president in one of America's closest and most contentious elections, in large part because of efforts by the NRA and their campaign to allow unfettered purchases of semiautomatic rifles. "This election was crucial for the Second Amendment," said NRA executive vice president Wayne LaPierre. "The NRA stands for freedom, our members are defenders of freedom, and we are proud to see that gun owners across the country came out and voted for freedom."

AS THE ASSAULT RIFLE ISSUE played out in the United States, the United Nations was also about to tackle the subject. Members of the world body, especially those from Africa, viewed these weapons not just as implements of war but as long-term impediments to economic growth and social progress in their countries. Other UN members saw these military-style rifles, especially the AK, as more of a threat to world peace than the atomic bomb and were determined to do something about it.

THE UNITED NATIONS TAKES ON THE TRUE WEAPONS OF MASS DESTRUCTION

On July 9, 2001, John Bolton stood before members of the United Nations and shocked them with what many considered the most vitriolic and unilateral stance seen at the world organization in recent memory. For a body that prided itself on being diplomatic and conciliatory, the members heard the U.S. undersecretary of state for arms control and international security affairs reel off a litany of forceful "No's"—lines in the sand that the world's only surviving superpower would not allow to be crossed when it came to small-arms control.

After lauding the concept of the UN's first Conference on the Illicit Trade in Small Arms and Light Weapons—SALW as it's often called—Bolton proceeded to lay out the U.S. minority position. "We do not support measures that would constrain legal trade and legal manufacturing of small arms and light weapons. . . . We do not support the promotion of international advocacy activity by international or nongovernment organizations, especially when those political or policy views advocated are not consistent with the views of all member states. . . . We do not support measures that prohibit civilian possession of small arms."

As his speech continued, Bolton dashed the hopes of officials from many countries, especially those in Africa, who had hoped for strong international support to help rid their nations of small arms, especially AKs, that were responsible for many of the continent's problems. As Bolton continued, it was becoming clear to many attendees that the U.S. position would not soften or change. Any agreement, if one were even to be reached during the two-week conference, would end up being inadequate and watered down. Perhaps most damaging to countries pulled apart by low-level conflicts fueled by cheap small arms was his statement, "We do not support measures limiting trade in SALW solely to governments." Calling this concept "conceptually and practically flawed," Bolton said it would "preclude assistance to an oppressed nonstate group defending itself from a genocidal government. Distinctions between governments and nongovernments are irrelevant in determining responsible and irresponsible end users of arms." In other words, there was no difference between legitimate governments and other groups in terms of who should be able to buy small arms, even in large quantities. While this stance played well to the National Rifle Association and pro-gun groups in the United States—a country not coping with well-armed rebel groups—it was a stab in the back to countries trying to keep AKs out of the hands of terrorist groups, drug cartels, and insurgents.

Bolton capped his remarks by stating that the United States would not commit to any binding agreements.

As he uttered his last words, most of the audience sat in stunned silence, astounded at how sharp and un-UN-like his presentation had been. Moreover, insiders who had read his speech the day before were totally shocked that he had changed it at the last minute to make it even more venomous. It was not the same speech approved for delivery by the State Department.

One group was not quiet. As members of the UN sat dumbfounded by Bolton's harsh words, cheers rose from the gallery where National Rifle Association representatives sat. To all present, it was clear that Bolton had carried the gun lobby's message.

After the meeting ended, Georgia congressman Bob Barr held a news conference. This move also surprised attendees, as no one could recall another time when a U.S. legislator had convened such an event at the UN. Barr, an NRA board member, reiterated Bolton's "Red Line" issues: "If the conference can concentrate on the central issue of the flow of illicit weapons then we're in agreement. But if it drifts off into areas that are properly the area of national level decision-making, then I think there will be difficulties." Barr threatened to cut funding to the United Nations if the body did not limit itself to the issue of illegal weapons flows.

As he hailed a cab outside the UN building, Barr pointed to a bronze sculpture titled *Non-Violence* by Swedish artist Carl Fredrik Reutersward, which depicts a .45-caliber pistol with a knot tied in its barrel. The pretzel-like symbol struck Barr as ridiculous. "You'd at least think they'd put an AK-47 out there. That's a standard firearm."

After Bolton gave his bombshell speech, he returned to Washington, leaving Lincoln Bloomfield Jr., the State Department's assistant secretary for political-military affairs, to handle the remainder of the conference. Although Bloomfield was a twelve-year veteran of the State Department, he had been in his current job for less than two months. Representatives from other nations viewed Bolton's hard-line speech, quick exit, and replacement by the inexperienced Bloomfield as dismissive and disrespectful to the United Nations and the conference's work.

Bolton's remarks had done their job. They stopped cold the UN's move to limit illegal small-arms trafficking, which had begun in earnest after the breakup of the Soviet Union.

TO UNITED NATIONS POLICYMAKERS, it was becoming clear that small arms were not just about little tribal wars. They were directly blamed for the deaths of more than half a million people annually both from armed conflict and domestic violence. They enabled drug wars, terrorism, and insurgencies. But small arms did much more long-term damage to countries. They increased the worldwide burden on health care systems and allowed the spread of infectious diseases by preventing medical caregivers from entering conflicted areas. Excesses of small arms led to severe economic consequences by destabilizing governments and destroying economic infrastructures. After having dealt with the specter of nuclear weapons for the previous decades, and with that shadow now gone, the UN had turned its attention to small arms and how to destroy them.

Small arms were the UN's new bogeyman.

Individual countries and regional groups had tried with mixed results to decommission large numbers of small arms. Most of these guns were remnants of past conflicts and now were embedded in the culture. In other areas, they were owned for protection in lawless regions untouched by government control that offered open terrain for bandits and thieves. For example, in areas like Kenya's Northeastern Province, which shares a four-hundred-mile border with Somalia, small arms used as protection were so ingrained in the day-to-day lives of the indigenous clans that efforts to have people turn them in, mainly AKs, proved unsuccessful. At the time of the UN conference, the only weapons relinquished there were ancient, unworkable, or barely able to function. "We are finding that if a weapon is surrendered voluntarily, that person has already acquired a better one," said Maurice Makhanu, provincial commissioner. This reluctance to turn in small arms, especially cheap and durable AKs, was common throughout the world, a point not lost on UN officials.

In a presentation a year earlier about the role of the UN in the twenty-first century, Secretary-General Kofi Annan had presented the world body's strongest attack on small arms when he said, "The death toll from small arms dwarfs that of all other weapons systems—and in most years greatly exceeds the toll of the atomic bombs that devastated Hiroshima and Nagasaki. In terms of the carnage they cause, small arms, indeed, could well be described as 'weapons of mass destruction.' Small arms proliferation is not merely a security issue; it is also an issue of human rights and of development. The proliferation of small arms sustains and exacerbates armed conflicts. It endangers peacekeepers and humanitarian workers. It undermines respect for international humanitarian law. It threatens legitimate but weak governments and it benefits terrorists as well as the perpetrators of organized crime."

For many U.S.-based pro-gun groups, the United Nations now had gone too far, and the agenda against SALW threatened their Second Amendment right to bear arms. Reports circulated throughout the pro-gun community that the UN was considering a one-gun-per-person strategy in addition to a ban on handgun possession by anyone other than government officials. There were rumors of plans for worldwide licensing of firearms with a database kept at the United Nations. None of these assertions were true, but many gun owners in the United States believed they were, and they inundated the United Nations with letters and phone calls voicing their concerns.

Even before the conference began, UN officials were forced to respond to the deluge with a public statement outlining their position. They reiterated that they were not planning to take away privately owned guns and that the conference's focus was on illicit trade in small arms and not the legal trade, manufacture, or ownership of weapons. They even cited the UN's own charter, which prohibited it from interfering in matters within a member state's domestic jurisdiction. This included gun laws.

The UN statement also noted that the organization was inviting 177 nongovernmental organizations (NGOs) from five continents to offer their views and opinions. These included anti-gun groups such as the International Action Network on Small Arms (IANSA) as well as pro-gun groups such as the National Rifle Association. All NGOs had the same rights and privileges.

Despite these clarifications, the U.S. pro-gun groups' fears were not assuaged, and they pressed Bolton to take his hard line at the

United Nations. Not that Bolton needed any persuading. He was widely known as a strict constitutionalist and someone who had shown great disdain and disrespect in the past for the United Nations. "If the UN secretary [secretariat] building in New York lost ten stories, it wouldn't make a bit of difference," he had told a conference seven years earlier. "There is no such thing as the United Nations. There is an international body that occasionally can be led by the only real power left in the world, and that is the United States when it suits our interest and we can get others to go along."

At a press conference during the UN meeting, Bolton refuted the constant din of allegations that his delegation's position was scripted by pro-gun groups. "I am not a member of the NRA. I have never been a member. Let me start over," he said firmly. "I am not now and never have been a member of the NRA, and I have no idea who on the delegation is a member of the NRA. The NRA did not write our position and that's that."

Tensions were rising among delegates. Just as the pro-gun groups could not be convinced that the UN had no designs on their weapons, anti-gun groups believed that the NRA wrote the U.S. stance.

NGOs played a more pronounced role in this conference than in most other UN proceedings, and their participation was a major factor in how the two-week confab worked. A coalition wanting to stem the proliferation of small arms was the largest group present, representing about three hundred groups. The second largest was represented by the World Forum on the Future of Sport Shooting Activities, with the NRA as its most outspoken member. One of the more interesting facets was how some countries, China and Algeria for example, sought to restrict participation by NGOs, because they feared these groups would bring up human rights issues. Other countries, like Canada, Ireland, and the United Kingdom, included NGO representatives in the delegations because they were a source of data and information. One thing that most anti-gun delegates believed was that the pro-gun NGOs exerted a large influence on the U.S. position. For the NRA, the UN conference represented an opportunity to raise funds and enter the international arena in a way never before possible. Although the NRA had been active internationally, the UN conference propelled it to a higher level.

The U.S. hard-line posture seemed out of place considering that the United States was a world leader in transparency of arms sales and accountability. Compared to many countries, U.S. domestic gun laws were solid and workable, and the country was in the forefront of monitoring weapons transfers, maintaining security of weapons caches, licensing of brokers, and setting standards for weapons markings. The U.S. delegation did not push for international standards even in cases where U.S. laws exceeded worldwide proposals. To some people, it seemed as though the U.S. delegation was being confrontational for no apparent reason.

Perhaps this should not have been a surprise to astute observers, however. The Bush administration regularly took pains to dismiss any UN initiative that it felt would limit its future options. For example, the United States has not signed the Kyoto Protocol on limiting greenhouse gases despite the fact that the nation's air was actually getting cleaner and many U.S. environmental laws are tougher than those elsewhere. And the United States has repeatedly refused to sign agreements that ban the use of land mines although it has not used antipersonnel mines since 1991. (President Clinton failed to sign the 1997 Mine Ban Treaty, but he did create a policy that would put the United States on track to join the treaty by 2006. The Bush administration has rejected the treaty outright.)

Although the United States appeared to go it alone with its stonewalling stance, other nations such as Russia and China tacitly agreed. For example, China, which supplied more AKs to the world than any other country, fought UN standards to mark weapons so they could be traced. Behind the scenes, Russia opposed restrictions on sales to nongovernmental entities, but was content to let the U.S. delegation take the heat. These three nations were not necessarily aligned on all issues, but the U.S.

delegates were publicly vocal, distracting attention from the other two, who kept a low profile.

As the conference progressed it was becoming clear that the entire exercise might come to nothing over two main sticking points: supplying nongovernmental entities with weapons, and restrictions on civilian ownership of military-type weapons, issues on which Bolton would not compromise. The African bloc of nations, which had suffered the most from small-arms proliferation, held fast, insisting that these two provisions remain.

At 6 a.m. on the conference's last day, the African states capitulated to the U.S. position rather than have the conference go up in flames. Some positive changes had come from the meeting, and they did not want to lose any momentum, albeit small. They knew that the U.S. position was absolutely intractable, because Bolton would be content if the conference did not produce *any* agreement whatsoever. In return, however, the African bloc insisted that conference president Camilo Reyes of Colombia publicly describe why they gave in and who was to blame. Reyes agreed and noted in part, "I must . . . express my disappointment over the conference's inability to agree, due to the concerns of one State [the United States]. . . . The States most afflicted by this global crisis, Africa, had agreed only with the greatest of reluctance to the deletion of . . . these vital issues. They did so strictly in the interests of reaching a compromise that would permit the world community as a whole to proceed together with some first steps at the global level to alleviate this common threat."

Although the conference's final document, the *Programme of Action*, did little to stop the illegal trade in arms, some considered it a success anyway, because it raised awareness of the issue on a global level. This consciousness-raising may have been the conference's most important legacy, according to many delegates who were optimistic that the meetings put in motion a long-term commitment to address the issue.

.   .   .

ONE TOPIC THAT DREW MUCH attention was that of universal standards for weapons marking to make tracing possible. At the time of the conference, the issue was thwarted because it could not get buy-in from countries like China, which sold many arms that ended up in the wrong hands. In fact, UN experts suggest that because more than 60 percent of illegal small arms started out as legal transfers, a marking and tracing system could go a long way to stop human rights abuses perpetrated at the end of a gun. Because no state was willing to institute worldwide restrictions at the national level on civilian possession of arms, this too was left out of the final document, but there was some movement at subsequent biennial meetings.

Unlike during the original conference, the United States became supportive in this area, mainly because U.S. gun makers already adhered to strict marking and record-keeping of firearms. Publicly, countries like Egypt, Syria, and China opposed marking and record-keeping because of increased scrutiny of their legal gun sales. Weapons from these countries often find their way into illegal channels.

For a worldwide marking system to be useful, each weapon must have a unique serial number that designates the country of origin, the manufacturer, and the year of production. As arms are transferred, a marking upon importation is also helpful. It offers investigators a starting point for any search by telling them the last country of import and also acts as a backup to the original markings if they become obliterated or if registry data become faulty or missing. Even if a trafficker were to imprint a false import marking, it could still be traced to the original country.

Politics asides, marking is a technical issue. Stamping is the traditional and most common marking technique. It is cheap and simple. Current-day marking usually takes place on large, flat areas such as the side of the receiver. On the AK, for instance, some typically seen symbols are an upward arrow within a triangle, which designates the Russian Izhevsk factory, and a five-pointed star, which is stamped on AKs from Russia's Tula Arsenal. There are

AK-47
MANUFACTURER MARKINGS

 Izhevsk Factory (Russia)

 Tula Arsenal (Russia)

 North China Industries (NORINCO)

 Bulgaria

several variations of these symbols, such as placing them inside triangles and other geometric shapes. Another common AK marking is the number 66 inside a triangle, which designates AKs produced by China's North China Industries (NORINCO), and the number 21 inside two concentric circles, placed on AKs from Bulgarian arms factories. Along with these shapes are numbers, letters, and other characters that identify the firearm and its point of origin.

Stamping has limitations, however. Newer, harder composites won't accept stamping at all, and imprinting through injection molding does not allow enough detail in a small area to be practical. Laser marking has become the state of the art because of its precision and ability to imprint a lot of information, even bar codes. NASA and private industry have developed a two-dimensional digital image matrix that contains tiny black and white squares representing binary digits that describe a part number. NASA's goal was to place these identification markers on even the tiniest parts used in the space program. Unlike bar codes, these matrix Unique Identifications, or UIDs, are scalable; they can be produced very large or microscopically small and still maintain their readability. They can hold more than one hundred times the amount of information of a typical bar code. The U.S. Army Armament Research and Development Center is testing these UIDs on M-16s and other matériel, because they can be read even after they have been damaged.

Lasers also allow marking on more expensive-to-replace, harder-to-reach parts of a firearm so that any grinding down of the area to obliterate the marking would make the firearm unusable. Some suggest placing laser markings on the breechblock or bolt. This would serve several purposes: it would be hidden until the gun was broken down; erasing the marking might render the part unusable; and replacing it with an unmarked bolt would be costly.

Many U.S., Canadian, and European gun makers routinely employ laser marking to imprint weapons quickly, about three firearms per minute. Costs are low, too, a few cents per weapon in large quantities once the imprinting machine is amortized at a cost of between $40,000 and $60,000. Stamping is less susceptible to erasures because the molecular structure of the metal is deformed much deeper by stamping than from a laser. On the other hand, laser marking is faster and some companies imprint markings with tiny laser holes that can go much deeper than a stamped imprint.

Although marking is one solution to illegal arms trafficking, it would be meaningless without a worldwide database and registry. Such a registry would require that all markings become standard—harmonization, as it's called—but chances are slim of this occurring in the near future because mandatory participation among all nations would be difficult to obtain.

At the 2001 UN meeting, Bob Barr noted that the United States has some of the world's most stringent laws concerning firearms marking, mandating the inclusion of the location, manufacturer's name, and serial number. He suggested that other countries would do well to follow the U.S. lead in controlling exports. Barr held firm against an international registry, though, which he compared to internationally forced gun registration. "That is completely unacceptable, and I and others in the Congress will work to ensure any system of marking firearms focuses on eliminating illegal firearms trafficking, and does not allow the United Nations to create any system which registers or tracks U.S. gun owners or sales."

At a June 2005 UN small-arms working group meeting on marking and tracing, attendees spent a great deal of time discussing the subject of ammunition marking. Proponents argued that while firearms were rarely left at the scene of crimes, shell casings often were, and bullets could be retrieved from victims' bodies. If these bullets could be traced to the buyer, investigators would have a solid tool at their disposal.

Although many ammunition makers argue that marking each round would be prohibitively expensive, those in favor of marking note that cartridges are already imprinted successfully with some letters and numbers, sometimes the caliber size, manufacturer's symbol, or some other identifier. German and Brazilian military ammunition buyers insist on further identification from their suppliers. They require that 5.56 × 45mm rounds for AK-102 and M-16 rifles be marked with the caliber and a ten-digit code composed of six numbers and four letters identifying the manufacturer, year and month of production, lot size, and a unique lot identifier.

Such intricate marking does impose additional expense. Simple markings such as manufacturer or year are traditionally applied by a piston that mechanically presses numbers and letters when the primer pocket is being formed by the same thrusting motion. These stamps only need changing annually. Not so with stamping of lot numbers. Assembly lines, which can hold up to ten thousand cartridges during the assembly process, must be stopped, current cartridges taken off the line, new stamps inserted, and the process begun anew. This is the only way to make sure that lot numbers are not mixed together, but it is time-consuming and slows production lines.

Brazil has decided to buck convention, however. Effective in January 2005, a Brazilian law required identification of eleven different calibers of ammunition to include the lot number as well as a code that identifies the buyer as armed forces, police, private security services, or sport shooting organizations. The calibers were those used in small arms including handguns, assault rifles, and machine guns. In addition, ammo boxes had to contain a bar code so the manufacturer and purchaser could be traced.

This move was in response to Brazil's high rate of domestic gun-related murders. About thirty-five thousand to forty thousand Brazilians are killed annually by guns. Gun murders, mainly using handguns, are the leading cause of death in that nation, according to a recent study of fifty-seven countries conducted by the United Nations.

At the time of writing many of these shootings take place in the favelas, or shantytowns, of Rio de Janeiro. The government has lost control of these makeshift neighborhoods, some eight hundred or so with 1.2 million inhabitants, and gangs have taken over. Armed youths carrying automatic weapons patrol their turfs; some belong to paramilitary groups, while others are part of drug gangs. Still others belong to loose amalgams of poor people trying to protect what little they own with whatever small arms they can afford. Often, military police raid these shantytowns, looking for drug dealers and criminals, and hundreds of innocent people are killed each year by stray bullets from both government and non-government shooters.

Amid this dreadful situation, Brazilian officials have instituted some of the most restrictive gun laws in the Western Hemisphere. Only police and other law enforcement officials are permitted to carry firearms in public (some hunters are exempt). The minimum age for owning weapons has been raised from twenty-one to twenty-five, and those caught carrying weapons are subject to prison sentences of two to four years. The government also established a gun buyback program that made it more expensive to register a weapon than to turn it in for cash, $30 for handguns to $100 for assault rifles. One woman reportedly received $65,000 in 2004 for her deceased father's collection of more than twelve hundred guns.

More important, at the time of writing, it is now possible in Brazil to trace ammunition used in crimes. One manufacturer, Companhia Brasileira Cartuchos (CBC), has already begun imprinting ammunition in compliance with the new marking law. The company uses lasers to imprint a five-digit code into the cartridge's extractor groove, which provides a tiny grip for the gun's extractor to pull the empty case from the chamber after firing. Using computer-directed lasers to imprint the codes does not slow down the assembly process, because once a lot has been produced, it is set aside for imprinting. Once the lot is finished, another lot can be imprinted with its own specific code. Numbers are recorded automatically by a computer for record-keeping purposes. Because marking is accomplished after production, even imported ammunition can be easily imprinted once it enters the country. To ensure tracing capabilities and prevent stealing, producers and importers are required to give "read-only" database information immediately to police and military commands. It is too early to tell if the new gun- and ammunition-marking laws will prevent gun violence, but legislators have high hopes.

So do California legislators and law enforcement officials who are scrutinizing the Brazilian ammunition-marking law for ideas. Instead of focusing solely on the firearm, they decided to look at ammunition for solutions to the state's poor homicide closure rate. During 2003, 45 percent of California's homicides remained unsolved. Although law enforcement officials in the state, as elsewhere, routinely collected bullets and empty cartridges left at crime scenes, nothing linked these remnants to a particular weapon until the shooter and the weapon were apprehended.

To help catch these people, the state senate passed a bill requiring all handgun ammunition sold or owned after 2007 in California to be marked, identifying the box from which it came. Ammunition dealers would be obligated to keep a record of sales, thus identifying each bullet shot and pegging it to the buyer. Gun owners were so incensed at the plan (cleverly labeled SB 357 after the .357 Magnum) that a Sacramento shooting club barred Department of Justice agents from firing on their range because of the attorney general's support for the bill. The Sporting Arms and Ammunition Manufacturers' Institute (SAAMI) opposed the bill, saying that implementation would cost hundreds of millions of dollars in new investment and raise the cost of each cartridge from pennies to dollars.

Law enforcement officials were split down the middle; some opponents suggested that the costs involved would not yield a worthwhile payoff, because criminals would simply use out-of-state ammunition. Law enforcement agencies were also concerned about the increased cost of ammunition that they would have to buy.

Another bill that attracted less controversy required that semi-automatic handguns imprint a microscopic stamp on casings as they were shot. In a criminal case, investigators would be able to match the gun (and presumably the owner) to the casings left behind at the scene. A company doing work in this area is NanoMark Technologies of Londonderry, New Hampshire, which holds a patent for "ballistic ID tagging." Company officials contend that the ID tag is unambiguous—unlike bullet comparisons using conventional CSI-type ballistics methods—and leads directly to the weapon. The only shortcoming of the system is that the shooter could pick up the shell casings after firing, assuming the luxury of time and the presence of mind to collect them all.

To get around this problem, Seattle-based Ammunition Coding System developed a way of coding both the bullet *and* the cartridge casing. The company's laser system imprints a unique identifying code on the inside of cartridge cases as well as the bullet. Both can be read with a magnifying glass. The company claims that the number can be read with as little as 20 percent of the bullet intact after firing. Testing by the San Bernadino County Sheriff's Department showed that they were able to read identification numbers in twenty-one of twenty-two instances. The only downside of this scheme is the high price of the engraving/handling equipment, from $300,000 to $500,000 per machine plus a per bullet licensing fee.

The implications of such bullet-tracing systems could be far-reaching. They could even keep small skirmishes from turning into regional wars. For example, UN officials had only casings to go on when they investigated a massacre at the Gatumba refugee camp in Burundi on the border of the Democratic Republic of the Congo. Beginning between 10 and 11:30 p.m. on August 13, 2004, refugees heard the sound of drums and religious chants approaching. Several survivors reported hearing a whistle and orders being shouted just before the attack. Witnesses disagreed on the number of assailants—the figure varied from one hundred to three hundred—but their composition was not in doubt. The attackers' ranks included armed men, women, and children, some wearing complete or partial military uniforms and others in street clothes. They spoke several different languages, including those common to Congo and Burundi, and shouted slogans such as "kill these dogs, these Tutsis," and "down with the Banyamulenge" (Tutsis from the Congo communities of South Kivu).

When the attackers finished their raid, 152 refugees were dead, and 108 were wounded. Eight refugees were never found. Of the dead and missing, 147 were Banyamulenge. The attackers did not target other groups in the camp. The tents housing Burundian returnees had been left untouched.

The massacre occurred during a fragile time. After six years of war in the Democratic Republic of the Congo and eleven years of war in Burundi, all sides were in the midst of winding down tensions both internally and externally when the attack occurred. Many people in the region considered the Banymulenge as pro-Rwandan even though they fought on both sides of the civil war in Congo. UN investigators suggested that the attackers' goal was to reignite regional fighting and weaken transitional governments.

The plan began to work. The governments of Burundi and Rwanda threatened to attack Congo and ferret out those responsible for the massacre. Strong evidence indicated one group, the National Liberation Front (FNL), which may have been part of the attacking group, but they did not organize the action or carry it out alone, judging by the different languages spoken during the melee. Leaders of the Burundi-based FNL at first admitted participating in the attack but later recanted. The Hutu group justified the massacre, saying that the Tutsis were heading up a new war in Congo that would destabilize a region that had been working toward peace.

After Burundi's first democratically elected president was assassinated in 1993, after only four months in office, war between the Hutus and Tutsi caused 200,000 deaths and displaced more than 1.3 million people both inside and outside the country. A massive wave of refugees entering Congo from Burundi and the concurrent genocide in Rwanda in the early 1990s sparked tribal wars and an overthrow of the Congolese government in 1997. When the newly installed regime was challenged by Rwandan and Ugandan rebels, the result was a regional war—pulling in additional countries—that left more than a million Congolese displaced. In addition, Rwandan rebels used Congo as a base to attack Rwanda, prompting Rwanda to invade.

The regional war surrounding the Democratic Republic of the Congo, formerly Zaire, has been dubbed "Africa's first world war," because it involved six nations, each with its own reasons for involvement, and at least twenty separate armed groups. Since the outbreak of large-scale fighting in 1997, at least 3.8 million people have died, mostly children, women, and the elderly, mainly due to starvation. (Some estimates put the figure as high as 4.5 million.) The prolonged war forced 2.25 million people from their homes, some into refugee camps like Gatumba. The war was the deadliest conflict since World War II, and it was fought mainly with small arms, AKs being the most popular weapon. Although hostilities officially ended in 2002, many of the armed groups continued to fight at the time of writing. To help maintain the delicate stability in the region, it was crucial for the United Nations to find physical evidence of the perpetrators and bring them to justice. This would go a long way to preventing further conflicts born from rumor and unsubstantiated facts.

Unfortunately, by the time investigators arrived at Gatumba camp, the area had been cleansed. Many bodies had been buried in mass graves without forensic examination. Evidence was contaminated and injured victims had been taken to hospitals, where workers rejected UN access to patients from the camp.

Investigators had little solid evidence to go on except some cartridge casings that had not been swept up. Of the thousands of rounds fired, four different cartridge types were found. Markings showed that one was manufactured in Bulgaria in 1995 by Arsenal Kazanlak, two from the People's Republic of China in 1998 by an unknown armory, and one from Prvi Partizan in Uzice, Serbia.

Without any way to trace the ammunition to their buyers, UN investigators were stymied. Not even the manufacturers were able to identify the original recipients of the ammunition. Based on the cartridge configurations, however, the Bulgarian and Chinese cartridges were probably fired from AKs. Beyond that, nothing else could be determined, and the attackers remain at large.

The incident at Gatumba camp remains a flash point for the region. Fighting continues. Some FNL troops have confessed to the Gatumba murders, and may be tried for their crimes. Without additional physical evidence, however, most participants may never be brought to justice.

Proponents of marking and tracing claimed that linking ammunition to buyers might curtail such attacks—and subsequent mistaken retaliations escalating to regional war—if perpetrators believed there was a high probability they would be caught. Opponents contended that unscrupulous gun brokers will *always* find a way to sell unmarked goods, and a black market in unmarked ammunition and guns will undoubtedly develop.

Even if marking and tracing were to begin tomorrow, however, there simply are too many older guns and caches of ammunition around to make any difference for the foreseeable future. Particularly in the case of AKs, it could take fifty years for some of today's weapons to cease working; that, combined with the guns' high tolerance for poorly made and deteriorating ammunition, means they could be functional and untraceable for decades. Johan Peleman, a Belgium-based arms investigator who has worked for the United Nations, put it starkly: "Tracing a twenty-year-old Kalashnikov, back to whoever delivered it, is virtually impossible."

Some of these twenty-year-old AKs surfaced in Iraq after the United States invaded that country in 2003 in an effort to oust Saddam Hussein and destroy his supposed weapons of mass destruction. Once again, the Soviet-designed AK would go head-to-head with the U.S.-designed M-16, just as it had done in Vietnam more than forty years earlier.

AK VERSUS M-16: PART 2

I N 1999, IRAQI PRESIDENT Saddam Hussein ordered construction to begin on what would be the world's largest
mosque. On a hundred-acre site, fifteen miles outside of the
capital city of Baghdad, the huge house of worship was part of the
dictator's plan to strengthen his iron-fist grip on the nation by
appealing to the region's Muslims even though his Baath Party had
a history of disavowing religion and regularly harassing and
killing Muslim fundamentalists.

The "Mother of All Battles" mosque was not only an attempt to
curry favor with Iraq's Muslims but also to pay homage to the Gulf
War of 1991. Hussein had dubbed it the Mother of All Battles, in
which Saddam's invasion of neighboring Kuwait prompted a
counterattack by a U.S.-led, UN-sanctioned coalition that drove
Iraq out of the small, oil-rich country but left him in office with
diminished military power.

Opened on April 28, 2002, Hussein's birthday, the mosque was
a tribute to its megalomaniac maker. The building housed a hand-
written Koran reportedly produced from three pints of Hussein's

blood mixed with ink and preservatives, a pool in the shape of the Arab world, and a twenty-four-foot-wide mosaic of the president's thumbprint. Outside, forty-three-meter-high minarets, symbolizing the forty-three-day conflict with the United States, reached skyward. These minarets were fashioned in the shape of Scud missiles, the NATO name for the R-11 missile built by the Soviet Union during the cold war. Hussein's military blasted Scuds into Israel and Saudi Arabia during the Mother of All Battles. These crude, inexpensive, but effective short-range missiles were often launched from trucks, and could deliver a conventional explosive warhead, a small nuclear bomb, antipersonnel bomblets, or biological or chemical weapons.

The mosque also sported four outer minarets. Like those closest to the main building, these towers were exact images of another Soviet-made, simple, inexpensive, and mobile weapon that Hussein revered. Standing thirty-seven meters high—signifying Saddam's birth year, 1937—these barrel-shaped minarets were replicas of Tabuk assault rifle barrels, Iraq's version of the AK.

Although Saddam's regime officially denied that the minarets were designed like either of these weapons, the look is unmistakable. In the case of the AK minarets, the towers even included the gun's distinctively shaped handguard that provides a tight grip on the barrel during automatic fire. Like Scud missiles, the AK offered Saddam Hussein simple weapons born from the Soviet utilitarian mind-set. They were cheap and deadly.

Although coalition bombings in 1991 destroyed much of Iraq's air force, Scud missiles, and tanks, Hussein's regime retained its arsenal of small arms, especially AKs. In fact, by March 2003 when the Iraq war, or Operation Iraqi Freedom, as it was called by the United States, commenced, Iraq's arsenals were brimming with small arms, perhaps as many as seven to eight million pieces. These weapons would prove deadly to U.S. troops once major hostilities ended, but were not considered a threat by military planners when the war began.

The war commenced with air and ground attacks led by Vietnam veteran General Tommy Franks. Believing that Iraq had violated UN sanctions against building and warehousing weapons of mass destruction—chemical, biological, and nuclear arms—President George W. Bush gave Franks the go-ahead. Although military pundits had expected lengthy air bombings as a prelude to entering ground forces, as in the 1991 Gulf War or the U.S. invasion of Afghanistan, Franks instead ordered ground troops to enter the southern tip of Iraq through Kuwait and make their way to Baghdad as fast as they could. Just as the German army motored swiftly through the Ardennes in 1940, bypassing small villages on the way to Dunkirk and Paris, U.S. troops traveled at top speed, ignoring small towns on their way north to the capital city. Pentagon planners believed that by attacking Baghdad and destroying the nation's command-and-control capabilities, they would cause the regime to disintegrate, and the Iraqi people would overwhelmingly support the invaders as liberators. Once Baghdad was under U.S. control, Pentagon strategists believed that these bypassed towns and villages would fall into line.

As U.S. forces advanced across Iraq, one of their first objectives was to secure the Rumaila oil fields, an area that extends underground into Kuwait. During the Gulf War, Hussein's soldiers ignited theses wells not only to hide their movements amid the dense smoke but to distract coalition forces. Franks was determined to prevent Iraq's army from burning the oil wells again and ordered GIs to secure the fields. This action would also pay postwar benefits, because President Bush hoped that the country's valuable oil supply would help defray the costs of Iraq's reconstruction.

One of the groups assigned to the area was the 1st Battalion of the 5th Marines. Wearing bulky and hot chemical protection suits, Alpha Company was one of the first large ground units to make its way across the Kuwaiti border. After an eight-hour drive, it reached Pumping Station No. 2. Once a base for an Iraqi brigade, the station was largely abandoned save for a few die-hard fighters. The marines took several Iraqi prisoners during skirmishes, but then something unexpected occurred.

A half dozen Iraqis, possibly from Hussein's elite Republican Guard, took off in a brown Toyota pickup truck, in what several marines later said resembled a drive-by shooting. The retreating Iraqis fired AKs wildly out the windows, hitting Second Lieu-tenant Therrel "Shane" Childers, in the lower abdomen. Childers, a thirty-year-old marine from Harrison, Mississippi, and a gradu-ate of the Citadel military college, died almost immediately. He was the first U.S. casualty of Operation Iraqi Freedom. For most of the marines in his company, it was their first look at the AK in combat, but it would not be their last. What perhaps frightened them most was the way these soldiers used their weapons. While U.S. troops were highly trained and disciplined and taught to make every shot count, these soldiers fired indiscriminately, with-out regard to whom they would hit. They were successful. They had killed one marine and injured several others. How could a professionally trained force engage and win against this type of soldier?

Other advancing troops avoided major cities except when nec-essary to gain control of strategic bridges across the Tigris and Euphrates. The first indication that the U.S. plan was running into trouble—although it was eclipsed in the news by the stunning and swift march toward Baghdad—occurred in the bypassed city of Basra, Iraq's second largest city, just north of the Kuwaiti border. As U.S. troops pushed onward, British troops were sent to secure it. To the surprise of military brass, it took two weeks of fighting for the British to enter the city, a conflict that included the largest tank battle the British had seen since World War II. Once Iraq's tanks were destroyed, however, fighting still continued, turning into close-quarter urban warfare. British troops found themselves under constant small-arms attack from Iraqi army regulars and fedayeen fighters.

Fedayeen is the plural of an Arabic word meaning "one who is ready to sacrifice his life for his cause." The first fedayeen in the eighth to fourteenth centuries were a group of Ismali Muslims belonging to the Shia sect of Islam, who terrorized the Abbasids, the Sunni Muslims who ruled Baghdad. This religious group was also known by the name *hashishin* because it was claimed that they put themselves into a fierce fighting-frenzy state by taking hashish before battles. (The modern word "assassin" is derived from their name, as many of their terrorist tactics involved murdering rulers.)

There have been several notable fedayeen groups throughout history. This latest group of fighters, Fedayeen Saddam, were handpicked by Hussein's regime and put under control of his son Uday. Their loyalty to Hussein and the Baath Party assured they would fight to the death against any invader. This paramilitary group, whose numbers may have reached thirty thousand to forty thousand fighters, were used by Hussein to put down opponents and smuggle arms and drugs in the region. Despite their numbers, the international community knew little about them until Hussein pressed them into military service during the U.S. invasion. Their weapon of choice was the AK.

As the U.S. military pressed toward Baghdad, their supplies lagged behind. At about the 250-mile mark, supplies on the front lines became scarce—food, water, and fuel—and supply convoys had to play catch-up. These lightly armored trucks were easy prey for fedayeen ambushes. Although many of the convoys were given cover by helicopters, others were attacked by hit-and-run raids. Fuel tankers were favorite targets because they were slow-moving, and exploding, burning fuel had a dramatic effect.

American troops entered Baghdad certain that total victory was near. When the city fell on April 9, 2003, the fedayeen were in disarray, but many of them carried on the fight, mainly armed with AKs and RPGs. Something else occurred, however. Despite the Bush administration's contention that the war would be over quickly, and the Iraqi people would welcome the coalition forces as liberators, what followed was a protracted guerrilla war for which U.S. forces were not properly outfitted.

The days following the taking of the capital city were marked by looting and an inability of American forces to maintain order. To Secretary of Defense Donald Rumsfeld, the Iraqi people, oppressed for decades by Hussein, were simply letting off steam.

Street violence continued. As U.S. forces attempted to contain it, many Iraqi people grew tired of what they saw as a growing American occupation. In addition, Hussein had gone into hiding and many citizens were afraid that the Americans would abandon them as they had done in the 1991 Gulf War, leaving an opening for Hussein to return to power, more vengeful against opponents than before. Moreover, many Iraqis were still angry about U.S. bombings during the 1991 war that had destroyed large sections of the country's infrastructure. Electricity was flowing at less than a quarter of its prewar amount and damaged water treatment plants allowed raw sewage to flow into the Tigris River, a prime source of freshwater for many Iraqis. Many Iraqis blamed the United States for the widespread disease that followed. Although most Iraqis despised Hussein's rule, at least they had had freshwater, electricity, and other basic services, none of which existed now.

During the uncertainty and chaos that followed the coalition's swift victory, millions of small arms, mainly AKs, were looted or sold from Hussein's huge armories. One of the main occurrences took place in May 2003, when L. Paul Bremer, head of the Coalition Provisional Authority, decided to dismiss all Baathist members from government positions and disband the Iraqi army. Although it may have been a correct decision—and perhaps the only logical one considering circumstances at the time—it caused major social disorder and violence as these groups let loose the nation's small arms to almost anyone. Not unlike the situation during the disbanding of the Soviet Union, military officers and government employees sold the country's weapons as a way to make money, and also to foment opposition against the government in power; in this case, the U.S.-run provisional government. The weapons landed in the hands of law-abiding but nervous civilians. They also reached Baathists loyal to Hussein and other opponents of the U.S. occupation who used them to run a protracted urban war.

As we've seen in many other countries, the street price of the AK is an accurate indicator of the degree of social order and citizen anxiety. In the months prior to the invasion, the price of an AK varied but stayed within a range of $150 to $300, with Chinese models on the lower end and Russian models at the high end. Oddly enough, despite Hussein's dictatorship, private gun ownership in Iraq was fairly high, especially among the loyal Sunni Muslims, for whom a $150 license fee permitted as many small arms as they wanted. It was not unusual for households to maintain several small arms, almost always an AK among them, even in the large cities such as Baghdad and Fallujah. During the worst disorder just after the fall of Baghdad in March and April 2003, prices plummeted as military inventories flooded the market. In Basra, AKs were so ubiquitous that they were almost worthless, one of the causes of the British difficulties maintaining control of that city.

About six months later, as Baghdad settled down and coalition forces got a better handle on widespread looting and street violence, AK prices reverted to previous levels. By then, the bulk of AKs from military arsenals either had been destroyed by coalition forces or distributed to Iraqis. As the summer progressed and insurgent groups coalesced behind political and religious leaders in opposition to the Provisional Authority, demand grew again to the point where small arms were being imported from the neighboring countries of Iran and Syria.

As U.S. forces prepared for an unexpected and extended guerrilla urban war in Iraq, their own small arms seemed unsuited to the task. GIs were issued the standard M16A2, which followed the M16A1, the official and more formal name of the M-16, from the Vietnam era. The A2 had improved sights, a modified handguard, and a different "twist rate" in the barrel. It fired a three-round burst, but the most important difference was the ammunition. The A1 fired the standard U.S. 55-grain, 5.56 × 45mm round, designated as the M193 cartridge. NATO altered the round to fire a 62-grain bullet instead of the 55-grain and classified the cartridge as the SS109. The U.S. designation was the M855. (A grain is a unit of mass equal to 64.79891 milligrams. It is used for measuring bullets and gunpowder in the United States, while most other countries use the metric system.)

The SS109/M855 could not be fired from the old M-16 rifles because the bullet would not stabilize in the M16A1's 1:12-inch twist rate. The A2 twist rate was 1:7-inch to accommodate the longer, heavier SS109/M855 bullet. (A 1:7-inch twist rate means that the bullet makes one complete twist in seven inches of travel.)

One of the most important advances in small arms is the concept of rifling, the purpose of which is to stabilize a bullet in flight and improve accuracy. As firearms developed, designers noticed that bullets would wobble once they left the barrel. By adding spiral grooves in the barrel, they could make the bullet spin and be more stable in the air, especially at high speeds. This is the reason why quarterbacks throw a football with as much spin as they can on the ball; it gives a longer and more accurate pass. It's also why a fast-spinning top has stability while slow-spinning tops wobble and fall over sooner.

Like everything else in arms design, there is a trade-off. Too low a twist rate and the bullet does not stabilize enough. But spinning the bullet too much accentuates even the most miniscule manufacturing defects, causing it to be unstable. Arms designers use complex computer models to find the best twist rate based on barrel length and bullet mass, but field experience usually yields the best data.

And there was another problem adapting the A2 to urban combat. Troops engaged in street fighting in the cities of Somalia years earlier noticed that they spent a great deal of time running in and out of infantry vehicles like Humvees, helicopters, building doors, and passageways. For these kinds of highly mobile situations, their rifles were too long and cumbersome. The quick fix was to outfit soldiers with carbines, rifles with shortened barrels, to make moving around easier. Just prior to their combat roles in Afghanistan and Iraq, soldiers of the 82nd Airborne and 101st Air Assault divisions had their A2s replaced with M-4 carbines, which were shortened versions of the A2. Although the M-4 barrel was only about six inches shorter than that of the A2, the weapon was much easier to handle in confined spaces because it was lighter and had a collapsible stock.

There was still another trade-off, however. The shorter barrel of the carbine gave the bullet a lower velocity compared to the longer-barreled A2. For the M855 bullet to be lethal, it must hit its target at more than 732 meters per second. As with its predecessor, the M193 NATO round penetrated human flesh and spun, causing devastating tissue damage. This only worked at high velocities, however. When fired from a long-barreled A2, the M855 bullet left the barrel at 914 meters per second and entered the target at 732 meters per second at a distance of about 200 meters. With the M-4 carbine, however, the bullet left the barrel at only 790 meters per second and after only 50 meters it had already dropped below the 732 meters per second threshold needed to inflict catastrophic damage. Specially equipped troops have complained that while the weapon was excellent for close-in fighting, it was ineffective at stopping enemy soldiers farther away. The problem was mitigated by the army's adoption of the MK262 Mod 0 cartridge that fired a slightly heavier 77-grain bullet with a tiny hollow point that fragmented inside the body. GIs reported more kills with this combination.

With more wars being fought in urban environments, the U.S. military eventually had to come up with a new type of weapon that would combine the lightness and shortened length of a carbine with the firepower of the standard M-16. Clearly, the M-4 was an interim, stopgap weapon. Although it was good for close quarters, it overheated on fully automatic fire and became unreliable because of the great stresses placed on its parts. Like Kalashnikov years ago, U.S. military planners had been looking for a new rifle for a new kind of warfare.

A plan for such a rifle, dubbed the XM-8, had been in the works for several years. Prototypes had been tested during 2003 and 2004 and deployment had been hoped for in 2005 but had been held up by the Iraq war and technical issues. Like all new army rifles, political and financial arguments surrounded it. In the case of the XM-8, Congress was reluctant to spend billions to outfit soldiers with new rifles while the war was draining the treasury—not to mention the task of training soldiers on a new weapon on the fly. Adding to the argument was that the new rifle came from Heckler & Koch, a German company, which would mark the first time that a non-U.S. design was used for GIs' rifles. Some suggested that because Germany had tried to block the U.S. invasion of Iraq, Congress would be remiss in rewarding a German company even though the rifles would be built inside the United States. As the war progressed, the XM-8 was gaining more and more favor with military planners and the soldiers who tested it, but until it was to come online American GIs had to fight the war in Iraq with the weapons they had available, and that included, ironically, AKs. (Many firearms experts, even those inside the military, contend that the XM does nothing significantly better than the current family of small arms. Nevertheless, Defense Department officials want a new weapons system to replace the M-16 series.)

Early reports from the front found GIs using AKs that they had picked up during raids. Unlike Vietnam, where GIs were afraid to use AKs for fear of drawing friendly fire because of the unique sound of the weapon through the dense jungle, where the enemy could be a few feet away and you couldn't see them, soldiers in Iraq had no such trepidation. In this war, they were rarely close to enemy combatants without knowing it. In many instances, combatants could see each other across open terrain.

One of the first stories to surface was that of the 3rd Battalion, 67th Armor Regiment of the 4th Infantry Division, which operated tanks in the city of Baquba in the summer of 2004. Along with Fallujah, Ramadi, and Samarra, this city of 280,000 people, about thirty miles northeast of Baghdad, and within the so-called Sunni Triangle, saw some of the heaviest ground action of the war.

In general, four-man tank crews were issued two M-4 carbines and four 9mm pistols in the belief that the group would mainly stay inside and fire the tank's turret-mounted machine gun. But as often occurs, real-life combat is not what Pentagon brass envisioned. While on patrol, the tankers found themselves trying to squeeze their vehicles through streets too narrow to accommodate them and over roads barely wide enough for a person to walk down. They were forced to leave their tanks and patrol on foot. "Normally, an armor battalion fights from tanks," said Lieutenant Colonel Mark Young. "Well, we are not fighting from our tanks right now." With each tank group short at least two rifles, the soldiers routinely used AKs, confiscated from raids or checkpoints, and put them to good use. Like their enemy brethren in Vietnam, they appreciated the gun's simplicity, reliability, and knockdown power, qualities absent from their M-16s and M-4s.

In some instances, even soldiers with the newer M-4s chose the AK because of its fully automatic fire that allowed them to "spray and pray" into hidden enemy positions such as areas of tall grass. They also preferred to have automatic fire inside buildings where the heavier 7.62mm round penetrated wood and thin stucco walls with ease. Soldiers also reported that sometimes it was easier to obtain ammunition for the AKs. During raids they would routinely find hundreds of new rounds in boxes available for the taking.

While some officers had considered prohibiting troops from using the AKs—to comply with army regulations concerning standard firearms—most allowed their soldiers to use them, especially because they would have had no small arms at all beyond their issued pistols.

Soldiers found that unlike their M-16s, the AKs resisted dust and sand from frequent storms that turned the landscape red and then pitch black. During these periods, M-16s clogged easily and did not fire until they were stripped down and cleaned. Troops learned quickly to cover their weapons with plastic wrap or place them in duffel bags. Some fit condoms over the barrel ends, to keep out sand particles that jammed their weapon's action. The AKs did not require similar handling. The GIs who used them appreciated their performance under adverse desert conditions.

Using the AKs also gave GIs a better understanding of the weapon they encountered most often. All too frequently, though, they learned about the AK's power when the 7.62mm rounds pierced their body armor.

IN THE LATE 1990s, soldiers were issued the Interceptor Multi-Threat Body Armor System that provided protection against shrapnel and 9mm rounds fired from low-velocity handguns. It was better than the twenty-five-pound Vietnam-era "flak jackets" that protected only against shrapnel, but it was still not up to the demands of Iraq as it offered no protection against 7.62mm rounds fired from AKs.

What could stop heavy fire, however, was the Interceptor with ceramic plates inserted into pockets on the vest. The pockets were strategically placed to offer protection for vital organs. Although their exact composition is classified, these Small Arms Protective Inserts—known to the soldiers as SAPI (Sappy) plates—can stop AK rounds and even light machine-gun rounds. The full vests cost about $1,500 each retail and can be bought with neck- and crotch-protection attachments. Even with the plates, the vests weigh 16.4 pounds, much less than the Vietnam-era flak jackets.

When the war in Iraq began, few soldiers had the protective inserts. Even months into the fighting, well after the fall of Baghdad as urban warfare escalated, about 30 percent of soldiers had not been issued the new vests. By the summer of 2003, congressional offices were receiving letters from soldiers and their families asking why these protective vests were not given to their soldiers even though Congress in April had specifically earmarked $310 million in the $87 billion appropriation for the Iraq war to buy 300,000 vests.

At hearings, lawmakers read letters from angry parents who had bought the inserts for their children with their own money and mailed them to Iraq. Small towns paid for vests with neighborhood fund-raisers and bake sales. Congressmen also brought up reports about GIs who duct-taped plates sent them by family members to old-style flak jackets. Soldiers complained that they were forced to share SAPI plates and vests, offering them to comrades who were heading into immediate combat.

The protective plates were so crucial to GIs' survival that they were touted in the raw lyrics of the rap album *Live from Iraq* produced by members of Taskforce 112 of the 1st Calvary Division who called themselves 4th25 (pronounced "fourth quarter," like the do-or-die period of a football game). Recording in a plywood shack with old mattresses for soundproofing, the group expressed their frustration at poor equipment and lack of army support for their mission, which included protecting Baghdad airport. Thousands of albums were sold over the Internet and through regional music stores around the Fort Hood, Texas, area where the men were based. The song "Stay in Step" told a story of survival: "Bloody desert combat fatigues, dusty and ammoless M-16 with a shredded sling . . . Hit in the head and shoulder but still taking deep breaths/Cause I'm in Kevlar and Sappy plates in my flak vest . . ."

Members of Congress wrote letters to Donald Rumsfeld demanding an explanation. "Not only did the Pentagon fail to provide U.S. soldiers with adequate lifesaving armor prior to the start of combat operations, but it took your Department seven months after hostilities began to even approach Congress with a request for funding for this essential equipment," wrote Ohio congressman Ted Strickland. "This is particularly startling considering that the latest-model Kevlar vests, which receive 'rave reviews' from field commanders, reportedly cost only $517 per unit [just for the plates]. This seems like an incredibly small price to pay in exchange for equipment that has been credited with saving at least 29 U.S. lives so far."

In response, Chief of the U.S. Central Command General John Abizaid testified, "I can't answer for the record why we started this war with protective vests that were in short supply." In private, Pentagon officials reiterated their surprise at the guerrilla war they found themselves fighting. Abizaid promised that all ground troops would have the vests and plates by year's end.

Body armor was not the only problem. AKs were making Swiss cheese out of vehicles, too. The High Mobility Multipurpose Wheeled Vehicle (HMMWV), commonly known as the Humvee, had become the Jeep of the modern military. With four-wheel drive, automatic transmission, a low center of gravity, and even a snorkel that allowed it to operate under sixty inches of water, the Humvee was the major transportation vehicle for American troops. It was designed to quickly bring troops to the front lines, but the Iraq war had no front line and no predictable point of contact with the enemy. Combat was wherever the insurgents decided it was. The Humvee proved to be a liability in many situations. Although its standard armor plating made it much safer for passengers than the standard army Jeep, it was vulnerable to close-range AK fire as well as IEDs, or improvised explosive devices, that were being deployed by enemy soldiers. The Humvee armor was designed for far-off AK fire and shrapnel but not close-in assaults.

Enterprising GIs raided junkyards and scrap heaps to find steel plates and other heavy metal pieces to bolt to their Humvees in an attempt to protect themselves from attack. Sometimes they would fill buckets with sand and hang them from the vehicle's side panels. The soldiers dubbed this jury-rigged setup "hillbilly armor" and "gypsy racks," and as pictures of these makeshift vehicles reached the U.S. public, it was becoming clear that GIs were fighting under conditions that Department of Defense officials had not anticipated. At a town hall–type meeting in Kuwait with Secretary Rumsfeld in December 2004, a National Guard soldier asked why soldiers had to rummage through local landfills for scrap metal and other materials to up-armor their vehicles.

The ever cryptic and aloof Rumsfeld shrugged. "You go to war with the army you have," he said, a response that reverberated throughout the United States as angry members of Congress continued to question the Department of Defense's planning and execution of a war that was growing unpopular as the U.S. death toll rose.

The controversy grew as the military retrofitted, or "uparmored," Humvees that were not designed to carry the extra weight. This additional burden produced excessive wear and tear and mechanical breakdowns, even rollovers and accidents, not to mention the additional fuel consumed by the heavier vehicles, which increased the burden on supplies.

It seemed to many that the war in Iraq was being fought with too few soldiers, inadequate small arms, subpar body armor, and ill-matched vehicles. And there was more embarrassment ahead. The newly forming Iraqi army, trained by the U.S. military and civilian contractors to defend their country, refused American-made M-16s or M-4s. They insisted on being issued AKs, and the United States was forced to comply.

THE COALITION PROVISIONAL AUTHORITY published an RFP, or Request for Proposal, for "brand new, never-fired, fixed stock AK-47 assault rifles with certified manufacture dates not earlier than 1987." In addition, each rifle had to include four magazines, magazine pouches, a bayonet, sling, and cleaning kit. Officials said they wanted a single source of the weapons. The ultimate shipment was to be thirty-four thousand rifles.

The request appeared ludicrous and humiliating on several levels. First, it bolstered the belief that the M-16 and M-4 were not up to the new realities of war. If so, why were GIs using these weapons? Second, if the Iraqis wanted AKs, why not issue them from the hundreds of thousands of AKs found in arsenals and stockpiles throughout the country? (Before the contract was awarded, the nascent Iraqi army was being outfitted with AKs from Iraqi stockpiles and from Jordanian army stocks.) Around the same time that the RFP went out, U.S. troops found about a hundred thousand AKs in Tikrit, a city north of Baghdad. Reports of similar discoveries were coming in almost daily. Some of these weapons were used but many were new and unused, purchased by Hussein's regime and stored in their original boxes.

Some U.S. gun makers were furious with the proposed purchases, saying that it not only demeaned the M-16 but that taxpayer money should not be going overseas at a time when the war was expected to cost in excess of $80 billion annually. Buying AKs for the Iraqi army also prevented them from being synchronized with U.S. weapons, an important issue for joint maneuvers.

Coalition Provisional Authority officials made strong arguments, however, for their purchase. "For better or worse, the AK-47 is the weapon of choice in that part of the world," said Walter Slocombe, senior advisor to the CPA. "It turns out that every Iraqi male above the age of 12 can take them apart and put them together blindfolded and is a pretty good shot."

Another reason, and perhaps more important, was value. AKs could be bought for around $60 each in these quantities, while M-16s cost $500 to $600 apiece. Still, it was never made clear why the AKs had to be bought when hundreds of thousands of unused weapons were being uncovered throughout the country.

Even the Russians were angry. Officials of Rosoboronexport expressed frustration that the United States would buy non-Russian AKs from other countries, a move tantamount to aiding piracy, they said. They claimed that no other country had a license to make the AK, and that the U.S. purchase encouraged continued violations. (This was not entirely true. The former Soviet Union had licensed production to Warsaw Pact countries and China and North Korea.

This controversy will be discussed later.) "We would like to inform everybody in the world that many countries, including the United States, have unfortunately violated recognized norms," said Igor Sevaastyanov, head of a Rosoboronexport division.

The story took an even stranger turn when the contract was finally awarded and slated for May 2005 delivery. The contract went to International Trading Establishment, a Jordanian conglomerate that received a $174.4 million deal for all sorts of weaponry including communications gear and night vision equipment in addition to AKs.

One of the subcontractors was China-based Poly Technologies, one of the world's largest munitions manufacturers. For its part, Poly received $29 million for various weapons, including almost 15,000 AKs, 2,300 light and heavy machine guns, and 72 million rounds of ammunition.

Poly Technologies had a checkered past, however. Officials of the company, which operated under the name Dynasty Holdings of Atlanta, had been indicted in May 1996 for attempting to smuggle 2,000 AKs into the United States along with 4,000, thirty- to forty-round magazines. The U.S. district attorney for the Northern District of California estimated the street value at more than $4 million and said the weapons were headed for street gangs. The weapons had markings from China (NORINCO) and Korea.

The arrests and indictment of fourteen people from NOR-INCO, Poly, and independent companies followed a sixteen-month investigation during which U.S. agents paid more than $700,000 for 2,000 AKs that were smuggled aboard the ship *Empress Phoenix*, owned by the China Ocean Shipping Company. Several of those involved pleaded guilty and at the time of writing are awaiting sentence. Others had not yet been charged and one official, Bao Ping Ma, listed in the indictment as president of Dynasty, fled to China and is still considered a fugitive, according to the U.S. government. Dynasty's Beijing account received 38 percent of the down payment and a portion of the final payment. U.S. Army officials noted that they had done a background investigation on Poly Technologies but not Dynasty Holdings, because the company no longer existed.

As attacks on U.S. troops in Iraq increased, the army was paying closer attention to the importance of the AKs wielded by insurgents. On several occasions, U.S. troops instituted weapons buyback programs to try to eliminate the large number of arms in the streets. During an eight-day period in May 2004, for example, U.S. troops distributed $350,000 daily for everything from pistols to surface-to-air missiles in Sadr City's Shiite district. They collected nearly 4,000 AKs, at $125 each, 9,000 mortar rounds, other assorted weapons, and ammunition, paying out a total of more than $1.3 million for the period.

Even though one less gun on the streets was considered a victory, the program barely made a dent in the country's overall supply. Because Iraqis were not required to turn in weapons, many decided to keep them. Also, by law, Iraqi families were permitted to own one registered gun (although many owned multiple unregistered guns), usually an AK kept for personal protection. Citizens were allowed one thirty-round magazine as well. Again, many had multiple magazines. Additionally, as happens in buyback programs, not just in Iraq but other countries as well, people brought in several older arms and used the money to buy a single better model on the black market. Black-market prices of AKs varied during the buyback programs, and U.S. troops adjusted their payment accordingly to stay just above the going rate on the street.

In another bow to the AK's widespread popularity, U.S. troops began systematic and official training on AKs to familiarize themselves with the weapon they would be encountering most often—both in enemy hands and in the hands of Iraqi soldiers who often patrolled side by side with American troops. Although special operations troops had always been trained on a number of foreign weapons, regular troops now were practicing with AKs both in Iraq and at stateside facilities like Quantico.

Marines who participated in "fam fire" practices were generally not impressed by the AK's looks. Compared to their own M-16s, the Kalashnikovs were crudely finished, heavy, and inaccurate. When they had the opportunity to fire them, though, they understood the effectiveness at close range of these "bullet hoses." Like their Soviet counterparts of the cold war, the marines learned to take apart the AK and put it back together in less than thirty seconds.

As civilian contractors working for security companies entered Iraq, they too were trained to fire AKs, and many were issued these weapons by their companies instead of Western arms. The AK's automatic fire was better suited to non-soldiers who did not have intensive training time or gun skills. It was also ideal for civilians in non-security jobs who wanted an easy-to-fire gun for protection while traveling to their worksites.

As U.S. troops became acclimated to street warfare, their opponents made more and more use of IEDs, homemade devices rigged to explode with a timer or by cell phone command. The charges were often made from explosive materials taken from large pieces of ammunition like mortars.

A favorite tactic of the guerrilla fighters was to place an IED in the path of a Humvee or other unarmored vehicle, and when troops stopped to check the vehicle's condition, they would find themselves facing a barrage of AK fire. This was reminiscent of similar mujahideen tactics against Soviet soldiers in Afghanistan. In many cases, the GIs would win the firefight but still lose soldiers. This tactic worked especially well against civilian employees traveling in convoys that were not heavily armed. Even though it was not particularly effective in terms of killing large numbers of coalition forces, it eroded troop morale and made soldiers edgy and suspicious of all Iraqi civilians. This in turn sometimes led to rougher handling of civilians at checkpoints and on the street—sometimes humiliating innocent Iraqis in the process—which played into the hands of insurgents looking to turn everyday Iraqis against U.S. forces.

With the continuing violence in Iraq, media reports focused on troops killed by IEDs. While these instances were dramatic, an army report made public in spring 2005 concluded that the most deadly threat to U.S. troops, Iraqis, and civilian contractors was small arms, mainly AKs and machine guns, and not roadside IEDs. The report noted, "Firing small arms in close combat remains the number one casualty-producing tactic." The report added that Iraqi militia often patrolled in unarmored vehicles, like pickup trucks, and were particularly vulnerable to ambush tactics that stopped a convoy either with bombs or road debris, then sprayed the occupants with automatic fire. By the middle of 2005, insurgents had turned their focus away from U.S. soldiers and trained their sights on Iraqi civilians. One particular group, physicians, were targeted by insurgents to prevent medical care of Iraqis and further cripple the country's infrastructure. In addition, criminals regularly attacked medical centers, because surgical supplies and medicines brought high prices on the black market. Since the fall of Baghdad, twenty-five doctors had been murdered and three hundred kidnapped. For their protection, the Health Ministry directed physicians to carry AKs along with their stethoscopes.

As the violence continued into 2006, Iraqi officials were beginning preparations to put Saddam Hussein on trial. He had been captured two years earlier in a remote farmhouse near Tikrit by soldiers of the 4th Infantry Division during Operation Red Dawn, a concerted effort to find where the dictator had been hiding since he left Baghdad. After searching one location, based on a tip, and coming up empty, troops turned their attention to a small walled-hut compound with a metal lean-to-type structure. They spied an entrance that had been camouflaged with bricks and dirt. The hole itself was six to eight feet deep, and Hussein was hiding at the bottom. Along with the now bearded dictator, troops found a pistol and $750,000 in U.S. currency.

Lying next to Hussein in his "spider hole" were two AK rifles, weapons that he revered and honored in the Mother of All Battles mosque but that failed to protect him from capture by American troops.

As the Iraq war continued, GIs began to appreciate even more the brilliant simplicity of the AK. As for Kalashnikov, however, this brilliant simplicity had not translated into money. Kalashnikov was hoping to change this, not by selling the AKs as a deadly weapon but as an icon of popular culture.

9

THE SECOND SELLING
OF THE AK

B Y THE MID-1990S, Kalashnikov begrudgingly accepted
the hard truth about his life. Even though he had
invented the world's most popular weapon, and received
numerous accolades, he would never become rich from his efforts.
Kalashnikov had always considered himself a simple, peasant man
who embraced the Communist ideal that duty was more important than money, but wouldn't it be nice to have a few extra rubles
in one's pocket? He wished there was a way to cash in on the AK's
growing popularity as a cultural icon if not as a military weapon.
Was there some way to make money off of his name?

Living on a meager pension, he made pocket money by appearing at arms shows, trotted out as a celebrity to help Russia move
more military hardware. While this helped his financial situation,
what he really wanted was some kind of royalty deal like Eugene
Stoner, who had made millions from his M-16. Kalashnikov
wanted financial recognition for his invention.

With the dissolution of the Soviet Union, Russian officials desperately tried to raise hard currency by exploiting Kalashnikov

and the AK. Besides sending him to arms shows as a spokesman, they continued to strong-arm AK-producing countries into paying royalties. Officials claimed that if it were not for the prolific and illegal manufacture of the weapon, they would be back in the manufacturing business and able to compete and thrive in the current market. They said that the large number of cheap AK knock-offs undermined their products by selling for one-fourth the price of their own. The Russians had already stopped production of military AKs, and were selling off their large stockpiles. Had it not been for the illegal gun makers, they contended, the stockpiles would be drawn down and they could engage in new production.

Licensing rights to the gun itself now was impossible. Kalashnikov had never patented the rifle's design—the thought had never occurred to him or anyone else under the Soviet regime—and now it was too late. Izhmash had won Russian patent rights to the AK after persuading the highest Russian patent court that they were the rightful inventors of the rifle. While this was a victory within Russia, enforcing such a patent outside the country was a non-starter. Kalashnikovs were being manufactured in almost twenty countries, and only a handful—China, Slovenia, and Turkey—were paying royalties, totaling less than $1 million. These were token payments designed to keep political relationships between the two countries friendly. Kalashnikov saw nothing from them.

Legally, unraveling the license agreements was an impossible task. For one thing, it was not clear if the then Soviet Union had actually signed license agreement documents with Soviet bloc countries or informally given them technical knowledge in exchange for their political friendship. Legal experts suggest that if such contracts existed they might have expired, or, on the other hand, might have been signed in perpetuity allowing continued and free manufacture. The Russian government has not made public any documents backing these claims. (Some international law scholars also argue that today's Russia is a different legal entity from the former Soviet Union and previous agreements may not carry over.)

More important, each country put its own spin on the AK, altering it to suit its particular interests and needs. It might be argued that these changes made the new versions no longer close enough to the original design to be relevant. Additionally, intellectual property scholars and attorneys contend that some products have become so ubiquitous that any claims of ownership are impossible to prove. With so many AKs and variants in circulation, a case for public domain probably might be argued successfully in court.

Out of financial desperation, Kalashnikov got his feet wet in the world of branding in 1998 by lending his name to vodka. "Vodka Kalashnikov," produced by the Glazovsky liquor and vodka distillery in the city of Glazov, was packaged in many different bottles, including one shaped like a hand grenade. Another in the shape of an AK displayed individually numbered dog tags on a chain around the bottle's neck. Intended for export, the vodka was based on recipes approved by Kalashnikov and claimed to be the first vodka ever to be created by combining salt, sugar, vanillin, and glycerin as flavor enhancers. Unfortunately, sales were poor.

The vodka won several medals and honors, mostly within Russia, but it still lacked international marketing and promotion savvy. In hindsight, the company that employed the AK-shaped bottle, VRQ International, may have played the military angle a bit too heavily for Western tastes. Advertisements boasted, "It looks like the legendary AK-47 rifle, but it holds several rounds of the finest original Russian vodka."

Consumers in the West enjoyed the antiestablishment nature of the AK, as long as it didn't remind them of the dirty side of war. There was a fine line between reality and fantasy, and the Russian distillery was unable to successfully exploit it.

As the years rolled on, however, the phenomenon of the AK as a popular icon continued to grow. Kalashnikov and his invention became the subject of several documentaries, including *Automatic Kalashnikov* from widely known German filmmakers Axel Engstfeld and Herbert Habersack, in which they sympathetically portrayed the eighty-year-old designer living in relative obscurity and resigned penury while his weapon was changing the world. The film, released in Germany in 2000 and shown worldwide on the Sundance Channel, offered the parallel, somewhat disjointed story lines of the aging Kalashnikov, living quietly in his modest apartment on his fifty-dollar-a-month pension, juxtaposed with mujahideen thanking him for his invention that drove out the Russians, to Los Angeles police officers talking about how they were outgunned by street gangs with AKs.

The film portrayed a sad, conflicted man. "Like it or not," he said, "you have to live with it, like a grenade splinter inside your body. I've got one in my body, long surrounded by scar tissue. You forget about it as you go about your daily routine, but then what do you do when a small twist or turn causes sudden acute pain?"

Years earlier, Kalashnikov had felt that pain as he stopped for a traffic light in his town. He saw an empty AK cartridge roll down the pavement. "It might have been hurled by a wheel of a car or blown by the wind," he thought. He found another cartridge and realized that there had been a shootout the previous night in the middle of town. "No one gathers the blank cartridges. No one cares anymore." He was so lost in thought that a police officer asked if he was all right, having missed the green light. "Armaments which should be kept in arsenals under the close watch of sentries are now freely bought and sold . . . yet it is not arms makers and not politicians that continue to be enemies of the people," Kalashnikov mused.

Although the film gave Kalashnikov's son Viktor only a cameo, he was an accomplished arms designer in his own right. Named after Kalashnikov's brother Viktor, his son designed the PP-19 Bizon, a 9mm submachine gun used by military special forces and tactical police units in close-quarter environments. The weapon

used many of the AK's well-proven aspects, including its trigger
mechanism and receiver cover. Its most unusual element was the
magazine, which was helical and placed underneath the forestock
instead of perpendicular as on other assault rifles and submachine
guns. This feature gave the weapon a low profile, allowing it to be
more easily concealed under clothing or held close to one's side
without being observed.

As a child, Viktor wanted to design aircraft, but the Kazan Aviation School where he applied did not accept him. Instead, he
enrolled at the Izhevsk Institute of Mechanics, where he majored
in small arms and received his PhD in 1980. Earlier, in 1967, his
design bureau had moved to Izhmash, where his Alexandrov
group competed against his father's group for the 5.45 × 39mm
rifle—a competition that his father's group won.

Viktor was more outspoken and bitter than his father about not
being paid royalties for the AK. "My father and I could have been
millionaires, just like the U.S. inventor of the M-16 assault rifle,
Eugene Stoner, who received a dollar for each gun sold."

About the same time that the documentary hit the screens, a
cutting-edge T-shirt company called OK47 began its growth into a
three-continent, hundred-boutique source of fashion alternatives.
The company admitted to playing on the surreal contradiction of
its name and the AK, as OK47 considered itself a counterpoint to
cookie-cutter clothing producers. Not only were its designs
unique, but the Toronto-based company bucked the trend of offshore manufacturing and exploitation of workers in less developed
countries by making all its clothing in North America. Like the
AK, OK47 was rebellious in its fashion and business practices.

The gun was popping up in movies like *Jackie Brown*, directed
by Quentin Tarantino, in which Samuel L. Jackson announced,
"AK-47. The very best there is. When you absolutely, positively
got to kill every motherfucker in the room." In the HBO TV hit
The Sopranos, Tony Soprano armed himself with an AK after a
bear was discovered roaming his New Jersey backyard. Just like

Shakespeare had an actor walk onstage and kick a dog to indicate to the audience that he was the antagonist, Hollywood has used the AK to show the antihero, the terrorist, the bad guy.

Artists were discovering the powerful symbolism of the AK. Because it was the definitive icon of protracted, dirty warfare, they incorporated the weapon into their work both as an ironic accent and as a symbol of protest against conflict. In Cambodia, a group of artists funded in part by the actresses Angelina Jolie and Emma Thompson worked almost exclusively in the medium of decommissioned AKs. Students at Phnom Penh's Royal University of Fine Arts participating in the Peace Art Project took thousands of AKs collected by the government and turned them into sculptures. After decades of war, including the genocide perpetrated by the Khmer Rouge depicted in the book and movie *The Killing Fields*, the country still remained smothered in weapons, mainly AKs, but the artists hoped to send a peaceful message with these rifles. Changing Kalashnikovs into artwork seemed as natural as Western artists turning their everyday cultural items like cars and soup cans into avant-garde art.

"Taking the weapons and turning them into art seems to be the perfect symbolism of a step away from a post-conflict society towards a society with a culture of peace," said David de Beer, head of a European Union arms decommissioning program in Phnom Penh. Because of Cambodia's tradition of sculpture, the weapons turned art seemed a natural. Animals such as elephants, horses, birds, chickens, and snakes were popular subjects. More than a hundred thousand AKs were turned over to authorities. Ones that were not turned into art were burned, many of them in public "Flames of Peace" bonfires that attracted hundreds of onlookers.

The project was loosely fashioned after a similar program in Mozambique called Swords to Ploughshares that offered implements such as plows, bicycles, and sewing machines in exchange for small arms after that country's civil war ended. Art played a role there, too, as several artists, including Feil dos Santos, turned

AKs and land mines into sculptures. Christian Concern, a non-governmental organization, collected the guns for dos Santos, which he welded together into a display titled *From Weapons to Art* that has traveled throughout Africa. The sculptures depicted the artist's stress and sadness at living in a war zone. One sculpture in particular, *Dual Surrender*, showed a man with outstretched arms, begging for charity, resigned to his decrepit situation. AK trigger handles formed his ears; cartridge shells made his hair. Another work by dos Santos, *Melody*, depicted a man whose limbs were formed from AK parts. The man was playing a harmonica because many in Mozambique found comfort in music, filling the quiet void left by the long war.

For citizens of countries in which the AK killed millions, seeing the weapons turned into harmless, sometimes stunning and beautiful art pieces has gone a long way toward healing the wounds of war.

Even high-end commercial artists and designers joined the AK design movement, mainly for shock value and to titillate Western consumers. At the Milan Furniture Fair in 2005, world-renowned designer Philippe Starck revealed high-end table lamps fashioned from replicas of AKs, M-16s, and Beretta pistols. Black shades lined with crosses sat atop the lamps. Said Starck, "I am a designer, and design is my weapon. I want my furniture to show that everything, even furniture, can be a political choice."

The founders of the online photography magazine *AK47* used the name to grab attention in the overcrowded Internet space. "The AK47—and those four symbols A-K-4-7 are iconic. So from an Internet magazine's point of view, where you want to stand out on a search page—AK47 just grabs the eye," said editor Joerg Diekmann. "Coming from South Africa, the AK47 has always played a terrifying role in our history. Bank robbers, burglars, carjackers, an angry disenfranchised people—it's the AK47 that puts real fear into people. They cost about $30 in the streets. Using the name AK47 for a photography magazine is hopefully an affirmation that those dark days are nearing an end. It's a signal of change.

An icon from a different era. Yet it is still edgy and raw, and churns up emotions. I like photography that induces an emotional response—it can remain murky—but there has to be an emotion."

KALASHNIKOV ATTEMPTED TO CASH in on the growing momentum. In 2003, he signed an agreement with Marken Marketing International (MMI) a Solingen, Germany, company that offered to market consumer items under the inventor's name. For lending his moniker, Kalashnikov would receive a one-third stake in the venture. The company planned an ambitious line of goods including pocketknives, flashlights, snowboards, umbrellas, and tennis rackets. The goal was to transfer the Kalashnikov reputation for solidness, simplicity, and rugged design to these products in much the same way that Harley-Davidson sold branded clothing and the Dannon yogurt company had a line of bottled water. Although neither of these companies knew anything about clothes or water, consumers associated them with quality, and that made product extension possible and profitable. Kalashnikov had hoped for the same outcome.

The fact that AKs enjoyed an antiestablishment cachet would help sales of products aimed at youths and those who liked to think of themselves as outside the mainstream. Harley-Davidson had successfully fostered an outlaw biker patina even though most Harley riders were males over forty, who had wives and children and enjoyed high family incomes from straitlaced jobs. For masculine sports and camping gear, the Kalashnikov name probably could move products if the marketer was skillful. "The articles are very similar to my rifle," Kalashnikov said. "Reliable, easy to use, and indestructible."

The announcement was met with great fanfare and media attention, but nothing ever became of the scheme. The company simply disappeared, and once again Kalashnikov failed to make money on his invention.

Still, the AK mystique grew stronger. *Playboy* magazine in 2004 listed the AK-47 as number four in its feature "50 Products That Changed the World: A Countdown of the Most Innovative Consumer Products of the Past Half Century." That the AK was considered a consumer item, behind the Apple Macintosh desktop computer (number one), the Pill (number two), and the Sony Betamax VCR (number three), was a true indication of the gun's seminal and long-lasting effect on the modern world. Citing a July 1999 State Department report mentioning the weapon, *Playboy*'s editors noted, "In some countries it is easier and cheaper to buy an AK-47 than to attend a movie or provide a decent meal." The magazine also cited a *Los Angeles Times* article calling the gun "history's most widely distributed piece of killing machinery."

Amid the AK hype, museums began looking at the rifle's effect on civilization and culture in a more somber and thoughtful way. The Dutch Army Museum in 2003 and 2004 hosted an exhibit on the AK called *Kalashnikov: Rifle without Borders* that offered visitors a look at multimedia displays on wars in which the rifle had played a deciding role. It showed combat children holding AKs in Africa and elsewhere. One exhibit dramatically illustrated the weapon's destructive ability by showing a bullet pattern in a porous block. However, even a serious museum could not ignore the Kalashnikov's pop culture side: attendees saw AKs that had been chrome-plated; others were covered with hot pink fabric and glitter. Even a military-oriented museum could not escape the fact that AKs had become so ingrained in world culture that people adorned them with bright colors, perhaps to defuse some of their power. Kalashnikov himself opened the exhibit amid fanfare. Again, as he had done at every public opportunity in the past, he used the forum to blame politicians for misusing his invention and to absolve himself of the AK's terrible legacy.

At home, his countrymen were preparing to honor their most famous inventor, too. In 1996, construction of a Kalashnikov museum in Izhevsk began but was suspended due to insufficient funding. With pleas for money throughout Russia and on the Internet, the $8 million Kalashnikov Weapons Museum and Exhibition Center opened on the arms maker's eighty-fifth birthday in 2004. The museum was designed not only to honor Kalashnikov's work, but also to jump-start the decaying city of Izhevsk, a boomtown during World War II and the cold war years, now fallen on hard times. Isolated and far from much of Russia's commerce, the city existed for the production of arms, which it made at the rate of more than ten thousand a day during World War II. Later during the cold war it continued to produce weapons, mainly AKs in great numbers, providing employment and prosperity.

Since the fall of the Soviet Union, with no more AKs being made, Izhevsk officials hoped that the museum would attract tourists. In what was once a top-secret location, closed to outsiders and casual tourists alike, city officials were hoping for urban renewal and better times based on the AK's star power. During speeches, the mayor conveyed that the museum embodied the strength of the city in that it produced a dependable product, one that worked reliably and was revered worldwide. Like commercial marketers hoping to make money off of Kalashnikov by selling consumer items with his name and endorsement, his adopted town was relying on his celebrity status, too, to help jump-start its economy.

So far, the results have been lukewarm.

PERHAPS THE INVENTOR'S GREATEST chance at financial success came in 2003, when British entrepreneur John Florey was looking for his next big thing. Florey reasoned that Russia was known for its vodka, the way France was known for wine, the Caribbean for rum, and Scotland for scotch whiskey. Russia was also known for producing the AK, and the Kalashnikov had already achieved global cult status. For Florey, the mix of Russia's favorite spirit and favorite celebrity seemed the perfect concoction. Over dinner one evening, the idea of Kalashnikov's AK and vodka seemed like a sure shot.

Florey had been a representative for chess champ Gary Kasparov and understood how to promote Russian culture. He had also helped to establish the Moscow Business School, so he was introduced to Kalashnikov in 2001 through the school.

Kalashnikov was interested albeit wary of the idea. He had been burned several times before. The failure of Kalashnikov's first excursion into the world of vodka branding was not lost on Florey, who approached this project with a showman's vision for big, bold promotions but without leaning too heavily on the gun angle. He believed that the previous vodka deal did not "extend" the Kalashnikov brand. He also brought a solid business plan. Kalashnikov was named honorary chairman of the "Kalashnikov Joint Stock Vodka Company (1947) plc." and was to receive a small equity stake and 2.5 percent of net profits for using his name and likeness on the bottle. A 1947 picture of a young and vibrant Kalashnikov was etched into the bottles, and non-rolling shot glasses, invented by Kalashnikov himself for the Russian navy, were slated for use at bar promotions.

Florey assembled an all-star cast including David Bromige, the creator of Polstar Vodka, an Icelandic spirit that played on the motto "Strength Through Purity" along with a polar bear logo. Bromige also was a director of Reformed Spirits Company, owners of Martin Miller's Gin, a product that had received a lot of attention for its citrus, pear, and clove flavors in Icelandic glacial water, all contained in a hip, angular bottle that bartenders liked to handle as they imitated Tom Cruise's dexterous motions in the movie *Cocktail*. Although the brand had come into existence only in 1999, it boasted using "England's oldest copper still." With the opening of the former Soviet Union, vodka was growing more popular in Europe and North America as venerable vodka makers like Stolichnaya, Absolut, and Finlandia (the last two were not from Russia) were wooing younger drinkers with offbeat flavors, edgy bottles, even edgier advertisements, and higher prices that pushed prestige appeal. Florey hoped to catch the wave.

The Kalashnikov 41-proof vodka was going to be produced by a distillery in St. Petersburg, with bottling done in England. Florey had to position the product just right for it all to work. Too much on the military angle would turn off drinkers. Too little and it was just another vodka. Florey pushed a well-honed message: "Kalashnikov stands for Russian design, integrity in so far as the product is true to itself, comradeship and strength of character, which epitomizes the General's life and the role he has played in Russian culture."

The company's public offering went well with investors—it was oversubscribed—and listed on the United Kingdom's JPJL market, a junior market to the OFEX, the country's independent market focused on small and medium firms.

Florey's approach was spot-on. Having Kalashnikov as your pitchman guaranteed that the story would be picked up by the world's major media. By the summer of 2004, Kalashnikov, clad in his honorary general's uniform complete with colorful ribbons, graced the pages of magazines and newspapers worldwide. Instead of holding an AK across his chest with his traditional two-handed grip, Kalashnikov delicately raised a martini glass up to the camera in a mock toast. This was a brilliant promotional trick; even though vodka was usually served in regular glasses, the martini glass's unique triangular shape was instantly recognizable as a cocktail drink, whereas a normal cylindrical glass could have contained any ordinary liquid. There was no doubt that the AK-47's inventor was enjoying a shot of liquor.

At the official launch at London's Century Club, Kalashnikov stayed on message, too. In Russian, he said to the crowd, "I would like the product we are about to launch to be as reliable and easy to use as my gun." It would be a message that he would repeat on many other occasions.

The reception included samples served to the crowd by Natasha, Anoushka, and Ivana, models clad in white,

In an effort to cash in on his weapon's newly established status as a cultural icon, Kalashnikov lent his name to a branded vodka. "I'm not interested in war anymore—only my military-strength vodka," he said. *The Kalashnikov Joint Stock Vodka Co. (1947) plc.*

military-type uniforms and short skirts and known as the "Nikita Girls." Their role was to visit bars during promotional efforts to push the Kalashnikov brand.

In interviews after the reception, Kalashnikov said, "I am to blame only for having designed a reliable weapon. . . . I am very sad when I see my weapon being used when they shouldn't be used, but the designer is not to blame. It's the politicians who are to blame." Like a good soldier, he also stuck with his commercial message during public appearances touting the new brew. "I've always wanted to improve and expand on the good name of my weapon by doing good things," he said. "So we decided to create a vodka under my name, and we wanted that vodka to be better than anything made up until now in both Russia and England."

In less public moments, however, he expressed his resigned reluctance at becoming a shill, saying, "What can you do? These are our times now." As he had been for most of his later life, Kalashnikov found himself torn between the capitalist reality of making money in the New Russia and holding firm to his lifelong Communist belief that what matters is doing your duty for the motherland without any thought of financial compensation.

Propelled by Florey's skill and Kalashnikov's notoriety, the vodka juggernaut was on a tear. Hip magazines like *FHM* placed it among the top ten best vodkas in their staff taste tests. Talk Loud PR, a public relations firm that had worked on the Polstar Vodka account, convinced bartenders to create trendy drinks using the vodka and submitted them to magazines. The London *Sunday Times Style* magazine displayed a picture of actress Julia Roberts with the caption reporting her interest in a drink called a Scorpino that contained Kalashnikov Vodka. The soft-porn men's magazine *ICE* featured an irreverent Q&A with Kalashnikov along with a pictorial titled "Raise Your Glass the Ruskie Way," on how to drink vodka in the traditional Russian style.

The initial $90,000 public relations blitz was paying off. The company was on the way to its goal of selling forty-four thousand cases by 2006 to bars and restaurants before targeting the retail trade. Florey even hoped to place a new phrase into the English drinking lexicon: "I went out last night and got Kalashed."

Then a problem arose.

Alcohol Focus Scotland, a group dedicated to "changing Scotland's drinking culture," complained to the Portman Group, a regulatory body funded by the drinks industry. It claimed that Kalashnikov Vodka "suggested an association with bravado, or with violent, aggressive, dangerous or anti-social behavior," and therefore violated the group's code of practice.

Complaints of this nature were fairly common as drink makers pushed the envelope as far as they could to create interest in their products, especially among younger consumers. For instance, during the time that the Portman Group was deliberating possible action against Kalashnikov Vodka, it was considering other breaches including whether a line of "tube drinks" named Blow Job, Orgasm, Foreplay, and Bit on the Side violated regulations because they implied a connection between alcohol use and sexual behavior, a group no-no. Another complaint at the time was that a pair of vodka drinks named Rocket Fuel Vodka and Rocket Fuel Ice, in concert with their prominent positioning of their very high alcohol content, 42.85 percent, were clearly using the intoxicating effect to sell themselves, another breach of the code. Both were found to be violations.

Of the more than 140 complaints dating back to 1996 (the group was started in 1989), the vast majority of upheld complaints concerned blatant sexual content in labels or packaging or false and misleading labels. Until Kalashnikov Vodka came along, only two actions had been taken against companies for violent content: a beer named Heist (even though the group conceded that it was American slang for a robbery), and a product named TNT Liquid Dynamite designed to represent a stick of dynamite with a fuse in it.

Florey argued that the Kalashnikov brand was based on "comradeship" and not military imagery. Company officials admitted that the brand was "funky" and "in your face," but that it "didn't cause people to take up armed conflict."

Florey put Kalashnikov out front to help spin public opinion their way. He gave interviews saying that it was wrong to associate the AK with aggression. Wearing an AK tie clip, Kalashnikov told *Financial Times* reporters, "The gun serves peace and friendship because it is used to defend one's country. Look how many countries have been liberated using this gun."

His arguments did not persuade the Portman Group, and they found that Kalashnikov Vodka violated the industry's own rules.

The group's assessment was both good and bad news for Florey and Kalashnikov. Although the Portman Group upheld the complaint, it officially recognized the pop icon status of the AK to the Western world. Even though the vodka's packaging did not look like an AK or contain any violent or antisocial references, the Kalashnikov name alone was enough to provoke a passionate response in the hearts of consumers. To marketers, this was a good thing. The panel said in its January 21, 2005, report, "Having considered the product as a whole, including its packaging and overall presentation, the Panel concluded that a name that primarily evoked an image of a contemporary gun, namely the AK, which was one of, if not the most widely used firearm in the world, was an unacceptable choice of brand name for an alcoholic drink, because it indirectly suggested an association with violent and dangerous behavior."

In true entrepreneurial flip style, Florey told those around him that *any* publicity was *good* publicity. At the same time, however, he took Portman to task publicly, complaining that other alcoholic beverages were named for weapons, including Spitfire beer, Bombardier beer, and Claymore scotch, and they had not been banned.

Florey had no choice but to begin negotiations with the panel to find a solution, which probably would mean changing the name in the United Kingdom. The company could still keep it for export. In fact, the vodka was doing extremely well in the Middle East. "There's an affinity in the Middle East with the gun," Florey noted. "And we're setting up a franchise in South Africa called 'AK-47 Freedom Vodka.'"

With negotiations going nowhere and bottles banned from shelves, the situation was looking grim until a journalist at a Portman-held news conference—convened to explain its decision—suggested a name that Portman chairman Sir Paul Condon admitted would probably work. By fall 2005, "General Kalashnikov Russian Vodka" was slated for a comeback in England and a push toward North America.

ALTHOUGH MANY PEOPLE (like the Portman Group) considered exploiting a deadly weapon for financial gain in bad taste, even more bizarre examples began to crop up. No longer only part of the military, counterculture, or Middle Eastern "Kalashnikov Culture," the AK was being seen and mentioned almost daily in mainstream movies, books, and on TV. What once was a horrible but everyday item in some parts of the world was now a solid part of contemporary global culture.

Rapper Eminem, whose rise to notoriety was portrayed in the hit movie *8 Mile*, used the powerful image of the AK to express his anger at the U.S.-led war in Iraq and to convince young people to vote against President George W. Bush in the 2004 election. In an animated video titled "Mosh," Eminem was seen leading a group of disenfranchised citizens wearing hooded sweatshirts through the dark "police state" streets of America. The keyed-up mob entered a government building, but instead of rioting, the group quietly lined up to register to vote. Eminem attacked President Bush as a liar and thief for putting his own agenda before that of the country. Along with an animation of Bush holding an AK, Eminem sang, "Let the president answer our high anarchy / Strap him with an AK-47 / Let him go fight his own war / Let him impress daddy that way." By invoking the AK image, Eminem brought his controversial message home.

Perhaps the weirdest consumer item to hook into the AK's iconic status was the AK-MP3 Jukebox from UK audiobook publisher AudioBooksForFree.com. The music player was built into a

banana-shaped magazine of the rifle and could be attached to the
Kalashnikov rifle instead of the regular magazine or played on its
own. It could hold up to nine thousand songs or three thousand
hours of audiobooks. "This is our bit for world peace," said Russian ex–rock star Andrey Koltakov, founder of the successful company. "We hope that from now on many militants and terrorists
will use their AK-47s to listen to music and audiobooks. . . . They
need to chill out and take it easy." The company featured the product on its web site along with camo-bikini-clad models holding the
weapon and player/magazine in provocative stances.

In India, the vibrant Bollywood dream factory played on the
AK's drawing power with a terrorism potboiler titled *AK-47*. At
the time of its release, reviewers chided it for being formulaic,
base, and too violent. Drawn by its name, however, audiences
flocked to see it. It didn't seem to register with moviegoers that
India had been undergoing frequent, severe, and large-scale hit-
and-run attacks on rural oil, chemical, and mining facilities by
Maoist terrorist groups wielding AKs.

That same year, the AK had reached another cultural mile-
stone. *Stuff* magazine, which appealed to young men with pictori-
als and text about gadgets, semiclad women, and the latest video
games, featured the gun in a two-page spread along with a Q&A
with the inventor. The automatic rifle was held up as a hip classic
tool, a cool accessory like a fast motorcycle, a beautiful woman, an
edgy video game, or the latest earphones. As expected, Kalashnikov seized the platform to blame politicians and not weapons
designers for the misuse of his weapon. He also assured U.S.
troops in Iraq that he didn't have them in mind as targets when he
made his rifle.

Kalashnikov used the opportunity to push his latest branding
venture. "I'm not interested in war anymore—only my military-
strength vodka. I like to sit and toast friendship. If the world did
more of that and little less fighting, it would be a better place."

THE LAST DAYS
OF THE AK?

IN 1980, SOVIET OFFICIALS searched for a remote place to exile Nobel Prizewinner and dissident scientist Andrei Sakharov. Hoping to contain him and his democratic rhetoric, they sent him to Gorky, a city sequestered from the rest of the world for decades. Despite his being relocated to this remote location, however, his beliefs and writings spread throughout the world, leading to his release in 1986 and fueling the eventual downfall of the Communist superpower.

When Russian military officials in 1993 sought a venue to display a radically new assault rifle to select government officials and engineers, they chose the same city. By then it had reverted to its prerevolutionary name, Nizhni Novgorod, but still maintained an air of isolation. In an attempt to keep information about the weapon from spreading, soldiers manning the arms fair booth offered nothing about the rifle beyond what was printed on a small caption card.

Just as Sakharov's ideology could not be contained by this isolated location, neither could information about the new rifle. Speculation grew among military officials worldwide, who were abuzz about this new entry in the world of small arms. Russian officials remained mum about plans for the rifle, and it would not be shown again for another three years, but anticipation in military circles grew.

Finally, Russian officials announced that the AN-94 would replace the venerable AK as the standard infantry weapon in the Russian arsenal. Many had predicted this, but even so, members of the world military elite still were stunned by the pronouncement.

This change had been in the works for a long time. As mentioned earlier, when the Soviets built the AK-74 in order to accommodate the smaller 5.54 × 39mm round, the rifle was a compromise, a way to get them into the small-cartridge game in a hurry by adapting Kalashnikov's design. Not that the design was substandard—the weapon and its "poison bullet" had proven itself in Afghanistan—but the Soviet Union's military was not satisfied with the AK-74. They desired accuracy on a par with the M-16 to go along with the AK's awesome killing power.

Any new design would have to wait, however. The Soviet economy was then falling into disarray—largely because of the high cost of the Afghan war—and research money was scarce. On the other hand, the Soviets were lagging in small-arms technology, and something had to be done.

The economical answer was a contest that would pit the nation's best arms designers against each other. The main requirement was for the new rifle to have a "hit ratio" of one and a half to two times better than the AK-74—in other words, one and a half to two times more accurate in automatic mode. It would also have to be reliable and easy to use by troops. Although the AK-74 was a superior weapon in many ways, it was still hard to control in automatic mode (although greatly superior to its predecessor the AKM with its larger 7.39mm round). While it was perfect for poorly trained troops who could "spray and pray," the Soviets realized that greater lethality could be achieved with greater accuracy—hitting the same spot several times in rapid succession. This was particularly important in confrontations with enemy soldiers wearing the newest body armor.

Recoil was the age-old enemy of accuracy. When a soldier fired his rifle, the recoil from the first bullet would always make the following shots less accurate. Not even the best marksmen can fire several shots rapidly in a row exactly on target because the weapon moves from the recoil of the preceding shot.

There were several standard ways to mitigate recoil. First was to use a smaller, less powerful round; however, designers believed they had made it as small as they could while maintaining its lethality. Other methods included a counter-recoil system like in the AL-7 that lessened the recoil blast with springs. While this greatly reduced recoil—and was cutting-edge for the time—it was still not what military planners sought. Other obvious possibilities included different types of shock absorbers in the shoulder stock, and even having the shooter wear more cushioning in his shoulder.

None of these "inside the box" ideas proved satisfactory. A totally new design was necessary if military officials were to realize their dream of zero recoil. This meant jettisoning the Kalashnikov design all together.

Many arms designers believed that a truly zero-recoil assault rifle was akin to designing a perpetual motion machine. According to the law of physics, it could not be done. In fact, through the years the Soviets had touted the AK-74 as recoilless because its recoil had been greatly diminished. True, it was better than those before it. Now they were reaching for the sky in the hope of designing a weapon that, like the Kalashnikov, could one day become an arms classic: no recoil, light, dependable, and easy to use by troops.

Code-named Abakan (a town in south-central Russia), the contest began in the late 1970s with about a dozen design groups competing against each other. Izhmash, where Kalashnikov held the post of senior designer (although it was more of an emeritus position), threw two design groups into the fray. His son Viktor headed one design bureau and the other group was headed by Gennady Nikonov, a well-established arms maker who had worked at Izhmash since he graduated technical school at eighteen. Both Nikonov's parents worked at Izhmash and early in his career he had distinguished himself by designing a trigger mechanism for an underwater rifle. He had also worked on sporting weapons and won accolades for the accurate and smart-looking Izbur (Buck Deer), a high-end carbine that was produced in limited quantities for discriminating shooters. During his tenure at Izhmash, Nikonov snared two prestigious awards, the Company's Top Designer and the Top Designer of the Ministry, and he was awarded more than forty patents. His wife, Tatiana, worked as an engineer in the same design center.

Kalashnikov lobbied heavily for his son's team to win the contest. Even after the winning rifle received its official name, AN-94—Automatic Nikonov 1994—and its adoption appeared certain, the elder Kalashnikov continued to push for his son's design. He wanted to carry on the family tradition, but his efforts at calling in political favors were of no use. Viktor's group came in second.

To add further insult to the dean of Russian weapons makers, Nikonov further separated himself from the AK by announcing publicly that his designs were influenced by the legendary designers Evgeny Dragunov and Azariy Nesterov, not Kalashnikov. The AN-94 looked and acted nothing like the AK.

One of the startling differences of the AN-94 was the muzzle attachment. Called a flash eliminator, this asymmetrically shaped muzzle device featured two vent holes on either side plus a vent hole in the upper right side of the first of two chambers. The upper vent hole was configured like a dog whistle, designed to produce a sound out of the range of human hearing caused by the fast-moving air pushing out of the barrel.

The AN-94 and a thirty-round magazine weighed nine and a half pounds, about two pounds more than an AK-74, and the furniture was produced from fiberglass-reinforced polyamide, similar to the newer AK models and most modern rifles. The rifle had improved sights and safety switch ergonomics, but the most dramatic difference was in how it worked.

The gas-operated system employed a design that the Russians called "blow-back shift pulse" that fired in two-shot bursts, instead of the usual three, with no recoil from the first to second shot. In addition, the first two shots fired at the astounding rate of 1,800 rounds per minute (about three times that of the AK's 600 round-per-minute rate) when in the two-shot burst mode. When the gun was placed in automatic operation, the first two rounds fired at 1,800 rounds per minute before decreasing to 600 for the remaining bullets.

Nikonov's groundbreaking design was genius, because he freed himself from traditional arms design conventions and the limiting configuration of the AK. While the AK's design was simple, the AN-94 was complex because it solved the problem of recoil with the help of extra components such as a pulley and cable configured in a way never seen before. Nikonov also realized that while a balanced system was easily accomplished for smaller rounds, if his rifle was to become the standard design for a family of Russian military guns it also had to accommodate larger rounds, such as those used in heavy stationary machine guns. The pulley and cable system allowed the mechanism to be scaled up for larger rounds while retaining its recoilless nature.

In traditional automatic weapons, including the AK, the bolt carrier must travel its full length so it can both eject the cartridge from the previously fired round and "strip" or remove the next cartridge from the magazine and put it into place before it can be fired. This trip takes time, and recoil occurs because the second bullet is always fired after the first bullet has left the chamber and is on its way out the barrel. Each firing cycle produces the same progression: a fired bullet, recoil, the next fired bullet. There was no way to prevent recoil with that step-by-step cycle, so Nikonov decided to break this linear progression—at least for the first two bullets.

In the AN-94, the pulley and cable came into operation when the bolt assembly began its rearward motion. The pulley and cable quickly reversed the bolt's rearward motion, pulling it forward from the rear and partially loading the next round into the chamber by means of a special feeding tray. As the bolt traveled forward again, this "half loaded" round was already chambered and ready for firing. The result was that two shots felt like one, and there was no recoil until after the second round was fired.

With no recoil for two full shots, a soldier could hit the same exact spot twice, a feat previously impossible for all but expert marksmen It was essentially a two-round-burst rifle that fired faster and more accurately than any other assault rifle with one pull of the trigger.

In semiautomatic mode, the rifle operated as any other, but with very low recoil. On full automatic, the results were similar, but with the selector switch pushed into two-shot mode the shooter could become one of the most feared adversaries faced by enemy infantry, even those wearing the most sophisticated body armor. With armor-piercing rounds, a salvo of well-placed two-shot bursts could even penetrate tank armor.

The rifle was more reliable than the AK, with tests showing the mean number of rounds between failures at forty thousand, compared to thirty thousand for the AK. The rifle had flaws, however. It was not as easy to maintain, and some users said that the sights caught dirt in battle environments. Testers also complained that it could not be fired when the stock was folded over because it covered the trigger. This was an important feature to soldiers in urban situations, because they kept their rifle stocks folded to save space in cramped quarters but they wanted to be ready for action when they emerged. Others grumbled that the pistol grip was not as comfortable as it should be.

All of these shortcomings were more than made up for by the two-shot burst feature. What could not be overlooked, though, was the price: about five times more expensive to produce than the

AK. Although the Russian army adopted the AN-94 as its official infantry rifle in 1997, budget constraints prevented it from being fully deployed. Unless economic conditions improve it will remain in limited production and distribution. So far, only Russia's SPET-sNAZ special forces and elite units police have been issued the AN-94, mainly to fight terrorists.

Even though his weapon was far superior to the AK, Nikonov's firearm will never unseat the Kalashnikov as the world's most deadly and popular rifle, especially among those fighting against establishment armies. It could be decades or more before the AKs now in circulation become decommissioned; and new ones are still being produced, especially by China, Bulgaria, and Romania. These weapons of mass destruction will be with us for a long time.

AND THEY HAVE BECOME EASIER and cheaper to obtain than ever. Almost anyone can buy one with little effort. During the late summer of 2005, the movie *Lord of War* was released, starring Nicolas Cage as Yuri Orlov, a Ukrainian immigrant to New York who starts his gun brokering business by dealing a few AKs and ends up a millionaire. Director Andrew Niccol was astonished when he shopped for three thousand replica AKs. Niccol, who also directed *Gattaca* and *The Truman Show*, found that he could buy real AKs cheaper than the fakes. All it took was a phone call. When filming ended, Niccol sold the firearms. Without trying, he had become an arms dealer of the world's most trusted weapon.

The AK's longevity may be why Nikonov's death in May 2003, at age fifty-three, barely made news, even in Russia. Despite his designing arguably the world's most advanced assault rifle, the official state obituary simply noted, "It is a tremendous loss to the Izhevsk arms-making school."

As for Kalashnikov himself, despite his age and growing feebleness, he continues to be the touted celebrity at military and even nonmilitary gun shows. His mission is to drum up interest in

Izhmash's weapons, including the AK-100 series, his son Viktor's Bizon submachine gun, and even the AN-94, which is often referred to by the name Abakan—but never as the Nikonov.

In 2002, while he was opening a weapons museum in Suhl, eastern Germany, Kalashnikov's demeanor changed. In marked contrast to his usually defiant defense that politicians and not arms designers caused wars, he displayed uncharacteristic sorrow and responsibility by announcing, "I'm proud of my invention, but I'm sad that it is used by terrorists. I would prefer to have invented a machine that people could use and that would help farmers with their work—for example, a lawnmower."

Unfortunately, Kalashnikov's lawnmower, an odd-looking, three-wheeled contraption that looks like a weed whacker with a locomotive cow catcher in front, was never manufactured. He built it before lawnmowers were plentiful in the Soviet Union, but he still uses it to cut the grass at his dacha. A model sits on display at the Kalashnikov museum next to his other inventions including a gadget that holds shish kabobs for grilling.

With its different-sized wheels and blue gaffer's tape holding its components together, Kalashnikov admits that the clunky lawnmower looks ancient, but he says it functions perfectly.

It gets the job done.

NOTES

EPIGRAPHS

v *In some places, an AK-47 assault rifle* Kofi A. Annan, "Small Arms, Big Problems," *International Herald Tribune*, July 10, 2001.

v *That rifle hanging on the wall* George Orwell, "Don't Let Colonel Blimp Ruin the Home Guard," *Evening Standard*, January, 8, 1941.

v *I'm proud of my invention* Kate Connolly, "Kalashnikov: 'I Wish I'd Made a Lawnmower,'" *Guardian* (UK), July 30, 2002.

INTRODUCTION

2 *As the Apaches hovered in position* Mary Beth Sheridan, "Ground Fire Repels Copter Assault; Two Crewmen Seized by Iraqis as Apache Goes Down," *Washington Post*, March 25, 2003.

3 *Why the U.S. military* Ibid.

3 *This "way we go to war"* Interview with Major General William J. Livsey Jr. at Fort Benning, 1978.

4 *Consider the U.S. Rangers in Mogadishu* Jonathan Fryer, "Jingoism Jibe over Black Hawk Down," BBCNews.com, January 21, 2002.

CHAPTER 1. PROTECTING THE MOTHERLAND

12 *Mikhail Timofeevich Kalashnikov was born* Much of the personal information about Kalashnikov's early life comes from his autobiography, *From a Stranger's Doorstep to the Kremlin Gates* (Moscow: Military Parade, 1997), translated from the Russian. Where possible, all incidents were confirmed with those involved and with other objective historical accounts.

13 *Only a few weeks after shipping out*   Ibid., 50, 92.

20 *The U.S. military was oblivious*   William H. Hallahan, *Misfire: The History of How America's Small Arms Have Failed Our Military* (New York: Charles Scribner's Sons, 1994), 402–404.

23 *In addition, rather than build components*   See Kalashnikov, *From a Stranger's Doorstep*, 231.

CHAPTER 2. A REPUTATION BORN IN THE RICE PADDIES

32 *One of the champions of the .30 caliber*   Edward Clinton Ezell, *The Great Rifle Controversy: Search for the Ultimate Infantry Weapon from World War II Through Vietnam and Beyond* (Harrisburg, PA.: Stackpole Books, 1984), 49–51.

34 *But the Americans did not keep their promise*   Hallahan, *Misfire*, 435–437.

41 *Stoner would not have known*   Much of the material about Stoner's efforts to push forward the AR-15 project and resistance from the army came from the Ichord hearings (see page 44 note below) into M-16 malfunctions during the Vietnam War. Stoner also did a series of videotaped interviews for the Smithsonian Institution (as did Kalashnikov) in which he talked about his battles with the army. Also, *The Great Rifle Controversy* and *Misfire*, both referenced above, contain extensive documentation about this period. This particular quote can be found in the History Channel's series *Tales of the Gun: The M-16*, in which Stoner explains on camera the genesis of the M-16 rifle.

43 *Their luck turned*   From an October 3, 1968, press conference where George Wallace announced that LeMay had agreed to serve as his vice presidential candidate.

44 *Boutelle's farm was a shooter's paradise*   *Report of the Special Subcommittee on the M-16 Rifle Program of the Committee on Armed Forces,* House of Representatives, 19th Congress, First Session, October 1967. This was dubbed the Ichord hearings after Missouri representative Richard Ichord, who championed Congress's inquiry into failures of the M-16 during the Vietnam War.

47 *Whatever his reason, McNamara was clearly angry*   Report by Preparedness Investigating Subcommittee of the Committee on Armed Services, U.S. Senate, on M-14 Rifle Program, 1961.

CHAPTER 3. PANDORA'S BOX

55 *The war that Soviet president Mikhail Gorbachev* Lester Grau, "The Soviet-Afghan Wars: A Superpower Mired in the Mountains," *Journal of Slavic Military Studies*, March 2004.

57 *Strategically, the invasion was brilliant* Ibid.

58 *The Soviets with their tanks* The CIA's operations in Afghanistan during the Soviet invasion have been well documented. Sources include congressional testimony on CIA operations as well as Charles G. Crogan, "Partners in Time," *World Policy Journal*, Summer 1993; and Steven Coll, *Ghost Wars: The Secret History of the CIA, Afghanistan and Bin Laden from the Soviet Invasion to September 10, 2001* (New York: Penguin, 2004), 58.

58 *Soviet weapons designers* Val Shilin and Charlie Cutshaw, *Legends and Realities of the AK* (Boulder, CO: Paladin Press, 2000), 38.

59 *Kalashnikov, well aware of the move* Kalashnikov, *From a Stranger's Doorstep*, 292.

59 *Making a smaller-caliber weapon* Much of the technical data for this section is drawn from Shilin and Cutshaw, *Legends and Realities of the AK*.

60 *Again, Western intelligence underestimated* Edward Clinton Ezell, *Kalashnikov: The Arms and the Man: A Revised and Expanded Edition of the AK47 Story* (Cobourg, ON: Collector Grade Publications, 2001), 121.

61 *The new bullet consisted of a thin-jacketed point* Galen L. Geer, "Jihad in Afghanistan," *Soldier of Fortune*, September and October 1980.

62 *Another tactic of the mujahideen* David Rooney, *Guerrilla: Insurgents, Patriots and Terrorists from Sun Tzu to Bin Laden* (London: Brassey's, 2004), 227–228.

63 *The covert pipeline managed by the CIA* Bobi Pirseyedi, *The Small Arms Problem in Central Asia: Features and Implications* (Geneva: United Nations Institute for Disarmament Research, 2000).

64 *As more and more AKs flooded the region* See Coll, *Ghost Wars*.

65 *Despite the graft, corruption, and skimming* *The State of the World's Refugees 1995: Conflict and Reconstruction in Afghanistan*, UNHCR. See also Chris Smith, "Light Weapons and Ethnic Conflict in South Asia," in Jeffrey Boutwell, Michael T. Klare, and Laura W. Reed, eds., *Lethal Commerce: The Global Trade in Small Arms and Light Weapons* (Cambridge, MA: Committee on International Security Studies, American Academy of Arts and Sciences, 1995), 64.

66 *Regardless of the large troop numbers* See Grau, "Soviet-Afghan Wars."

67 *Economically, the war's drain on the faltering* A. Z. Hilali, "Afghanistan: The Decline of Soviet Military Strategy and Political Status," *Journal of Slavic Military Studies* 12, no. 1 (March 1999): 102.

68 *Just prior to the Soviet withdrawal* Henry Kamm, "Pakistani Arms Dealers Hail God and the AK-47," *New York Times*, March 8, 1988.

68 *A 1988 story in the* Los Angeles Times Mark Fineman, "Ethnic Tensions Grip Hyderbad; Pakistanis Fear for Lives in Kalashnikov Culture," *Los Angeles Times*, October 5, 1988.

68 *In Peshawar itself, people reportedly could rent* Mary Williams Walsh, "Guns and Gunmen Rule in Pakistan's Wild West," *Wall Street Journal*, June 30, 1987.

69 *This economic and social reliance on AKs* Ibid.

70 *When the Albanian government fell* Chris McNab, *The AK47* (St. Paul, MN: MBI Publishing, 2001), 60.

70 *Now, with the Soviets gone* *Jane's Intelligence Review*, August 1, 1997.

70 *When the Soviets attacked Afghanistan* For an excellent and concise summary of bin Laden's rise, see Rooney, *Guerrilla*, 229–241.

73 *In essays from al-Qaeda writers* From English translations of al-Qaeda essays cited in Michael Scheure's "Al-Qaeda's Tactical Doctrine for the Long War," *Terrorism Focus*, March 14, 2006. Scheuer also addressed al-Qaeda doctrine in his book *Imperial Hubris: Why the West Is Losing ther War on Terror* (Dulles, VA: Potomac Books, 2005).

CHAPTER 4. THE AFRICAN CREDIT CARD

76 *"A few planeloads of arms"* PBS, *Frontline/World*, "Gun Runners," May 2002.

79 *Instead of ignoring Taylor* Howard Witt, "In Liberian Jungles, Teens Take Charge," *Chicago Tribune*, July 15, 1990.

80 *Taylor went further* Tom Kamara, "Children Remain Useful," *The Perspective*, January 24, 2001.

80 *Taylor's Small Boy Units* Jamie Menutis, "No End to the Ugliness in Liberia," *Alternet*, June 24, 2003.

81 *In a perverted context* "Up to 15,000 Child Soldiers in Liberia, UN Says," IRIN News, September 24, 2003. IRIN is the Integrated Regional Information Networks, part of the UN Office for the Coordination of Humanitarian Affairs.

81 *The Small Boy Units were often looked* Howard Witt, "In Liberian Jungles, Teens Take Charge," *Chicago Tribune*, July 15, 1990.

81 *Nobody knows how Taylor got the idea* Michael Klare, "The Kalashnikov Age," *Bulletin of the Atomic Scientists*, January 1999.

81 *During the capital's siege* "Liberia's Killing Goes On," *Economist*, September 15, 1990.

82 *Some international observers, including former U.S. president Jimmy Carter* Fadiru B. Koroma, "War in Liberia Threatens to Destablise Region," Worldpress.org, August 14, 2002.

82 *With the elections drawing world attention* P. W. Singer, *Children at War* (New York Pantheon, 2005), 56.

84 *Despite a UN embargo* Ken Silverstein, "Comrades in Arms," *Washington Monthly*, January 1, 2002.

85 *To maintain control of these diamond mines* Holly Burkhalter, Physicians for Human Rights, testimony before the U.S. House of Representatives Ways and Means Subcommittee on Trade, September 13, 2000.

85 *Taylor repeatedly denied any involvement* Tamam Ahmed Jama, "Soaked in Blood," *Al-Ahram Weekly*, January 23, 2003.

86 *As the years progressed, Taylor found* Alex Vines, *Hunting the Illegal Arms Traffickers*, report to Norwegian Initiative on Small Arms Transfers, December 6, 2003.

86 *One of the problems encountered by officials* Paul Salopek, "Disarming Sierra Leone," *Chicago Tribune*, December 23, 2001.

87 *The shame of blood diamonds* "A Region in Flames: West Africa Wars," *Economist*, July 5, 2003.

87 *One incident, not publicized at the time* Kim Sengupta, "British SAS Overpower West Side Boys with Military Precision," *Hamilton* (ON) *Spectator*, September 11, 2000. An entire book detailing the incident is William Fowler, *Operation Barras: The SAS Rescue Mission, Sierra Leone 2000* (London: Weidenfeld & Nicholson, 2004).

88 *Although many countries employed child soldiers* "Children of the Gun," Children in Crisis Report, Save the Children, September 2000. Also see Singer, *Children at War*, 15.

89 *Court testimony has stunned the world* Clarence Roy-Macaulay, "Sierra Leoneans Testify on Rebel Abuse," Associated Press, July 21, 2004.

90 *Reports from the war crimes court showed* *Terrorist Responses to Improved US Financial Defenses*, testimony by Douglas Farah before

the House Subcommittee on Oversight and Investigations, Committee on Financial Services, February 16, 2005. Farah is also author of an in-depth investigation into blood diamonds and their use by terrorist groups such as al-Qaeda. He makes a convincing case that the September 11, 2001, attacks were funded in part by illegal trading in these and other precious gems. See Douglas Farah, *Blood from Stones: The Secret Financial Network of Terror*; (New York: Broadway Books, 2004). See also "9/11 Funds Traced to Taylor," *Africa News*, July 22, 2004.

93 *In Somalia, as in many areas of the world* "Somali President a 'Man of Peace,'" *BBC News World Edition* (online), October 14, 2004.

94 *Kalashnikovs poured into Rwanda* Stephen D. Goose and Frank Smyth, "Arming Genocide in Rwanda," *Foreign Affairs*, September/October 1994.

95 *Most news accounts emphasized* Jeffrey Boutwell and Michael T. Klare, "A Scourge of Small Arms," *Scientific American*, June 2000.

95 *In mid-July, RPF forces* Carter Dougherty, "Rwanda Marks Geno-cide Anniversary," *Boston Globe*, April 8, 2004. See Linda Melvern, *A People Betrayed: The Role of the West in Rwanda's Genocide* (London: Zed Books; 2000), for a description of Boutros-Ghali's role.

96 *There was little public mention* Richard D. Hooker, *By Their Deeds Alone* (New York: Ballantine, 2003).

97 *Rwanda and other countries in Africa* Shapi Shacinda, "Tides of Guns Leaves Africa Awash with Misery," Reuters, November 14, 2004.

98 *The AK changed cultural patterns* Anthropologists and other re-searchers have studied the effect of AKs on pastoral people. For one case study, see Mustafa Mirzeler and Crawford Young, "Pastoral Poli-tics in the Northeast Periphery in Uganda: AK-47 as Change Agent," *Journal of Modern African Studies* 38, no. 3 (2000).

99 *One report had the Mozambican government* *Small Arms Survey 2001* (Geneva: Graduate Institute of International Studies, Oxford Univer-sity Press, 2002); 64.

100 *Even if the AK image is deleted* Tom Bowman, "The Father of Terror-ism: Kalashnikov Is a Trademark for Revolution," *Daily Telegraph* (Sydney), March 9, 2002.

CHAPTER 5. THE KALASHNIKOV CULTURE REACHES LATIN AMERICA

106 *These civil wars, fueled by AKs* The testimony of Adolfo A. Franco, Assistant Administrator, Bureau for Latin America and Caribbean,

U.S. Agency for International Development, Committee on House International Relations Subcommittee on Western Hemisphere, April 20, 2005, offers insights into the Latin American crime problem.

109 *The Israelis had built the Galil*   Chuck Taylor, "Galil: The World's Best Assault Rifle," *Guns*, August 1994.

109 *For Somoza, a major draw of the Galil*   "Israel Shows Off a New Rifle That She Says Rates with the Best," *New York Times*, April 15, 1973.

111 *As hostilities grew, small arms rushed*   Christopher Dickey, *With the Contras: A Reporter in the Wilds of Nicaragua* (New York: Simon & Schuster, 1985), 118–119.

112 *In August 1985, the Contras received*   George Gedda, "Contras Obtain 10,000 Polish AK-47 Rifles, US Officials Say," Associated Press, August 31, 1985.

113 *When soldiers reached the wrecked plane*   Michael S. Serrill, "Shot out of the Sky: A Captured U.S. Soldier of Fortune Spins a Tale of CIA Intrigue," *Time*, October 20, 1986.

114 *Calero testified that Secord and Singlaub*   Elaine Sciolino, "Contra Leader Discloses Bank Records," *New York Times*, March 6, 1987.

114 *Further media investigations revealed*   Some of the best reporting at the time was by the *Wall Street Journal*, in particular, John Walcott and David Rogers, "Ship Used to Send Arms to Contras Said to Aid Delivery of East-Bloc Arms," February 13, 1987.

116 *During this time, the FMLN had received large shipments of AKs*   Roy Gutman, "Bush Assails Soviets on Salvador Aid; He Says They're Exporting Revolution," *Newsday* (New York), May 3, 1989.

116 *As it turned out, the weapons came from an unexpected source*   "Grapevine," *Time*, March 27, 1989.

117 *This influx of AKs bolstered the rebels' morale*   Frank Smyth, "Mysterious Influx of Soviet and Chinese Arms for Salvador Rebels," *Sacramento Bee*, June 4, 1989.

120 *One incident in October 1999*   Report of the General Secretariat of the Organization of American States on the Diversion of Nicaraguan Arms to the United Defense Forces of Colombia, January 6, 2003.

122 *What makes this example*   *El Tiempo*, June 30, 2002. The first story on the arms diversion was published on April 21, 2002.

125 *Montesinos went into business with the country's drug dealers*   DEA unclassified document written August 27, 1996. Part of a FOIA request in the National Security Archive, George Washington University.

126 *As more details emerged about Montesinos's arming of Colombian rebels* Juan O. Tamayo, "Peru's Link to Arms Deals Worried U.S.," *Miami Herald*, September 20, 2000.

127 *A more intriguing possibility* For pricing information, see An Vranckx, "European Arms Exports to Latin America: An Inventory," *IPIS Background Report*, Antwerp, Belgium, updated January 2005.

128 *The only bright spot for the Colombian government* *El Tiempo*, June 16, 2004. See also Marcela Sanchez, "Guerrillas March to War in $100 Boots," *Seattle Post-Intelligencer*, June 25, 2004.

130 *U.S. officials paid less attention* "The Iron Fist of Hugo Chavez," FoxNews.com, February 4, 2005.

131 *Rumsfeld discussed the AK purchase* Pablo Bachelet, "Rumsfeld 'Concerned' about Venezuela's Plan to Buy AK47s," *Miami Herald*, March 24, 2005.

131 *Chávez did not immediately respond* Bill Gertz and Rowan Scarborough, "Inside the Ring," *Washington Times*, February 18, 2005.

CHAPTER 6. KALASHNIKOV AND HIS GUN VISIT AMERICA

134 *Fearful that government agents* See Kalashnikov, *From a Stranger's Doorstep*, 335.

134 *Over the following years, Ezell mailed Kalashnikov* Ezell, *Kalashnikov: The Arms and the Man*, 231–239.

135 *On May 15, 1990, Kalashnikov arrived* Author interviews with William Addison Hurst, September 2004.

137 *Over the following days* Sergeant Chris Lawson, "Top Weapons Designers Meet Here," *Quantico Sentry*, May 22, 1990.

137 *They also shared a sense of humor* Interviews with William Addison Hurst, September 2004.

138 *Kalashnikov received unexpected praise* Author e-mail and phone interview with Major General Matthew P. Caulfield (ret.), May 2005.

142 *Still friends, the two did not have much time* Stephen Johnson, "The Rifle Men; Meeting of the Minds Behind AK-47, M-16," *Houston Chronicle*, January 18, 1993.

143 *This small, modest man* J. Kampfner, "Kalashnikov," *Courier* (Queensland, Australia) *Mail*, March 5, 1994.

144 *Observers also took note of Kalashnikov* Celestine Bohlen, "Arms Fac-

tory Can Make Bricks, But, Russia Asks, Is That Smart?" *New York Times*, February 24, 1992.

147 *"It did not look like he was really angry"* "Five Children Killed as Gunman Attacks a California School," Associated Press, January 18, 1989.

150 *Even former president Ronald Reagan* Laurie Becklund, "Saddled Up, Reagan Vows to Speak on Issues," *Los Angeles Times*, February 7, 1989.

150 *President George H. W. Bush* Douglas Jehl, "Bennett Pressured by NRA on Gun Views, Officials Say," *Los Angeles Times*, March 18, 1989.

151 *He reassured gun owners* "Bennett Feels the Heat over Stand on Guns," *Chicago Tribune*, March 18, 1989.

157 *Within a few months of the ban* Interview with Ron Whittaker, *60 Minutes*, February 8, 1995.

158 *Gun magazines, which had opposed the ban* *Gun World*, August 2001.

158 *"If I could have gotten fifty-one votes in the Senate"* Interview with Dianne Feinstein, *60 Minutes*, February 8, 1995.

159 *On February 28, 1997* There are many accounts of the North Hollywood shootout. See Nancy J. Rigg, "Shootout in North Hollywood," *9-1-1 Magazine*, Sept/Oct. 1997, for a discussion from the dispatcher's point of view; "Botched L.A. Bank Heist Turns into Bloody Shootout," CNN.com, February 28, 1997; Beth Shuster and James Rainey, "The North Hollywood Shootout," *Los Angeles Times*, March 1, 1997; "Stunned Police, Residents Cope with Aftermath of L.A. Shootout," CNN.com, March 1, 1997; and *1997 LAPD Annual Report*. A recording of the police radio transmissions during the forty-four-minute incident is also available to the public from several sources on the Internet.

163 *Police were routinely issued shotguns* Mark Schlueb, "As Danger Grows, Orlando Cops Get Rifles with Punch," *Orlando Sentinel*, June 4, 2002.

165 *Some state assault rifle bans* Author interview with John Rosenthal, June 2005.

CHAPTER 7. THE UNITED NATIONS TAKES ON THE TRUE WEAPONS OF MASS DESTRUCTION

171 *As he hailed a cab outside the UN building* Mei-Ling Hopgood, "Gun Lobby Keeps Heat on U.S. at Conference," *Atlanta Journal-Constitution*, July 11, 2001.

172 *Individual countries and regional groups*   Mike Crawley, "Kenya Trade-In; Guns for Schools," *Christian Science Monitor*, January 2, 2001.

172 *In a presentation a year earlier*   Kofi Annan, *We the Peoples: The Role of the United Nations in the 21st Century, October 2000 Millennium Report*, April 3, 2000.

173 *Even before the conference began*   Setting the Record Straight, UN Conference on the Illicit Trade in Small Arms and Light Weapons in All Its Aspects, New York, July 9–20, 2001. Published by the United Nations Department of Public Information in cooperation with the Department for Disarmament Affairs, July 2001.

173 *Despite these clarifications*   Global Structures Convocation (3rd: 1994), February 2–6, 1994, Washington, D.C.

183 *The implications of such bullet-tracing systems*   Joint Report of the United Nations Organization Mission in the Democratic Republic of the Congo, the United Nations Operation in Burundi and the Office of the United Nations High Commissioner for Human Rights into the Gatumba Massacre, October 5, 2004.

186 *Even if marking and tracing*   Johan Peleman, "Tracing Arms Flows," presentation given at the international experts meeting on tracing illicit small arms and light weapons, organized by the GRIP and the European Cost programme, Brussels, October 22, 2004.

Chapter 8. AK versus M-16: Part 2

189 *One of the groups assigned to the area*   Gordon Dillow, "Battle Transforms Fresh Faced Troops," *Orange County Register*, March 23, 2003, in conjunction with Department of Defense Press Releases.

193 *As we've seen in many other countries*   Anna Badkhen, "Gun Market Thrives on Dread," *San Francisco Chronicle*, March 26, 2003. See also *Small Arms Survey 2004* (Geneva: Graduate Institute of International Studies, Oxford University Press, 2004), 48.

196 *Early reports from the front*   Andrew England, "US Troops Using Confiscated Iraqi AK-47s," Associated Press, August 25, 2003.

199 *Members of Congress wrote letters*   Ted Strideland, letter to Secretary of Defense Donald Rumsfeld, October 1, 2003.

202 *Coalition Provisional Authority officials*   William Matthews, "U.S. Officials Rap Rifle Buy for Iraqi Corp," *Defense News*, December 22, 2003.

202 *Even the Russians were angry* C. J. Chivers, "Who's A Pirate? Russia Points Back at the U.S.," *New York Times*, July 24, 2004.

203 *The story took an even stranger turn* Northern District of California indictment, U.S. District Attorney, May 23, 1996. See also Jonathan S. Landay, "Chinese Firm Linked to Smuggled AK-47s Picked to Supply Iraqi Army," Knight Ridder Newspapers, April 27, 2005.

205 *With the continuing violence in Iraq* Oliver Poole, "The Iraqi GP: Stethoscope and AK-47," *The Age*, May 19, 2005.

CHAPTER 9. THE SECOND SELLING OF THE AK

212 *Years earlier, Kalashnikov had felt* Kalashnikov, *From a Stranger's Doorstep*, 444.

213 *Viktor was more outspoken and bitter* "Kalashnikov Inventor Wants Peace; Recalls Soviets Nostalgically," Agence France-Presse, May 7, 2000.

215 *Even commercial high-end artists and designers joined the AK design movement* E-mail to author from Starck representative.

215 *The founders of the online photography magazine* AK47 E-mail to author from Joerg Diekmann.

216 *The fact that AKs enjoyed* Dave Graham, "Kalashnikov Sets Sights on Superbrand," Reuters, February 17, 2003.

217 *Still, the AK mystique grew stronger* *Playboy*, January 2004.

220 *The Kalashnikov 41-proof vodka* "Russian Routlette," *Growing Business*, June 2004.

222 *In interviews after the reception* Vicky Allan, "Kalashnikov Calls New Kinds of Shots," *Sunday Herald* (Scotland), September 26, 2004. See also "Kalashnikov Launches Liquid Weapon," CNN.com, September 20, 2004. (Notes 129–132 include material from an author phone interview with Florey.)

223 *Florey argued that the Kalashnikov brand was based* John Ness, "Swords into Vodka," *Newsweek International*, November 22, 2004.

224 *Florey put Kalashnikov out front to help* "Britain's Kalashnikov Vodka to Change Name after Anti-Violence Campaign," Reuters, January 15, 2005. See also Adam Jones, "Lobby Sets Sights on Kalashnikov Vodka," *Financial Times*, October 26, 2004.

224 *The group's assessment was both good and bad news* Report of Panel Meeting, January, 21, 2005.

226 *That same year* Billy Hidge, "Killing Machine," *Stuff*, April, 2005

EPILOGUE: THE LAST DAYS OF THE AK?

230 *Kalashnikov lobbied heavily* See Shilin and Cutshaw, *Legends and Realities of the AK*, 144.

234 *In 2002* Kate Connolly, "Kalashnikov: 'I wish I'd made a Lawn-mower,'" *Guardian* (UK), July 30, 2002.

INDEX

Page numbers in *italics* refer to illustrations.

Abidjan Accord, 89
Abizaid, John, 200
Afghanistan
  bin Laden, Osama, 70–73
  Soviet Union invades, 5, 55–71
  United States invades, 5, 71–74
Africa, 4–5. *See also specific African countries*
  AK-47, 76, 80–81, 86, 97–101
  cold war, 75–76
  Liberia, 4, 75, 76, 78–84, 87, 90–91
  Mozambique, 98–100
  Rwanda, 94–97
  Sierra Leone, 87, 88–89, 90–91
  Somalia, 5, 91–94
  United Nations arms control, 170, 176
Ahmed, Abdullahi Yusuf, 93–94
Aidid, Mohammed Farrah, 91
AK-47. *See also* ammunition and cartridges; ballistics
  Afghanistan war (Soviet Union), 55–71
  Afghanistan war (United States), 5, 71–74

Africa, 76, 80–81, 86, 97–101
arms trade, 86–87, 91
cartridges, 59–61
cold war, 29–30
criminal violence, 147, 153, 166
culture, 6, 97–101, *99,* 213–218, 225–226
design of, 23–24
effectiveness of, 2–3
Iraq war, 2, 190–207
Latin America, 116–118
law enforcement equipped with, 161–164
M-14 rifle compared, 37–38, 48, 50
modifications to, 25, *26,* 30, 59–60
M-16 rifle compared, 51, 54
proliferation of, 55, 67–70, 100–101, 211, 233–234
prototypes of, 24–25
replacement of, 228–233
Soviet Union, 25–26, 27–28
U.S. arms trade, 146, 152
Vietnam War, 3, 28, 48, 50, 51–52
warfare, 3–6
AK-47 (film), 226

AK-47 (magazine), 215
AK-47 Story, The (Ezell), 134
AKM (AK Modernized), *26*, 30,
    60
AK-MP3 Jukebox, 225–226
AK-74, 60, 72, *72*
Albania, 70
al-Qaeda, 71, 90
Amin, Hafizullah, 56, 57
ammunition and cartridges. *See also*
    AK-47; ballistics
    AK-47, 59–61
    Kalashnikov, Mikhail T., 59
    nomenclature of, 17–18
    North Atlantic Treaty Organiza-
        tion (NATO), 32–36
    physics of, 21, 23, 32–33
    Soviet Union, 19–20
    submachine guns, 16–17, 17
    United Kingdom, 32–33
    United States, 30–36
    weapons marking, 179–186
Andropov, Yuri, 66
Angola, 97
Annan, Kofi, 172–173
AN-94 (Russian assault rifle), 228,
    230–233
Apache attack helicopter, 1–2
Ap Bac, Battle of (Vietnam), 48
Arbulú, Guillermo, 124
AR-15 rifle, 40–48, 50, 51, 59
Arisaka round, 19–20
ArmaLite, 39, 41, 42, 43
arms trade. *See also* diamond trade;
    drug trade; gun control
    Afghanistan war (Soviet Union),
        61–69

Africa, 75–76, 84, 86, 90–91, 93,
    172
    AK-47, 86–87, 93–94
    Central Intelligence Agency
        (CIA), 126–127
    Colombia, 118–124
    Iran-Contra scandal, 113–115
    Latin America, 103, 105–106,
        115–118
    Peru, 123–128
    Russia, 129
    Venezuela, 128–131
art, AK-47, 213–216. *See also*
    culture
AR-10 rifle, 39–40
Arusha Accords, 95
ATACMS rockets, 1
atomic bomb, 5–6, 44
Automatic Kalashnikov (film),
    212–213
automatic rifles, Soviet Union,
    19–20

ballistics
    cartridges, 32–33
    submachine guns, 17
Bank of America siege, 159–161
Bao Ping Ma, 203
Barr, Bob, 171, 179
Batista, Fulgencio, 107
BBC network, 5
Belgium
    ammunition, 33, 34, 35
    World War II, 10
Bennett, William, 150, 151–152
bin Laden, Osama, 6, 70–73, 164
Black, Chris, 96

Black Hawk Down (film), 5, 92, 93

"Black Hawk Down" incident, 4–5, 92, 93, 131

Blair, Tony, 88

blitzkrieg tactic, World War II, 9–10

Bloomfield, Lincoln, Jr., 171

body armor, 198–201

Boland Amendment (U.S.), 112

Bollywood, 226

Bolton, John, 169–171, 173–174, 176

Bout, Victor, 84

Boutelle, Richard S., 38, 39, 43, 44, 46

Boutros-Ghali, Boutros, 96

Brady Center to Prevent Gun Violence, 164

branding, 216, 219–225

Brazil, weapons marking, 180–182

Bremer, L. Paul, 192

Brenes Jarquin, Carlos Alberto, 107

Brezhnev, Leonid, 66

Bromige, David, 219

Brown, Robert K., 61

Browning Automatic Rifle, 42

Browning pistol, 12

Bryansk, Battle of (Soviet Union), 11–12

Buchanan, James, 78

Buchanan, Thomas, 78

Bulgaria, 30, 69, 233

Bureau of Alcohol, Tobacco and Firearms, 153

Burkina Faso, 86

Bush, George H. W., 116, 117, 150, 151, 152

Bush, George W., 71, 165, 175, 189, 225

Cage, Nicolas, 233

Calero, Adolfo, 114

Canada, ammunition, 35

carbine, design of, 16

Carten, Fred, 34, 41, 42, 47

Carter, Jimmy, 57, 82, 108, 110–111

cartridges. *See* ammunition and cartridges; ballistics

Casey, William, 110–111

Castano, Carlos, 122

Castro, Fidel, 56

Caulfield, Matthew P., 138–139

Central Institute for Precision Machine Building (TsNI-ITochmash), 60

Central Intelligence Agency (CIA), 57–58, 61, 62

 Afghanistan war (Soviet Union), 56, 57–58, 61, 62–65, 66

 arms trade, 126–127

 bin Laden, Osama, 71, 73

 drug trade, 125, 127

 Iran-Contra scandal, 112–115, 116–117

 Langley, Virginia, shootings, 154–156

 Vietnam War, 50

Chamorro, Violeta, 117, 118

Chamorro Cardenal, Pedro Joaquin, 108–109

Chapman, Nathan Ross, 73–74

Chávez, Hugo, 128–131

Chernenko, Konstantin, 66

Childers, Therrel "Shane," 190

children
  Africa, 79–81, 83, *83,* 86, 87–89
  Latin America, 122–123
  South Asia, 73–74
China
  AK-47, 30, 63, 157–158, 202–204, 233
  arms trade, 67–68, 177
  Rwanda genocide, 96
  United Nations arms control, 175–176
  warfare, 27
  weapons marking, 177, 178
Cholm, Battle of (Soviet Union), 18
Churchill, Winston, 34
Clapsaddle, Eric, 163
Clinton, William J., 92, 96, 175
Coalition Provisional Authority (CPA), 201–202
Cocktail (film), 219
cold war
  Afghanistan, 56
  Africa, 75–76
  AK-47, 29–30
  Kalashnikov, Mikhail T., 135–136
  Nicaragua, 107–108
  Soviet Union, 29
  United States, 36–37
Collins, Joe L., 35
Colombia
  guerilla activities in, 118–124
  United Nations arms control, 176
Colt, Samuel, 19
Colt firearms, 43–48, 51, 157
Communism, 56. *See also* cold war
Condon, Paul, 225

Congo, 91
Cooper, William J., 113
Crane, Dave, 90
Cruise, Tom, 219
Cuba, 107, 116, 119
culture, 6, 97–101, *99,* 213–218, 225–226

de Beer, David, 214
diamond trade, 85–86, 90–91. *See also* arms trade; drug trade
Diekmann, Joerg, 215
Diem, Ngo Dinh, 49
Dien Bien Phu, Battle of (Vietnam), 36
Dirty Harry (film), 18
Dobrynski, Andrzej, 112
Doe, Samuel K., 79, 81–82
domino theory, 36–37
dos Santos, Feil, 214–215
Dr. Strangelove (film), 44
Dragunov, Evgeny, 230
drug trade. *See also* arms trade; diamond trade
  arms trade and, 119, 123
  Iran-Contra scandal, 113
  Latin America, 105–106
  Peru, 124–125
  Uzi submachine gun, 145–146
Duarte, José Napoleon, 116
Duffney, Bob, 2
Durant, Mike, 92
Dutch Army Museum, 217

East Germany, 30
Economic Community of West African States (ECOWAS), 82

Egypt
  AK-47, 63
  Rwanda genocide, 96
  weapons marking, 177
8 Mile (film), 225
Eisenhower, Dwight D., 35, 37
El Salvador, 116
Eminem, 225
Engstfeld, Axel, 212
Ezell, Ed, 133, 134, 135, 137

FAL cartridge, 34–36, 41
Farabundo Martí National Libera-
    tion Front (FMLN), 116, 117
Farell, Loren, 159
Federov, Vladimir, 19–20, 24
Feinstein, Dianne, 153, 158
FHM magazine, 222
Financial Times (newspaper), 224
Firestone Plantation Company, 78
Florey, John, 218–220, 222–225
FN-FAL cartridge (Fabrique
    Nationale-Fusil Automatique
    Léger), 34–36, 41
Forjaz, Jose, 100
France
  Rwanda genocide, 95, 96
  Vietnam, 36, 37
  World War II, 10
Franks, Tommy, 189
Frontline (TV show), 76
Fujimori, Alberto, 124–128

Gadhafi, Mu'ammar, 79, 89
Galili, Israel, 109
Galil submachine gun, 109
Garand, John, *22,* 31

Gattaca (film), 233
Gatumba refugee camp incident,
    182–186
Geer, Galen L., 61
genocide, Africa, 94–97, 183–186
Germany
  ammunition, 17–18, 20
  blitzkrieg tactic, 9–10
  Soviet Union invasion, 15
  submachine guns, 14–15, 16–19
Golding, William, 80
Goodman, John, 160
Gorbachev, Mikhail, 55, 66–67
Gourevitch, Philip, 97
Granda, Rodrigo, 130
Grau, Lester W., 5
grease gun (M3 submachine gun),
    42
Greenleaf, Simon, 78
Guinea, 84, 86
Gul, Haji Baz, 68
Gulf of Tonkin Resolution, 50
gun control. *See also* arms trade
  Gun Control Act of 1968, 145,
    146
  politics of, 151–167
  Stockton, California, schoolyard
    shooting, 149–150
  terrorism, 164–165, 166
  United Nations, 169–186
  Violent Crime Control and Law
    Enforcement Act of 1994, 156
  weapons marking, 177–186
Gun Control Act of 1968, 145, 146

Habersack, Herbert, 212
Habyarimana, Juvenal, 95

Hackworth, David H., 52
Harkins, Paul, 50
Hart, Howard, 58, 63
Hasenfus, Gene, 113, 114
Hassan, Yusuf, 5, 93
Heckler & Koch, 163, 196
Hellfire antitank missiles, 1
Hezbollah, *148*
Hitler, Adolf, 10, 15, 18, 19
Ho Chi Minh, 36
Holbrooke, Richard, 85
Humvee vehicle, 200–201, 205
Hungary
    AK-47, 30, 69
    Soviet invasion of, 27–28
Hussein, Saddam, 1, 6, 123, 125,
    187–188, 191, 192, 193, 206
Hussein, Uday, 6, 191
Hutu people, 94–97

ICE magazine, 222
Ichord, Richard, 51, 52
improvised explosive devices
    (IEDs), 205–206
India, 226
Interceptor Multi-Threat Body
    Armor System, 198–201
Iran-Contra scandal, 112–115,
    116–117
Iran hostage crisis, 110–111
Iran-Iraq war, 111, 123, 125
Iraq war
    AK-47, 2, 3
    conduct of, 188–192
    initiation of, 1–2, 188
    opposition to, 225
    U.S. occupation, 192–207

Israel
    arms trade, 120–121, 145–146
    Nicaragua, 109
Ivory Coast, 84, 86

Jackie Brown (film), 213
Japan, 19
Johnson, Lyndon B., 50
Johnson, Yormie, 82
Jolie, Angelina, 214

Kagame, Paul, 95, 97
Kalashnikov, Elena, 135, 136
Kalashnikov, Mikhail T., 100, *221*
    AK-47 design, 15–16, 19, 21,
        23–25
    biography of, 6–7, 12–14
    cartridges, 59–60
    commercial ventures of, 141, 144,
        209–213, 216, 218–225
    media and, 142–144
    personality of, 141
    politics and, 132
    travels of, 140–141
    U.S. visit of, 133–139
    World War II, 11–12, 13
Kalashnikov, Natasha, 140
Kalashnikov, Viktor, 140, 212–213,
    230, 234
Kalashnikov, Yekaterina, 140
Kalashnikov Joint Stock Vodka
    Company, 219
Kalashnikov Weapons Museum
    and Exhibition Center (Izhevsk,
    Russia), 217–218, 234
Kallay, Foday, 88
Kansai, Aimal, 154–156

Kasparov, Gary, 219

Kennedy, John F., 44–45, 47, 49, 50

Kennedy, Robert F., 145

Kenya, 172

Kerry, John, 166–167

Khan, Sardar Mohammed Daoud, 56

Khe Sanh, siege of (Vietnam), 138–139

Khomeini, Ayatollah Ruhollah, 56

Khrushchev, Nikita, 28

Killing Fields, The (film), 214

King, Martin Luther, Jr., 145

Klare, Michael, 81

Koltakov, Andrey, 226

Korean War, 27, 39, 45

Kouen-Hoven, Gus, 84

Kubrick, Stanley, 44

Kurz ammunition, 17, 18, 20

Kyoto Protocol, 175

LaPierre, Wayne, 167

laser weapons marking, 178–179

Latin America. *See also specific Latin American countries*

  arms trade, 115–118

  Colombia, 118–124

  drug trade, 105

  Nicaragua, 103–105, 106–115

  Peru, 123–128

  Venezuela, 128–131

law enforcement

  AK-47 equipment, 161–164

  weapons marking, 182

lawnmower, 234

Lee-Enfield rifle, 58, 61

LeMay, Curtis, 43–44, 45

Liberia, 4, 75, 76, 78–84, 87, 90–91

Libya, 79, 86

Livsey, William J., Jr., 4

Longbow radar systems, 1

Lord of the Flies (Golding), 80

Lord of War (film), 233

Los Angeles Times (newspaper), 68, 217

Luxembourg, World War II, 10

Macdonald, Bobby, 43, 46, 51

Mackey, Lori, 147

Makhanu, Maurice, 172

Mao Tse-tung, 27

Marken Marketing International (MMI), 216

Maschinenkarabiner (Mkb), 18–19

Maschinenpistoles (MP40, German submachine gun, Schmeisser), 11, 14, 18

Matasareanu, Emil, 159–161

McNamara, Robert S., 45, 46–48, 50, 53

Menutis, Jamie, 80

M-43 cartridge, 19

M-14 rifle, 35, 36, 37–38, 39, 40, 42, 44, 45, 46, 47, 48, 62

Mine Ban Treaty, 175

Minin, Leonid, 84

Mogadishu, Somalia, 4–5, 91–92, 93

M1 Carbine, 32, 42

M1 Garand (U.S. semiautomatic rifle), 16, 20, *22,* 29, 30–31, 32, 36, 42, 53

M1 steel helmet, 32

Monroe, James, 78

Montesinos, Vladimiro, 124–128

Mozambique, 4, 98–100
M-16 rifle, 3, 44, 48, 50–54, 59, 137
M3 submachine gun, 32
museums, 217–218

National Defense Authorization
    Act of 1997, 162
National Firearms Museum,
    National Rifle Association
    (NRA), 137
National Rifle Association (NRA),
    137, 140, 151, 165–167, 171,
    174–175
Nawroz, Mohammad Yahya, 5
Nesterov, Azariy, 230
Netherlands, World War II, 10
Newsweek (magazine), 34
New York Times (newspaper), 68
Nhu, Ngo Dinh, 49
Nicaragua, 103–105, *104,* 106–115,
    116, 117–118, 121–122
Niccol, Andrew, 233
Nigeria, 89
Nikonov, Gennady, 230, 231, 233
Nikonov, Tatiana, 230
nongovernmental organizations
    (NGOs), arms control, 173,
    174
North, Oliver L., 114–115
North Atlantic Treaty Organiza-
    tion (NATO), 32–36, 43
North Korea, 30, 202–203

Ofcansky, Tom, 76
Olin Mathieson Corporation, 53
Operation Desert Storm (Persian
    Gulf War [1991]), 2

Ordnance Department (U.S.), 39,
    41–42, 43, 44, 45, 46–47, 51,
    52–53
Ortega, Daniel, 112, 117

Pahlavi, Mohammed Reza Shah, 56
Pakistan, 57–58, 62, 63–65, 68–69
Palestinian Liberation Front, 147
Panama, 121
Panzer tank, 10
Pastrana, Andres, 119
Patton, George, *22,* 31
Perello, Martin, 159
Persian Gulf War (1991), 2,
    187–188, 189
Peru, 123–128
Phillips, Larry Eugene, Jr., 159–161
Pig Boards (tests), 33
Playboy magazine, 217
Ploter, Carlos, 128
Poland
    AK-47, 30, 63
    Nicaragua, 112, 113, 114
    World War II, 10, 11
Polstar Vodka, 219, 222
Poly Technologies, 203–204
Portman Group, 223, 224, 225
PPD34/38 (Soviet submachine gun),
    14–15
PP Kurz pistol, 17
PPSh41 (Soviet submachine gun),
    14–15, 24, 37
Purdy, Patrick Edward, 146–147,
    149

Reagan, Ronald, 62, 73, 110–111,
    113, 115, 123, 125, 150

recoil, 229, 231–232

Remington Arms Company, 40

Remington Model 8, 24

Republican Guard (Iraqi defense force), 1

Reutersward, Carl Fredrik, 171

Revolutionary Armed Forces of Colombia (FARC). *See* Colombia

Reyes, Camilo, 176

Ridgway, Matthew B., 35

Roberts, Julia, 222

Romania, AK-47, 69, 233

Rosenthal, John, 165

RPK-74, 61

Ruger, William, 140, 153–154

Rumsfeld, Donald, 130, 131, 192, 199, 201

Russia. *See also* Soviet Union
  arms trade, 129, 158, 202–203, 209–210, 228–233
  United Nations arms control, 175–176
  weapons marking, 177–178

Russian Revolution, 20

Rwanda, 94–97, 184–185

Saiga (hunting gun), 141

Sakharov, Andrei, 227, 228

Sandinista National Liberation Front (FSLN), *104,* 108, 110, 111–115, 116

Sandino, Augusto, 103, 107

Sankoh, Foday, 89

Saudi Arabia, 62

Schmeisser. *See* Maschinenpistoles (MP40, German submachine gun, Schmeisser)

Schmeisser, Hugo, 14, 18

Scott, George C., 44

Scud missile, 188

Secord, Richard V., 114

Sevaastyanov, Igor, 203

Sheikh, Aftab, 68

Shpagin, Georgy, 24

Sierra Leone, 87, 88–89, 90–91

Simonov, Sergei, 19

Singlaub, John K., 114

SKS (Soviet rifle), 37

Slocombe, Walter, 202

Smith & Wesson, 19

Soghanalian, Sarkis, 125–126

Soldier of Fortune magazine, 61

Somalia, 5, 91–94, 131

Somoza Garcia, Anastasio, 107–110, 111

Sopranos, The (TV show), 213–214

South Africa, 91, 98

Soviet Union. *See also* Russia
  Afghanistan, 5, 55–71
  AK-47, 6, 25–26, *26,* 27–28
  automatic rifles, 19–20
  cold war, 29, 56
  collapse of, 69, 142, 171, 218
  Hungary, 27–28
  Nicaragua, 107–108
  Russian Revolution, 20
  submachine guns, 13–15, 18, 19
  warfare, 25–26, 27–28
  World War II, 9, 11–12, 15, 18

Sporting Arms and Ammunition Manufacturers' Institute (SAAMI), 153–154, 182

Springfield Armory, 20, 28, 31, 34, 35, 42, 47–48, 53

Stalin, Josef, 19, 27, 140
stamping. *See* weapons marking
Starck, Philippe, 215
Stinger missiles, 65
Stockton, California, schoolyard
　　shooting, 146–147, 149
Stoner, Eugene M., 38–43, 51,
　　52–53, 133, 135, 136, 137, 142,
　　213
Stop Handgun Violence, 165
Strickland, Ted, 199–200
Studler, Rene, 32, 34
Stuff magazine, 226
Sturmgewehr (Maschinenkarabiner
　　[Mkb]), 18–19, 20–21, 31, 41
submachine guns
　　Germany, 16–19
　　Maschinenpistoles, MP40, 11, 14
　　physics of, 21, 23, 32–33
　　Soviet Union, 13–15, 18, 19
Sudayev, Alexei, 19
Sugarmann, Josh, 165
Sullivan, George, 38–39
Sunday Times Style magazine, 222
Syria, weapons marking, 177

Taliban, 71, 73, 90
Taraki, Nur Muhammad, 56
Tarantino, Quentin, 213
Taylor, Charles, 4, 75–76, 77, 78–86,
　　105
　　arms trade, 84, 90–91
　　biography of, 75, 78–79
　　child soldiers, 79–81, 83, 86
　　diamond trade, 85–86, 90–91
　　indictment of, 89
　　Liberia civil war, 82–83

　　Liberia invaded by, 75, 76, 77, 78,
　　　79
Taylor, Maxwell, 42–43
terrorism, gun control, 164–165,
　　166
T-44 cartridge, 34–35
Thompson, Emma, 214
Thompson submachine gun
　　("Tommy Gun"), 14
Togo, 86
Tolbert, William, 78–79
Tonkin, Gulf of, 50
Truman, Harry S., 34
Truman Show, The (film), 233
TsNIITochmash (Central Institute
　　for Precision Machine Building),
　　60
Turkey, AK-47, 63
Tutsi people, 94–97

Uganda, 97, 98
Ukraine, 15
　　AK-47, 70
United Kingdom
　　Africa, 87–88
　　ammunition, 32–34, 35
United Nations
　　Afghanistan war (Soviet Union),
　　　66, 67
　　AK-47, 4
　　arms control, 169–186
　　arms trade, 76, 84, 86, 87, 93, 100
　　children, 83
　　diamond trade, 85
　　Latin America, 117
　　Rwanda genocide, 95, 96, 97
　　Somalia, 91, 92–93

United Nations Children's Fund
  (UNICEF), 83
United States
  Afghanistan, 56
  Afghanistan invasion (Soviet
    Union), 57–58
  ammunition, 30–36
  AR-15 rifle, 40–43, 40–48
  AR-10 rifle, 39–40
  Iraq war, 188–207
  Liberia, 78
  M-14 rifle, 35, 36, 37–38, 39
  M1 Garand (U.S. semiautomatic
    rifle), 16, 20–21, 22
  Nicaragua, 106–115
  Peru, 123–128
  Rwanda genocide, 95, 96
  Somalia, 5, 91–94
  United Nations arms control,
    169–171, 173–175
  Venezuela, 128–131
  Vietnam, 36–37
  Vietnam War, 48–50
  warfare, 26–27
  weapons marking, 177, 179, 182
U.S. Army Materiel Command, 47
U.S. Drug Enforcement Adminis-
  tration (DEA), 125
Uzi submachine gun, 109, 145–146

Vance, Cyrus, 47
Venezuela, 128–131
Vietnam
  France, 36
  United States, 36–37, 46, 47
Vietnam War, 41
  AK-47, 3, 28, 48, 50, 51–52, 55, 138

AR-15 rifle, 46
  end of, 54
  Khe Sanh, siege of, 138–139
  M-16 rifle, 44, 48, 50–54, 137
  United States, 48–50
Vines, Alex, 86
Violence Policy Center, 165
Violent Crime Control and Law
  Enforcement Act of 1994, 156
vodka, 211, 218–220, 221, 222–225

Walker, William, 106–107, 116
Wallace, George, 43
Walther, Carl, 18
Walther PPK pistol, 18
warfare
  Afghanistan invasion (Soviet
    Union), 58, 62
  AK-47, 3–6
  China, 27
  Soviet Union, 25–26, 27–28
  United States, 26–27
  Vietnam War, 48–49, 49
Washington, George, 135
weapons marking, gun control,
  177–186
Westmoreland, William, 50
West Side Boys (child soldiers),
  87–88
Whittaker, Ron, 157
Williams, Willie, 161
Wolf, Bill, 3
Woolsey, James, 154
World War I, 10, 12
World War II, 38
  blitzkrieg tactic, 9–10
  end of, 20

World War II (*continued*)
  Kalashnikov, Mikhail T., 6
  M1 Garand (U.S. rifle), 16, *22,* 31,
    53
  Soviet Union, 9, 11–12, 18
Wyman, William G., 39–40

XM-8 rifle, 196

Yelinek, Shimon, 120–121
Yeltsin, Boris, 140, 143
Young, Mark, 197

Zingo, Nick, 161